CIVIL WAR, A to Z

Books published by The Random House Publishing Group are available at quantity discounts on bulk purchases for premium, educational, fund-raising, and special sales use. For details, please call 1-800-733-3000.

CIVIL WAR,
A to Z

The Complete Handbook of America's Bloodiest Conflict

Featuring illustrations, photographs,
a time line, and hundreds of entries on
battles, weapons, and personalities

Edited by
Clifford L. Linedecker

PRESIDIO
PRESS

BALLANTINE BOOKS • NEW YORK

2005 Presidio Press Mass Market Edition

Copyright © 2002 by Clifford L. Linedecker

Published in the United States by Presidio Press, an imprint of The Random House Publishing Group, a division of Random House, Inc., New York.

Presidio Press and colophon are trademarks of Random House, Inc.

Originally published in trade paperback in the United States by Ballantine Books, an imprint of The Random House Publishing Group, a division of Random House, Inc., in 2002, and simultaneously in Canada by Random House of Canada Limited, Toronto.

ISBN 0-89141-878-4

Printed in the United States of America

Presidio Press website address: www.presidiopress.com

OPM   9   8   7   6   5   4   3

It is well that war is so terrible,
or we should get too fond of it.
—GENERAL ROBERT E. LEE

Introduction

Fifty years ago, replicas of Civil War garrison caps, Yankee blue and Confederate gray, were selling to children and adults all over America. The horrors of World War II were already beginning to fade, and Americans were looking back to an older conflict fought on our own soil, a struggle that with the passage of time has become romanticized and glorified as the first modern war. The last of the old wars and the first of the new, the Civil War was a war of military innovations. It produced hot air balloons and the first aerial reconnaissance, the first battle between ironclad ships, the first submarine to sink a ship, water mines, land mines, machine guns, rail guns, antiaircraft fire, magazine rifles, wire entanglements, and the first battlefield use of the telegraph, as well as many other inventions and scientific developments that revolutionized warfare.

Most important, the tragedy of the Civil War marked a new beginning in our nation's history. Slavery, one of the defining causes of the war, was ended in North America once and for all by the Union victory and by President Lincoln's Emancipation Proclamation midway through the conflict. States' rights, the other major point of contention between North and South, is still fiercely debated today, but the quarrel is bloodless and carried out in the halls of Congress, rather than on the field of battle.

The Civil War produced brilliant and energetic new national leaders while it was ushering in advances in battlefield armaments and tactics. All the accomplishments were produced against a background of astonishing acts of individual heroism and self-sacrifice.

It was our nation's epic national conflict and the last war to be fought by land forces totally on American soil. American cities, towns, plantations, and farms were destroyed, and innocent civilians were killed, injured, or dispossessed and left without food or shelter.

The conflict claimed the lives of more American fighting men than all the nation's other wars combined. Billy Yanks and Johnny Rebs died on battlefields in cities and small towns and at isolated crossroads, rivers, and creeks like Petersburg, Gettysburg, Chickamauga, Bull Run, and Five Forks. Even more died of disease and infection spread by huge numbers of men massed together in unsanitary conditions, with insufficient medical care that too often was aggravated by malnutrition.

Two of every ten men who marched off to war never saw their homes again. Thousands of others returned without arms and legs, blind, or with other physical and emotional injuries that would plague them throughout the remainder of their lives. The Civil War was a ghastly four-year bloodletting between North and South that, after incredible pain and sacrifice on both sides, transformed a country at war with itself into a stronger, cohesive union that became the most powerful nation in the world.

The world's first modern war changed the Union and the Confederacy into the United States!

A

Abatis
One of the most formidable obstacles laid around defensive positions during the war, abatis were tangles of trees and large limbs carefully arranged with the branches pointed toward the attackers. Small branches and leaves were stripped away to prevent their use as cover for the enemy. Remaining branches were sharpened at the ends, and larger chunks were often covered with earth, staked to the ground, or nailed to cross-beams to inhibit efforts to dismantle the obstacles.

Abercrombie, Brigadier General John Joseph, U.S.
A West Pointer, Abercrombie served as a captain in Florida's Seminole Wars, before he was brevetted as a major for gallant conduct at the Battle of Okeechobee. After frontier duty and fighting in the Mexican War, where he was wounded at Monterrey and again cited for gallantry, he was promoted to lieutenant colonel. During the Civil War he fought at Falling Waters during the Shenandoah Campaign and served through the Peninsular Campaign as a brigadier general of volunteers. Abercrombie was wounded at Fair Oaks and fought at Malvern Hill, then participated in several skirmishes during the retreat to Harrison's Landing. During 1862 and 1863 he was engaged in the defense of Washington. He later served at Fredericksburg and fought against Hampton's Legion. Abercrombie was brevetted brigadier general at the end of the conflict.

Abolition

Religious fundamentalists in the North were convinced that slavery was a national evil, and they became the primary force that founded and shaped the abolitionist movement. In the South most whites considered abolitionists uninformed meddlers, who were attacking their lifestyle and economy. As the abolitionist movement took firm root, the American Anti-Slavery Society grew to more than 1,000 chapters and a membership of more than 250,000. Inevitably, the heated debate and partisan rancor led to bloodshed on both sides of the issue. Passage of the Fugitive Slave Act in 1850 and publication two years later of Harriet Beecher Stowe's melodramatic but scathing attack on slavery *Uncle Tom's Cabin* helped fan the flames of the growing enmity between the largely proslavery forces in the South and the abolitionists in the North. (See: Douglass, Frederick; Dred Scott Decision; and Stowe, Harriet Beecher.)

Adams, Brigadier General John, CS

The son of Irish immigrants, Adams graduated from West Point and served in the U.S. Army during the Mexican War. Brevetted for gallantry and meritorious conduct during the Battle of Santa Cruz de Rossales, he was commissioned first lieutenant in 1851 and promoted to captain five years later. Adams was serving at Fort Crook, California, when he resigned his U.S. Army commission and traveled to Tennessee to fight for the South. He was a captain of cavalry when he was placed in command at Memphis. In May 1862 he was promoted to colonel and in December became a brigadier general. When Brigadier General Lloyd Tilghman died in 1863, Adams assumed command of his Mississippi infantry brigade, fought under General Joseph E. Johnston at Vicksburg, and served with Lieutenant General Leonidas Polk in Mississippi. Transferred to the Confederate Army of Tennessee, Adams served with General John B. Hood after the fall of Atlanta, in the Nashville Campaign, and briefly with General Nathan Bedford Forrest's cavalry. Adams was leading his regiment in an attack against Union troops at the Battle of Franklin on November 30, 1864, when he was killed.

Adams, Brigadier General William Wirt, CS
A brother of General Daniel Weisinger Adams, William was a veteran of the Army of the Republic of Texas and a former Mississippi state legislator when he turned down an offer by President Davis to serve as the Confederacy's new postmaster general. Instead, Adams raised the 1st Mississippi Cavalry, and as the regiment's colonel he led it in battle in Mississippi and Tennessee. He was promoted to brigadier general for his performance at Vicksburg. Late in 1864, his brigade was attached to General Nathan Bedford Forrest's corps and served there throughout the remainder of the conflict. After the war he served as a state revenue agent and postmaster of Jackson, Mississippi, before he was shot to death by a newspaper editor he had quarreled with.

Admiral
Congress created the title of flag officer in 1857, but it wasn't until five years later, while the Civil War was raging, that the first American use of the admiral rank was authorized. (The same act also restored the title of commodore.) The first American naval officer to be named to the new rank was Admiral David G. Farragut. (See: Farragut, Admiral David Glasgow, USN.)

African Repatriation
Both President Lincoln and abolitionist Harriet Beecher Stowe, author of *Uncle Tom's Cabin,* toyed with the idea of repatriating the slaves to Africa. (See: Stowe, Harriet Beecher.)

Age of Soldiers, Average
The average age of Union soldiers was in the midtwenties. Most Billy Yanks ranged in age from 18 to 45, although some boys not yet in their teens managed to enlist. A few old men in their sixties or seventies also served, if only briefly, before their age and infirmities caught up with them. Con-

federate records are missing or incomplete, but the ages of
Johnny Rebs are known to have been in the same general
range as those of their foe. (See: Clem, Major General John
Lincoln, U.S.)

Air-to-Ground Communication

Information about enemy strength and troop movements was
relayed from the air to friendly forces on the ground for the
first time during the Civil War. Aeronauts communicated intelligence through telegraph wires attached to the baskets on
hot air balloons. (See: Balloons, Hot Air; and Telegraph.)

Alabama, CSS

The most notoriously successful commerce raider of the
war, the CSS *Alabama,* sailed the globe, gorging itself on
spoils from the Union's merchant fleet. Captain Raphael
Semmes was hobbled by an international crew that included
more mercenary adventurers than Southerners, and their reluctance to submit to strong discipline created problems during engagements with enemy warships. During a 22-month,
75,000-mile voyage touching in ports in Asia, Africa, South
America, North America, the Caribbean, and Europe the *Alabama* nevertheless captured 65 Union merchantmen, including 52 that were burned. By June 1864, the *Alabama*'s
boilers were burned out, her seams were splitting, and she
was badly in need of repair. Captain Semmes sailed his ship
to Cherbourg, France, sent 38 prisoners ashore, and requested permission from authorities to put the ship in dry
dock. (See: *Alabama,* CSS, and *Kearsarge,* USS, Battle of;
Semmes, Captain Raphael, CSN; and Winslow, Rear Admiral John A., USN.)

Alabama, CSS, and *Kearsarge,* USS, Battle of

It was like a picnic for the French who crowded Cherbourg
in June 1864 to watch the fun and root for the Rebels when
the *Alabama* sailed out of the harbor to do battle with the
Kearsarge. But it soon became hellish aboard the *Alabama.*
Commanded by Captain John A. Winslow, the *Kearsarge*

had sailed 300 miles from the Dutch coast in response to an alert from the U.S. minister in Paris and a bold challenge from Semmes delivered through the Confederate agent in Cherbourg to show up for a fight. It was an uneven battle, even though the *Alabama* drew first blood with a salvo of broadsides that disabled a gun crew. A third or more of the Confederate shells that struck the enemy ship failed to explode, and the *Kearsarge* began raking the *Alabama* with 11-inch shells that blew sailors to pieces, ripped away cannon, and tore gaping holes in the sides and superstructure. Injured in the right hand, Semmes was afraid his ship was about to sink when he ordered his executive officer, First Lieutenant John McIntosh Kell, to steer for the coast. It was too late, and when Kell told his superior that the stricken ship couldn't last another ten minutes, Semmes ordered him to haul down the colors. Winslow was suspicious and called for one more ghastly broadside before the *Alabama* ran up a white flag and boats from the *Kearsarge* and nearby civilian craft began picking up survivors and the dead. Captain Semmes and Lieutenant Kell were rescued by an English steam yacht, hidden from the Union sailors, and released in England. The notorious Confederate raider slipped beneath the waves at 12:24 P.M., just 90 minutes after the battle began. The *Alabama* suffered 43 casualties, about half of the deaths during battle or from drowning. One sailor aboard the *Kearsarge* died, and two were wounded. (See: *Alabama,* CSS; Semmes, Captain Raphael, CSN; and Winslow, Rear Admiral John A., USN.)

Albemarle, CSS

The Confederate ram was threatening the Union blockade in Albemarle Sound, North Carolina, in October 1864 when navy lieutenant William B. Cushing led a handpicked squad of Yankee volunteers up the Roanoke River in a 30-foot launch to sink the Southern ironside with a spar torpedo. Confederate sentries spotted the boat and opened fire at about 3:00 A.M., but Cushing crashed it over a log barrier, lowered the spar, pushed the torpedo under the ship, and pulled a lanyard to trigger an explosion. Both the ironclad and the launch were sunk, and Cushing was one of only two Union sallors who escaped capture or death. (See: Plymouth, Battle of; and Spar Torpedoes.)

Alcatraz
Several hundred captured Confederates were held at the fort and prison in San Francisco Bay.

Alexander, Brigadier General Edward Porter, CS
An engineer and expert artillerist, Alexander was a West Pointer who campaigned with the U.S. Army in the Utah Territory before resigning his commission to fight for the Confederacy. He served as a signal officer under General Beauregard at First Bull Run, fought with Stonewall Jackson at Chancellorsville, was chief of artillery for General James Longstreet, and participated in the Battle of Gettysburg and the Siege of Knoxville. In 1864 Alexander was promoted to brigadier general, becoming one of only three Confederate generals who were artillery officers. Alexander fought at Spotsylvania and Cold Harbor and was seriously wounded at the Crater. He survived the war and went into the railroad business. (See: Wig-Wag Signaling.)

Allen, Brigadier General Henry Watkins, CS
A native Virginian, Allen made his mark as a politician in Louisiana and as an implacable warrior for the Confederacy. After fighting in the War for Texas Independence as a volunteer, studying law, teaching school, and becoming a planter, he was elected a Mississippi state representative. He later moved to Louisiana, where he was also elected to the state legislature. When the Civil War broke out, he enlisted in the infantry as a private but was quickly elected lieutenant colonel of the 4th Louisiana Infantry. Allen was a colonel when he refused to leave the field at Shiloh, despite suffering a serious facial wound. In action again at the defense of Baton Rouge, he was wounded in both legs and one was so badly

shattered by a shell fragment that surgeons were prepared to amputate before he forbade the operation. But the damage was so severe that he used crutches for the rest of his life. Allen was promoted to brigadier general on August 19, 1863, and transferred to the Trans-Mississippi Department, where he proved his ability as an administrator, working to shore up the shattered economy of the area. Elected Louisiana governor, he served in the civilian job as chief executive while retaining his military rank until the end of the war. Allen, who had advocated freeing the slaves and arming them to fight the Union, initially opposed surrender but finally helped negotiate the capitulation of troops under General Edmund Kirby Smith. Smith was leader of the last significant force of Confederate soldiers still in the field. Then Allen fled to Mexico, where he established and edited an English-language newspaper until his death on April 22, 1866. (See: Smith, General Edmund Kirby, CS.)

Allen, Major General Robert, U.S.

A West Point graduate and Mexican War veteran, this native Ohioan served the Union as a major and colonel before being promoted to brigadier general in May 1862. He served as chief quartermaster in the Department of Missouri and quartermaster for the Mississippi Valley, then became quartermaster for all areas west of the Mississippi River.

Alvord, Brigadier General Benjamin, U.S.

A graduate and instructor at West Point who was also a paymaster, Alvord served in the Mexican War and the Seminole Wars. In April 1862 the native Vermonter was appointed brigadier general of volunteers, and he commanded the District of Oregon until March 1865.

Ambulance Corps

With thousands of gravely ill and wounded on both sides of the conflict, ambulance corps were organized to carry the helpless men to field hospitals and surgeons in the rear. Most of the corpsmen were boys or men who were too short or considered otherwise unfit for combat, and they came to their jobs with no formal training. Litter bearers who were as physically run-down and exhausted as the men they were trying to help often jostled or dropped the wounded, adding to the pain and injuries. Ambulances were horse-drawn two-wheel carts or crowded four-wheel open wagons with a canvas over the top to shield the sick and injured from the sun and dust. The wagons often had poor springs, and reckless drivers could make the ride to the rear an excruciatingly painful ordeal capable of rattling the remaining life out of patients. Hospital stewards assigned to aid stations had a smattering of specialized medical training that helped them assist surgeons and tend the wounded.

Ames, Major General Adelbert, U.S.

A West Point graduate and recipient of the Medal of Honor, Ames was a lieutenant of artillery at the First Battle of Bull Run. He was also assigned to the defense of Washington, served in the Peninsular Campaign, fought with the 20th Maine at Antietam and Fredericksburg, and was as an aide to General George G. Meade at Chancellorsville. Appointed a brigadier general of volunteers, Ames commanded a brigade at Gettysburg, was with the X Corps at Charleston, and led a brigade at Cold Harbor and Petersburg and a division at Fort Fisher. Ames was brevetted major general U.S. Volunteers on January 15, 1865, and major general U.S. Army on March 13, 1865. After the war he was provisional governor of Mississippi, served as a U.S. senator and state governor, and fought in the Spanish-American War. Ames died in 1933 at age 97 and was the last surviving Civil War general from either army.

Ammen, Brigadier General Jacob, U.S.

A graduate and instructor at West Point, this native Virginian fought in the Western Virginia Campaign, at Shiloh and Corinth. He was named a brigadier general of volunteers in 1862 and served on court-martial boards and in garrison commands.

Amputation

Amputation was the treatment of choice for most badly broken, lacerated or shattered limbs during the war, and so many arms and legs were severed by surgeons that they stacked up like cordwood until permanently disposed of. U.S. Army records show that almost 29,000 amputations were performed on Federal soldiers and sailors and about 7,000 of the patients died. Among the chief reasons for the high death rate were infection and gangrene, stemming from lack of knowledge on the part of the mid-nineteenth-century surgeons of the importance of clean, sterile surgical tools and hands. Only about 200 Bluecoats who had finger amputations died, but the bigger the limb the worse the chances of survival, and more than half the men who lost their legs died after surgery. Some field surgeons became so proficient that they could saw and cut off an arm or a leg in less than two minutes while the screaming patient was held down by a couple of strong orderlies. Injured Confederates endured amputations at an at least similar rate, and although records are scarce, probably suffered an even larger percentage of deaths after going under the surgeon's knife because of the critical shortage of care and facilities. Stonewall Jackson, one of the South's most gallant and skillful generals, died of pneumonia in a Richmond hospital after his left arm was amputated following the Battle of Chancellorsville. (See: Anesthetics; Jackson, Lieutenant General Thomas Jonathan "Stonewall," CS; and Minié Balls.)

Anaconda Plan

A strategy devised by Commanding General of the Union Army Winfield Scott at the beginning of the war that called for strangling the Rebels into submission by cutting off their supply lines and bringing them back into the fold with a minimum of bloodshed became known as the Anaconda Plan. As outlined to the protégé of President Abraham Lincoln, Scott, and Major General George B. McClellan, the plan focused on cutting off foreign commerce with a coastal blockade of Southern ports; taking control of the Mississippi River from

Cairo, Illinois, to the Gulf of Mexico with gunboats and 60,000 troops; and destroying the Confederate government by capturing the capital at Richmond. Scott's plan to squeeze the South into submission was considered by more militant Unionists too passive, and it was not wholly adopted at the time. But the first element of the plan was put into place on April 19, 1861, only six days after the surrender of Fort Sumter, by declaring a formal blockade of Southern ports extending along the Atlantic coast from South Carolina to Florida and along the Gulf Coast to the Mexican border. A few days later, after Virginia and North Carolina prepared to secede, the blockade was extended north to the Potomac River. Nearly three years of bloody warfare ensued before other similar, more aggressive elements of the original plan were employed by General Ulysses S. Grant, who kept the major Confederate forces tied up in Virginia and Tennessee while Major General William T. Sherman's fast-moving troops split the South with their destructive march through Georgia to the sea. (See: Boa Constrictor Plan; Scott, Lieutenant General Winfield, U.S.; and Sherman, Major General William Tecumseh, U.S.)

Anderson, Brigadier General Robert Houston, CS

After graduation from West Point, this Savannah native was assigned to duty in Upper New York State, then at Fort Walla Walla in the Washington Territory as an infantry lieutenant. As secession approached, Anderson switched to the Confederacy and was commissioned as a lieutenant in the artillery. In September 1861, he was promoted to major and named assistant adjutant general to Major General W. H. T. Walker of the Georgia State troops. Anderson fought at Fort McAllister in coastal Georgia before transferring to line duty and being promoted to colonel of the 5th Georgia Cavalry. On July 26, 1864, he was commissioned brigadier general. Attached to the Army of Tennessee as a cavalryman, he fought in the Atlanta Campaign. When Brigadier General John H. Kelly was killed near Franklin, Tennessee, Anderson temporarily assumed the division's command, but he resumed his former role as a brigade commander after the fall of Atlanta. He led his brigade against the Federals through the march to the sea and the Carolinas Campaign. After surrender, he became police chief of Savannah.

Anderson, Lieutenant Edwin Maffitt, CSN

Closely related to other famous Confederate Navy officers, Anderson served with Captain Raphael Semmes aboard the shipping raiders CSS *Alabama* and CSS *Sumter*. He was also acting master of the blockade runner CSS *Owl*. (See: *Alabama*, CSS; Semmes, Captain Raphael, CSN; and *Sumter*, CSS.)

Anderson, Lieutenant General Richard Heron, CS

"Fighting Dick" graduated from West Point and from the U.S. Army Cavalry School at Carlisle, Pennsylvania, before being posted to the Western territories. During the Mexican War he was brevetted first lieutenant for meritorious conduct. When Anderson's home state of South Carolina seceded, he resigned his commission to fight for the Confederacy. Appointed colonel of the 1st South Carolina Infantry, he served at the siege of Fort Sumter, then succeeded Brigadier General Beauregard as commander at Charleston. Anderson was promoted to brigadier general on July 18, 1861, and became senior aide to General Braxton Bragg during the Pennsylvania Campaign of 1862. He fought at Seven Pines, Gaines's Mill, and Malvern Hill. In July 1862, he was promoted to major general, and he led troops at Second Bull Run, Antietam, Fredericksburg, Chancellorsville, Gettysburg, Spotsylvania, and Cold Harbor. He had been advanced to the rank of lieutenant general when his command was shattered at the Battle of Sayler's Creek. When he returned to Richmond there was no command befitting his rank and he was relieved of duty the day before the Confederate surrender at Appomattox Courthouse.

Anderson, Major General James Patton, CS

A Tennessee native, Anderson was a man of many talents who was a physician, fought in the Mexican War, and served as a Mississippi state legislator, U.S. marshal in the Washington Territory, congressman, and was a Florida plantation owner before becoming a delegate to the Florida state secession convention. Anderson was commissioned as an army colonel in the Confederate Army but quickly rose to brigadier general. He fought at the Battle of Shiloh and commanded the Army of Tennessee during the Kentucky campaign and the Battle of Perryville. Anderson also fought at Stone's River, Chickamauga, and Chattanooga before promotion to major general on February 17, 1864. After briefly commanding the Confederate District of Florida, he returned to the Army of Tennessee, fighting at Ezra Church, Utoy Creek, and the Battle of Jonesboro, where he suffered a serious chest injury and was removed from command. Ignoring doctors' orders, he rejoined his troops and fought through their final battles in the Carolinas until the end of the war.

Anderson, Major General Robert, U.S.

This 1825 graduate of West Point from Kentucky who firmly supported the Union even though he was strongly proslavery became the North's first hero of the war after surrendering Fort Sumter. Anderson, who fought in the Black Hawk War, Seminole Wars, and Mexican War, was a major with the 1st Artillery when he was posted to Charleston on November 15, 1860. On December 26, Anderson reacted to South Carolina's secession by secretly moving his two-company garrison past Rebel picket boats in the dead of night from the nearly indefensible Fort Moultrie to the unfinished but stronger Fort Sumter in the middle of Charleston Harbor. In January 1861, he was under orders not to engage Confederate artillery as it fired upon the Union relief ship *Star of the West*. But during the bombardment of Fort Sumter on April 12–13 he held on for two days until lack of ammunition and food forced him to surrender. Although Anderson considered himself a failure for having been unable to prevent the war, he was appointed brigadier general on May 15, 1861, then placed in command of the Department of Kentucky. He continued in command when the department was merged with the Department of the Cumberland but was relieved of field duties after his health began to fail and worked at various assignments in the North. Anderson retired from the army on October 27, 1863, and was brevetted major general for his performance at Fort Sumter. When the Union recaptured Fort Sumter, he raised the Stars and Stripes. (See: Fort Moultrie; and Fort Sumter.)

Anderson, William T. "Bloody Bill"

One of the most notorious of the Border Ruffians who terrorized Missouri during the Civil War years, Bloody Bill had a pathological hatred of Union soldiers and Northern sympathizers. Although he enlisted with William Clarke Quantrill's irregular partisan raiders, Anderson later broke away to command his own ruthless band of 60 to 70 cutthroats. Riding at the head of the band with a string of scalps around his neck, he ravaged the Missouri countryside, burning homes, razing towns, murdering settlers, and cold-bloodedly executing captured Union soldiers. Scalpings, torture, cold-blooded executions, and other crimes were excused by the mounted terrorists as being justified by the Southern cause. Anderson met rough justice on October 27, 1864, when he was ambushed by Captain Samuel P. Cox, leading a contingent of Missouri State Militia, and riddled with bullets. Anderson's body was taken to nearby Richmond, where he was decapitated and his head impaled on a telegraph pole. Anderson's headless corpse was roped to a horse and dragged along the dusty streets, then dumped into an unmarked grave. (See: Centralia Massacre; Lawrence Massacre; and Quantrill, Colonel William Clarke, CS.)

Andersonville Prison

This huge prison in Sumter County, Georgia, became synonymous with brutality and horror after it was liberated by Federal troops during the closing days of the war. Emaciated survivors told stories of ghastly treatment by the brutal prison commander Captain Heinrich "Henry" Wirz, and investigators pieced together a shocking picture of starvation and endemic disease that claimed the lives of 13,000 prisoners. That meant a death rate of approximately 29 percent. The sprawling prison in southwest Georgia grew up almost overnight, until at its most crowded it held a wretched army of 33,000 Federal soldiers—a population that was exceeded by only four cities in the Confederacy. The grossly overcrowded prison was established to move Federal captives held at Richmond, Virginia, where the main prison was previously located, farther away from Union forces and to relieve the Confederate capital's critical food shortage. Prisoners began arriving at the camp, which initially covered 16 acres and was surrounded by a 15-foot-tall stockade, in February 1864. Although originally designed to hold 10,000 men, even after the camp was expanded to 26 acres it was soon jammed with three times that number. At its peak, nearly 400 prisoners were arriving at the camp every day. Critically short of food and medical supplies for its own troops and civilians, the rapidly crumbling Confederacy found it almost impossible to adequately feed, shelter, and provide health care for the prisoners. Proper sanitation was nonexistent, and the only freshwater for prisoners and guards was provided by Stockade Creek, a small stream that trickled through the prison yard. Waste was routinely dumped upstream, and downstream the creek was used as the prisoners' latrine. After the death from exhaustion of the first camp commander, Brigadier General John Henry Winder, helpless prisoners were routinely brutalized by guards and the sadistic, Bluecoat-hating new commandant, "Henry" Wirz. (See: Old Capitol Prison; Winder, Brigadier General John Henry, CS; and Wirz, Captain Heinrich "Henry," CS.)

Andrews, Brigadier General George Leonard, U.S.

After graduating first in his West Point class of 1851, this Massachusetts native supervised construction of fortifications in Boston Harbor before returning to his alma mater to teach. He returned to civilian life in 1855 to work as a civil engineer until he was commissioned as a lieutenant colonel at the beginning of the Civil War. Promoted to colonel, he led the 2d Massachusetts Regiment in the Shenandoah Valley and was in command of the rear guard during the retreat at Cedar Mountain. He served under General John Pope and fought at Antietam, was cited for bravery, and promoted to brigadier general. He later commanded a brigade while with General N. P. Banks and for more than eighteen months commanded the Corps d'Afrique. On March 26, 1865, he was brevetted major general of volunteers for distinguished service at Mobile, Alabama. After the war he served as U.S. marshal for Massachusetts and later accepted a teaching position at West Point.

Andrews, John

Governor of Massachusetts from 1861 to 1866, this Boston lawyer was a firm abolitionist and was strongly dedicated to recruiting black regiments for the Union. Andrews established the 5th Massachusetts (Colored) Cavalry and the 54th Massachusetts (Colored) and 55th Massachusetts (Colored) Infantry regiments. (See: Black Enlistment, Union.)

Anesthetics

Although great strides in development of painkillers and anesthesia were just over the horizon, it was still a primitive area of science during the Civil War, and soldiers often experienced incredible agony while being treated for injuries. Patients facing major surgery were lucky if they were in a field hospital or a medical facility in some nearby city where they could be put to sleep with chloroform, ether, or nitrous oxide. If they were at an aid station or battlefield hospital just behind the lines, they most often had to be satisfied with a stiff shot of whiskey or were told to bite down on a bullet or piece of cloth while the surgeon went about his grisly work with knife and saw. (See: Amputation; and Minié Ball.)

Angel of Fredericksburg

Nearly 6,300 Union soldiers had fallen at Fredericksburg in a disastrous frontal attack that was shattered by a surprisingly strong force of well-dug-in Confederates when help for wounded and dying came from an unexpected source. Richard R. Kirkland, a 19-year-old sergeant from South Carolina, was so touched by the pitiful cries of the injured men throughout the long December night that just after dawn the next morning he could stand it no longer. "Sir, I'd like to take those boys water," he told his commander. The commander's reply was blunt and to the point: "Son, you're a dang fool." But Kirkland got the permission he needed, and in minutes he was gathering up canteens. Moments later he leaped over the entrenchments, disregarding a hail of gunfire from startled Federals, and raced to the nearest wounded soldier. As the young Rebel leaned over and raised the canteen to the moaning Yankee's lips, the Union commander raised his arm and shouted to his troops, "Don't shoot that man. He's too brave to die!" Kirkland moved from one dying soldier to another, giving them water, whispering words of comfort, and covering one man with his own overcoat. When he had finally helped all those he could and turned to go back to his own lines, soldiers on both sides cheered. The Angel of Fredericksburg was killed less than a year later at the Battle of Chickamauga. (See: Fredericksburg, Battle of.)

Angel of the Battlefield

See: Barton, Clara Harlowe.

Antiaircraft Fire

The first antiaircraft fire in military history was directed at observation balloons when Confederate major E. P. Alexander elevated his artillery to fire at the airborne enemy during the Civil War. Both sides were known to camouflage their batteries and wait for balloons to drift nearby, then open up with artillery. Tom Rosser's battery of New Orleans's Washington artillery reportedly shot down one of General McClellan's balloons, but most Civil War historians say there is no record to back up the claim. There is no firm evidence that balloons were shot out of the sky by either side or that any daredevil aeronaut was killed by enemy fire. (See: Balloons, Hot Air.)

Antietam, Battle of

Robert E. Lee's first attempt to invade the North and capture the capital of Pennsylvania at Harrisburg ended on September 17, 1862, in the bloody Battle of Antietam. By a crippling stroke of bad luck, a copy of Lee's plans to split his forces and protect his supply lines through the Shenandoah Valley by sending Stonewall Jackson to take Harpers Ferry before rejoining the rest of the army for the march through Maryland into Pennsylvania fell into Union hands. The monumental blunder presented Union commander General George B. McClellan with a golden opportunity to win the war in 24 hours, but typically he frittered away his chances. McClellan waited until the next day to order his 90,000-man army to move against the Confederates, and by that time J. E. B. "Jeb" Stuart had notified Lee about the lost orders. Lee quickly assembled 19,000 men from General James Longstreet's division along the banks of Antietam Creek at the town of Sharpsburg. Major General Stonewall Jackson, who had just taken Harpers Ferry from a strong Union garrison, joined Lee with another 22,000 battle-hardened veterans. By the time the attack was finally launched, Confederate forces had more than doubled to 41,000 men. Jackson's men, including a division of Texans under General John B. Hood, met the initial charge with 8,700 men of General Joseph Hooker's Army I Corps in a cornfield, badly bloodying the Union troops. As fighting spread across the battlefield, first one side, then the other took the advantage, but the Confederate forces were gradually being drained by the overwhelming numbers of Union troops. By midafternoon a Union corps led by General Ambrose E. Burnside capped a costly daylong struggle by forcing its way across a bridge over Antietam Creek, pushing the Rebels back to a road leading to one of the shallowest areas of the Potomac River. The Fed-

erals appeared to have yet another opportunity to destroy
Lee's army, this time by shutting off the only escape route
across the river. But the opportunity was lost at the last mo-
ment by the timely arrival on Burnside's flank of General
Ambrose P. Hill with a division that Jackson had left to guard
Federal prisoners at Harpers Ferry. The fresh Confederate
force saved the day by driving Burnside's exhausted troops
back to the bridge. McClellan still had a tremendous advantage in men and equipment and at the end of the day lost yet
one last chance to crush Lee with a final assault and put an
end to the Southerner's march on the North. Typical of his reluctance to pursue and destroy retreating enemy forces, the
Union general failed to follow through. At the conclusion of
the bloody daylong battle, the Union had 12,350 casualties;
the Confederates, 13,700. Although basically a draw from a
purely military standpoint, the battle had halted Lee's first
Northern invasion and stifled Southern hopes of attracting
European intervention to put a stop to the war and guarantee
independence for the Confederacy.

Appalachians
This mighty mountain chain was the natural barrier that
divided North America into two theaters of war, the East and
West.

Appomattox Court House
If the condition of the uniforms of the two military commanders who met at Appomattox Court House on April 9, 1865,
told the story of winner and loser, General Lee would have
been the victor and General Grant would have been humbled
in defeat. Lee wore a clean, neatly pressed uniform set off
with his dress sword and a brilliant scarlet sash. Grant wore
the mud-smeared blouse of a Yankee private with the sewn-
on stars of a general. But it was Lee who was surrendering
his tattered and beaten Army of Northern Virginia to the
Union commander in chief. The Yankee victor, who earned
a reputation earlier in the war as "Unconditional Surrender
Grant," was surprisingly considerate. He proposed that Lee

order his men to surrender their arms and military supplies, while officers would be permitted to keep their swords and horses. When Lee asked that enlisted men be permitted to keep any horses they owned so they could be used for plowing and other civilian chores, Grant readily agreed. He also ordered that food rations be immediately distributed to the hungry Southerners, and told his own soldiers to cease firing their weapons to celebrate the surrender. Grant explained: "The rebels are our countrymen again." (See: McLean, Wilmer; and Unconditional Surrender Grant.)

Appomattox Station, Battle of

Time was rapidly running out for General Lee's tattered Army of Northern Virginia and the Confederacy when Union cavalry captured four trains filled with supplies for the hungry Rebel troops on the evening of April 8, 1865. After a brief skirmish nearby, the Yankees also captured 25 Confederate cannon and part of a wagon train.

Archer, Brigadier General James Jay, CS

After volunteering for the Mexican War, Archer was cited for gallantry at Chapoultepec and joined the regular army in 1855 with the rank of captain in the 9th Infantry. Resigning his commission at the outbreak of the Civil War, Archer was named a colonel of the 5th Texas. As part of a mixed brigade of Texans and Georgians under General John Bell Hood, Archer and the 5th Texas fought in the Peninsular Campaign. On June 3, 1862, after seeing action at Etham's Landing and Seven Pines, Archer was promoted to brigadier general. He was placed in command of three regiments, and in 1862 his brigade combined with five others to form the Light Division led by Major General Ambrose P. Hill. Archer led his brigade in the Seven Days Campaign, at Cedar Mountain, and at Second Bull Run. By September 1862 he was being troubled by ill health, and when the Light Division arrived at Antietam he was too sick to ride. So he directed his brigade from an ambulance while they broke through the Union flank and re-

captured a Rebel battery. Three days later Archer teamed up
with Brigadier General William D. Pender to defeat Union
pursuers, bringing an end to the Antietam Campaign. Still
ailing, Archer led his troops to victories at Fredericksburg
and at Chancellorsville. He and most of his troops were part
of a new division led by Major General Henry Heth when
Archer was captured and became the first general officer
taken prisoner since General Lee became the army's commander in chief. Archer was exchanged in mid-1864 after
imprisonment at Johnson's Island in Lake Erie and briefly
commanded two brigades. But his health continued to dete-
riorate, especially during imprisonment, and he died in Richmond on October 24, 1864. (See: Horses and Mules; and
Maloney, Private Patrick, U.S.)

Arlington National Cemetery

After Robert E. Lee resigned his U.S. Army commission to
fight for the Confederacy, his ancestral home just across the
Potomac River from Washington, D.C., was seized by the
Union Army. The U.S. government justified the seizure by
citing a law that required owners to show up in person to pay
their property tax. Lee owed $92.02. His mansion was used
as a headquarters for the supervision of Washington's defense, and in the spring of 1864 the expansive landholdings
were chosen by Quartermaster General Montgomery Meigs
as the location for a new national military cemetery. (See:
Meigs, General Montgomery C., U.S.)

Armistead, Brigadier General
Lewis Addison, CS

The son of a U.S. Army officer, Armistead was kicked out of
West Point after breaking a plate over the head of fellow
cadet Jubal A. Early. Despite that setback, the feisty North
Carolinian was commissioned as a lieutenant in the 6th U.S.
Infantry and brevetted three times for bravery during the
Seminole Wars. He was a widower in 1861 when he accepted
a commission in the Confederate Army, and eventually, after
his promotion to colonel, his only son served as his aide

Armistead was promoted to brigadier general on April 1, 1862, and fought gallantly at Seven Pines and in the Seven Days Battles before participating in the Battle of Gettysburg. With a yell of, "Boys, give them cold steel," Armistead led 150 men over Union breastworks during Pickett's Charge, and he temporarily broke through a line of Pennsylvanians under Brigadier General Alexander Webb. As the battle raged along the line, Armistead was killed leading his men in a headlong charge into the muzzles of a Union battery. (See: Early, Lieutenant General Jubal Anderson, CS; Malvern Hill, Battle of; and Pickett's Charge.)

Armstrong, Brigadier General Frank, CS
Before becoming a Confederate general, Armstrong led Federal cavalry troops as a captain at First Bull Run.

Army of Northern Virginia
When Robert E. Lee relieved the critically wounded General Joseph E. Johnston as commander of Confederate forces on May 31, 1862, he inherited an army that had been hastily cobbled together with bits and pieces from here and there. Lee consolidated the command, stepped up training, and named his new fighting force the Army of Northern Virginia. (See: Lee, General Robert E., CS.)

Army of Ohio
This army was renamed the Army of the Cumberland when Union major general Ambrose E. Burnside assumed command. (See: Burnside, Major General Ambrose Everett, U.S.)

Army Pay
Both the North and the South were in the grip of economic recessions when the war began, and army pay, as meager as it was, helped attract some jobless recruits on both sides. At the beginning of the war, Union privates marched and fought for a mere $13 a month. Rebel privates were recruited for $11 a month.

Army of the Potomac

After the demoralizing Union defeat at First Bull Run, President Lincoln named Major General George B. McClellan to command the forces protecting the capital. Called the young Napoleon by a fawning press, McClellan whipped the dispirited Billy Yanks into shape and named the 130,000-man fighting force the Army of the Potomac. In four years of fighting, the Army of the Potomac suffered the highest casualty rate of any Union troops. (See: McClellan, Major General George Brinton, U.S.)

Army of Tennessee, Confederate

Formed on November 20, 1862, by merging General Braxton Bragg's Army of Mississippi with General Edmund Kirby Smith's Army of Kentucky, the Army of Tennessee was the Confederacy's principal army in the Western Theater. After undergoing various reorganizations under different leaders, the army was being led by General Joseph E. Johnston for the second time and fighting in North Carolina when hostilities were formally ended on April 18, 1865.

Army of the Tennessee, Union

The Union's Army of the Tennessee was named after the Tennessee River, not the state. Thus the word *the* differentiates it from the Confederate Army of Tennessee, which was named after the state.

Army of the Valley

Short on troops to defend Richmond, General Robert E. Lee detached Lieutenant General Jubal Early's 2d Corps from the Army of Northern Virginia in 1864 and renamed it the Army of the Valley. Then Lee ordered Early to use his forces to keep the Yankees in the Shenandoah Valley off balance, throw an invasion scare into Washington, and gather up supplies from the enemy and the countryside to send to the Army of Northern Virginia in Petersburg. (See: Early, Lieutenant General Jubal Anderson, CS.)

Army of West Virginia

Famous Indian fighter George Crook commanded the Army of West Virginia and used many of the unconventional warfare techniques he learned on the frontier in his war against the Confederates. (See: Blazer's Scouts; and Crook, Major General George, U.S.)

Ashby, Brigadier General Turner, CS

After John Brown's ill-fated raid on Harpers Ferry, Ashby raised a company of volunteer cavalry in his native Virginia to patrol the Potomac River and guard against future attacks. But when his state seceded from the Union, the hardworking farmer became a partisan raider for the Confederacy and once disguised himself, then sneaked into Chambersburg, Pennsylvania, to gather information about enemy forces. A few weeks into the war, he was commissioned as a captain and he and his volunteers became part of the Confederate Army's 7th Virginia Cavalry Regiment. Quickly promoted to colonel, Ashby was known as an easygoing leader and was well liked and respected by his men. But he turned into a vengeful Yankee hater after his brother, Captain Richard Ashby, was killed in a clash with a Union patrol. In the spring of 1862 Ashby was named by Stonewall Jackson to the command of all Confederate cavalry in the Shenandoah Valley and was promoted to brigadier general. On June 6, 1862, Ashby was covering a Confederate retreat up the valley when he repulsed an attack and set up an ambush that led to the capture of Union general Sir Percy Wyndham. Ashby was later preparing another ambush when he encountered pursuing Yankee troops and his horse was shot from under him. Ashby scrambled to his feet and was urging his men forward when he was shot in the chest and killed. (See: Wyndham, General Sir Percy, U.S.)

Athens, Rape of

Citizens of Athens, Alabama, had the misfortune of crossing a Union colonel known as "the Mad Russian" when they aided partisan guerrillas conducting raids against Don Carlos Buell's Army of the Ohio. Colonel Ivan Turchin was so outraged after learning that civilians forbade blacks to rescue a Union soldier who was roasted alive when he was trapped between the tender and engine of a blown-up train that he told his troops: "I shut my eyes for one hour." On May 3, 1862, three regiments of vengeful Billy Yanks plundered the town, raping women, stealing silverware and jewelry, and setting fires. Turchin was court-martialed and sacked from the army for encouraging the atrocity and for taking his wife along with him to battle. (See: Turchin, Brigadier General Ivan, U.S.; and Turchin, Madam.)

Atlanta, Battle of

After months of bombardment by Union artillery, Atlanta was a wasteland. Civilian residents had gone underground when Sherman sent six corps to make a wide swing around to the south to cut off the last two rail lines into Atlanta and attack the city's vulnerable underbelly. On August 28, after the Federals moved on the Montgomery & Atlanta Railroad, Confederate lieutenant general John Bell Hood ordered an attack on the Union flank at nearby Jonesboro. It was the defenders' last gasp, and after losing a fierce battle Hood ordered his troops out of Atlanta on September 2. The last to leave was the cavalry, which had been given the task of destroying ammunition dumps and a huge rolling mill. The devastated city shook with fire and smoke when seven locomotives and 18 boxcars of ordinance exploded, while the cavalry rode down McDonough Road to rejoin other survivors of Hood's defeated army. The Federals marched into Atlanta the next day. Mayor Calhoun met the Yankees with a white flag and formally surrendered the city to Major General Henry Slocum. (See: Atlanta, Siege of; Hood, Lieutenant General John Bell, CS; McPherson, General James Birdseye, U.S.; and Sherman, Major General William Tecumseh, U.S.)

Atlanta, Siege of

General William Tecumseh Sherman's capture of Atlanta on September 3, 1864, demoralized the shattered South, strengthened the Union's fighting spirit, and practically guaranteed the reelection of President Lincoln. It also deprived the Confederacy of a vital manufacturing, transportation, and communication center deep within its own territory. The Union was fielding a formidable, well-equipped, and veteran army of 100,000 men, with each man firmly committed to Sherman's infamous scorched earth policy of destroying anything and everything that could possibly be used by the South to continue the war. On the other side, the able Confederate general Joseph E. Johnston's 62,000-man Army of Tennessee had neither the manpower nor the supplies and equipment to seek a head-to-head confrontation with Sherman. So Johnston devised a strategy of delay, aimed at holding back the enemy until after the November elections. If all went well, he reasoned, a Lincoln defeat might usher a new president onstage who was willing to talk peace and help negotiate an end to the devastating war. Beginning in early May, Sherman kept Johnston's forces on the run. The Army of Tennessee was forced to fall back from Rocky Face Ridge and Snake Creek Gap around Chattanooga, then was kept on the move after the Battle of Resaca, until Johnston finally formed strong defensive positions at Kennesaw Mountain, a short march from Atlanta. Johnston's forces were firmly dug along the steep, rocky slopes on June 27, when Union troops launched a frontal assault and were massacred by Rebel rifle and cannon fire. Sherman suffered 2,000 casualties and the Southerners just 500, but the Union was capable of absorbing such huge losses. The South's manpower reservoir was depleted, and Confederate casualties couldn't be replaced. Sherman determinedly forced Johnston's battle-weary defenders to continue falling back until they were only seven miles from Atlanta. Then Johnston withdrew even farther south to the Chattahoochee River and ordered his tired army to dig in. Alarmed by the cautious defensive battles being waged by Johnston, Confederate Jefferson F. Davis had him relieved by the far less able General John B. Hood. Hood was unpopular with his troops, but he was aggressive and ordered an attack at Peachtree Creek that cost 2,500 casualties. On July 20, Hood shifted his attack east against forces led by General James B. McPherson and lost another 4,800 irreplaceable men. The Confederate Army of Tennessee was forced to retreat into the city. Two days later the Confederates lost another 8,500 men in the Battle of Atlanta. Sherman followed up the battle, sending Major General Oliver Howard along the western edge of Atlanta with orders to sever communication and transportation lines, leading to the Battle of Ezra Church, which cost the Confederates yet another 2,500 casualties. With the Army of Tennessee whittled down to fewer than 45,000 combat-able men, Hood ordered the survivors to dig in behind the city's defensive lines and wait for the enemy attack. Sherman didn't take the bait by risking a frontal assault and instead laid siege to the city. For more than a month, Atlanta and its vital supply lines were bombarded by Union heavy artillery. Largely due to the valiant efforts of Confederate cavalry commander Joseph Wheeler, sufficient supply lines to keep the army lightly fed and equipped were kept in operation until August 28. On that date, Sherman ordered an attack on the Montgomery & Atlanta Railroad south of the city, and Hood responded with an attack on the Union flank at nearby Jonesboro. The exhausted Rebels lost the battle, and with their last remaining defenses shattered, they pulled out of Atlanta on September 2. Sherman's victorious troops rode and marched into the devastated city the following day. (See: Army of Tennessee, Confederate; Atlanta, Battle of; Ezra Church, Battle of; Hood, Lieutenant General John Bell, CS; Howard, Major General Oliver Otis, U.S.; Johnston, General Joseph Eggleston, CS; Kennesaw Mountain, Battle of; McPherson, General James Birdseye, U.S.; and Sherman, Major General William Tecumseh, U.S.)

Ayres, Major General Romeyn Beck, U.S.
A New York native and West Point graduate, Ayres was on garrison duty in Mexico before beginning his Civil War ser

vice as a captain in the 5th Artillery. He fought at First Bull Run and Antietam, and after promotion to brigadier general saw action at Fredericksburg, Chancellorsville, Gettysburg, the Wilderness, Spotsylvania, Cold Harbor, and Petersburg before being promoted to major general and ending his Civil War service at Appomattox.

B

Babcock, Lieutenant Colonel Orville, U.S.

A Vermont native and West Point graduate, Babcock helped construct defenses around Washington shortly after the beginning of the war, then was promoted to lieutenant colonel and fought at Vicksburg. In January 1864 he became aide-de-camp to General Ulysses S. Grant. After the war, then President Grant appointed Babcock as his personal secretary. When Babcock became involved in a scandal over skimmed whiskey taxes, Grant helped win an acquittal by testifying for him in court.

Bailey, Major General Joseph, U.S.

More than 40 Federal gunboats and transports were saved at the close of the disastrous Red River Campaign by Lieutenant Colonel Bailey's ingenious construction of a series of wing dams that enabled them to cross the rapids near Alexandria, Louisiana. The flotilla was retreating after Union ground forces were chewed up at the Battle of Mansfield, but the water level had dropped so low it was impossible for the boats to make the crossing. Ignoring bad advice from colleagues, the army engineer constructed dams on each side of the river, narrowing the channel to 66 feet and increasing the depth of the water level sufficiently for the flotilla to navigate the rapids. The Ohio native was commissioned as a captain in the Union Army in early 1861 and posted with his regiment to New Orleans. In December 1862, following the city's capture by Union forces, he was appointed acting engineer for New Orleans's defenses. After promotion to major, he joined

General N. P. Banks's Red River Campaign. Bailey was promoted to brigadier general in 1864 in recognition of his accomplishment at Alexandria, and on March 13, 1865, was brevetted to major general of volunteers. (See: Mansfield, Battle of; and Red River Campaign.)

Baker, Brigadier General Alpheus, CS

A native South Carolinian, Baker taught school and studied law before moving to Alabama. At the outbreak of war, he served as a captain with the Eufaula Rifles, then moved to the 1st Alabama Infantry, served briefly at Pensacola, Florida, and late in 1861 moved on to Tennessee. After election as colonel of a mixed regiment of Alabama, Mississippi, and Tennessee troops, he fought in the Battle of New Madrid and was taken prisoner in 1862. After exchange, he became colonel of the 54th Alabama, which he led at the Battle of Vicksburg. In 1863, he was seriously wounded at Champion's Hill but recovered and assumed command of an Alabama brigade. Baker was promoted to brigadier general on March 5, 1864, and fought in the Atlanta Campaign, until he was wounded again at the Battle of Ezra Church. After recovery, Baker was reassigned to the Department of the Gulf and his brigade fought in the Carolinas Campaign until the entire unit was captured at Bentonville, North Carolina.

Baker, Colonel Edward D., U.S.

A better politician than a soldier, Baker's inexperience in military matters cost him his life and helped lead to a humiliating Union defeat at Ball's Bluff. Baker was a U.S. senator from Oregon as well as a close friend of President Lincoln and newcomer to military command when he was put in charge of 1,700 men sent to test Confederate strength on top of the rocky outcrop over the Potomac River. Baker could have been a general, because his presidential pal offered to make the appointment, but he turned down the rank because he worried that it would interfere with his Senate duties. The clash at Ball's Bluff had barely been joined when Baker rejected the advice of a West Pointer to occupy some high ground, only to see Rebels stream into the breach a few minutes later and begin directing withering fire on the Yankees. Baker may have been a military neophyte, but he was no coward and he was boldly standing in no-man's-land between two skirmish lines urging on his men when a redhaired Rebel suddenly loomed in front of him and emptied a revolver into his head. Bluecoats fought hand-to-hand to repel a Confederate charge and recover their fallen leader's body. (See: Ball's Bluff, Battle of.)

Baker, Lafayette C.

Provost marshal of his own counterintelligence corps, Baker got the job by learning and working from the ground up. At the beginning of the war he convinced the Union's general in chief, Winfield Scott, that he had what it took to be a spy and traveled to Richmond posing as an itinerant photographer, carrying a broken camera and with no pictures to show. He was twice arrested by Union pickets and had to appeal to General Scott to obtain his release before he finally made it through Confederate lines, where he was again arrested. After being passed up the chain of command to Jefferson Davis, Baker was allowed to move around on his own. When Confederate authorities in Fredericksburg again accused him of spying, he fled back to the North, where he was rewarded for his information and performance by being put in charge of his own Secret Service agency. Baker became involved in so much political and other intrigue after the war that his agency was eventually disbanded and the country did without a counterespionage operation until 1917, when the Secret Service was revived under a new director.

Baldwin, Brigadier General
William Edwin, CS

A bookstore owner in Columbus, Mississippi, and member of the local militia, Baldwin joined the Confederate Army and was commissioned as a colonel of the 17th Mississippi Infantry. After brief duty at Pensacola, Florida, he was ordered to East Tennessee, then to Central Kentucky. He fought at Fort Donelson, where he was taken prisoner. After exchange, he was promoted to brigadier general and placed in command of a brigade of Mississippi and Tennessee regiments in the Confederate Army of West Tennessee. He was commended for gallantry at Coffeeville, Mississippi, and fought at Fort Gibson and Champion's Hill and in the Vicksburg Campaign. Baldwin was captured and paroled again, then assigned to the District of Mobile. He was killed in a freak accident on February 19, 1864, near Dog River Factory, Alabama, when a broken stirrup caused him to fall from his horse.

Balloons, Hot Air

Observation balloons used to spy on troop movements and obtain other intelligence were a Civil War innovation that played a major role in turning the tide in the Union's favor at the Battle of Fredericksburg. Professor Thadeus Lowe, Chief Aeronaut, Balloon Corps, Union Army, led a small contingent of daring balloonists, and his fleet eventually grew to seven balloons. The balloonists once used another new battlefield innovation, the telegraph, to direct artillery fire on Rebel positions. Curiously, the Union abandoned the Balloon Corps after the Battle of Chancellorsville. The Confederacy also experimented with aerial observation, and the Silk Dress Balloon was the most famous lighter-than-air craft in its fleet. The name was coined from silk dresses donated by Southern women to construct the balloon. It was captured by the Yankees in 1862. (See: Antiaircraft Fire; and *Intrepid*.)

Ballou, Major Sullivan, U.S.

A strong opponent of slavery, Ballou joined the 2d Rhode Island Volunteer Infantry in July 1861, and the regiment became part of Major General Irvin McDowell's campaign to take the Confederate capital of Richmond. On July 21, 1861, only one week into the campaign, Major Ballou was killed when he was struck by a cannonball at the First Battle of Bull Run. Nearly a century and a half later he became famous when a poignant letter he wrote to his wife, Sarah, only one

week before his death was featured in a public television
chronicle about the Civil War.

Ball's Bluff, Battle of

Green Yankee troops dispatched at General McClellan's or-
ders to make a show of force at Confederate positions near
Leesburg, Virginia, met with disaster when they ran into an
almost exactly equal number of battle-hardened Rebels at
Ball's Bluff. Leesburg was only 35 miles up the Potomac
River from Washington, D.C., and McClellan was hopeful of
occupying the area without a fight because the Confederates
had been slowly pulling back from their positions after the
Union's morale-shattering defeat at First Bull Run. The
Union debacle began when an inexperienced captain, Chase
Philbrick, led a scouting party of 20 men from the 15th Massachusetts Infantry on a probe and mistook fog-shrouded
haystacks reflected in the light of a full moon for Rebel
tents. When the faulty information was reported to General
Charles P. Stone, he ordered four companies of the 15th Massachusetts under Colonel Charles Devens to attack the camp.
Devens quickly confirmed there was no Rebel encampment
but was told to maintain his position while additional troops
under the command of Colonel Edward Baker were sent in
as reinforcements. The Rebels weren't in the haystacks, but
they were watching the activity from nearby, and early on the
morning of October 21, 1861, the two forces clashed. The
Southerners were not only more experienced, but they were
better led by a hard-drinking but militarily competent officer,
Colonel Nathan G. Evans. The Yankees were forced back
against the steep, rocky 80-foot-high (Ball's) bluff overlooking the Potomac when their overall commander, Colonel
Baker, was killed. Minutes later the Union retreat was sounded
and the panicked troops fled for their lives. Many who managed to scramble down the bluff drowned when they plunged
into the river and were dragged down by their heavy equipment. Others were picked off by Confederate sharpshooters
firing from the heights, and more than 500 were captured and
marched into nearby Leesburg. The six-hour clash began

with 1,720 Union soldiers and 1,709 Rebels. When the brief, bloody battle ended the Union had taken 921 casualties. The South had 155 casualties, including 36 dead, 117 wounded, and 2 captured. (See: Baker, Colonel Edward D., U.S.; Evans, Brigadier General Nathan G. "Shanks," CS; and Holmes, Colonel Oliver Wendell, Jr., U.S.)

Baltimore Riot, the

Maryland was a slave state when the North and the South began preparing for war, and citizens were so bitterly divided over the issue of secession that the first blood of the conflict was eventually shed in Baltimore. Pro-Confederacy sentiments were strong, and on April 19, 1861, a clash between citizens and soldiers known as the Baltimore Riot broke out when the 6th Massachusetts Regiment entered the city on the way to Washington to defend the nation's capital. Southern sympathizers first forced the soldiers to abandon transports, and when the troops attempted to march through the city the angry mob, led by secessionist rowdies known as "plug uglies," began throwing bricks and rocks. That led to panic, and soldiers fired blindly into the crowd. Most of the Massachusetts volunteers escaped, but they left much of their equipment behind, along with their marching band. Four soldiers and 12 civilians died, dozens were injured, and thousands of dollars in property damage occurred. During and immediately after the riot, telegraph wires to Washington were torn down, railroad bridges leading to Baltimore were ripped up, and state officials demanded that no more Federal soldiers be sent through Maryland. Washington responded by sending a strong force of Federal troops, including the 6th Massachusetts, back to Baltimore the next month. The Bluecoats declared martial law, arrested the police chief and other officials, and began an occupation that continued until the end of the war. (See: Barton, Clara Harlowe; and Border States.)

Bands

Bands performed on the home front to stir patriotism and spur recruitment and were used on the battlefield to inspire the troops. In May 1861 the U.S. War Department approved 24-man brass bands for each infantry or artillery regiment and 16-man bands for cavalry regiments. Confederates also had their own bands, and some nights during the lull between combat, musicians on both sides blended their music for the weary troops on both sides. By July 1862, the U.S. adjutant general ordered the volunteer regimental brass bands disbanded because they cost too much, and most units were left with just their drum corps.

Banks, Major General Nathaniel Prentiss, U.S.

Banks's life was a rags-to-riches story, but he was untrained in military matters and was a much better politician and administrator than battlefield leader. He rose from a job as a bobbin boy in a Massachusetts cotton mill to speaker of the state's lower house, his election as a U.S. congressman and, finally, governor. When the Civil War began, Lincoln appointed him as major general of U.S. Volunteers, which meant that the military neophyte was outranked by only three other officers in the Union Army. The move outraged senior officers because of his total lack of military training or experience. Banks was named to successive command assignments including the Department of Annapolis, Department of the Shenandoah, Military District of the Potomac, and the Army of the Potomac and others. In a face-off with Confederate general Stonewall Jackson in the breadbasket Shenandoah Valley, Banks's troops were so roundly defeated and he lost such a huge cache of supplies to the enemy that the Rebels nicknamed him Commissary Banks. Jackson gave Banks another drubbing at Cedar Mountain, and he fought at Bull Run before being transferred to the West, where he replaced General Benjamin F. Butler as commander at New Orleans. Banks finally succeeded in winning the bloody Siege of Port Hudson, after the fall of Vicksburg made it impossible for the Mississippi River garrison to continue resistance. But his inexperience as a military leader was widely blamed for causing excessive Union casualties during the siege and battles. Banks was soundly defeated by Confederate general Edmund Kirby Smith in his final major campaign, the Red River Expedition. At last replaced by Major General Edward Canby, Banks returned to Congress, where he became an unwavering opponent of President Andrew Johnson's Reconstruction policies. (See: Mansfield, Battle of; Port Hudson, Siege of; Red River Campaign; and Smith, General Edmund Kirby, CS.)

Barksdale, Brigadier General William, CS

A Mexican War veteran and former editor of a proslavery newspaper, Barksdale was a Mississippi congressman before resigning his post in 1861 to become the state quartermaster general. A short time later he was commissioned as a colonel in the 13th Mississippi Regiment, and he fought in many of the major battles during the early months of the war. He led his regiment through the Peninsular Campaign, and, after taking over a brigade command when the previous commander was wounded, was appointed to brigadier general. His original regiment and three others from his home state became known as "Barksdale's Mississippi Brigade." The brigade delayed a Union advance at Fredericksburg, which bought valuable time for General Lee to prepare for the Battle of Chancellorsville. Barksdale was taken prisoner after being critically wounded at Gettysburg and died behind Union lines on July 2, 1863.

Barry, Major General William Farquhar, U.S.

A New Yorker and West Point graduate, Barry served as a lieutenant of artillery on the Canadian border and fought in the Mexican War, Seminole Wars, and Kansas-Missouri Border War. He was promoted to major of artillery at the outbreak of the Civil War and was Brigadier General Irvin McDowell's chief of artillery during First Bull Run. When Barry mistook advancing Confederates for friendly forces, his position was overrun, but he was a courageous leader and rebounded from the error. Promoted to brigadier general, he became chief of artillery for Major General George B. McClellan and organized ordnance for the Army of the Potomac.

During the Peninsular Campaign, Barry fought at Yorktown, Mechanicsville, Gaines's Mill, White Oak Swamp,
and Malvern Hill. Barry later supervised forts and ordnance
surrounding Washington, D.C., then became chief of artillery for Major General William T. Sherman. He fought with
Sherman in Tennessee and during the march to the sea and
the Carolinas campaign.

Bartlett, Brigadier General William, U.S.

Bartlett was one of the few senior officers trapped in the Crater,
where his leg was blown away by a Confederate cannonball
during the siege of Petersburg. Moments later he was sitting
up and giving orders, because the shattered leg was cork. He
had lost his flesh-and-blood leg in an earlier battle. (See:
Crater, Battle of the.)

Barton, Clara Harlowe

The woman known to Union soldiers as "the Angel of the
Battlefield" and who later founded the American Red Cross
had no formal medical training. Her only experience with
patients prior to the Civil War was two years caring for an invalid brother. A onetime schoolteacher, she was a clerk for
the U.S. Patent Office in Washington when she organized a
relief program for volunteers with the 6th Massachusetts
Regiment after they were bloodied in the Baltimore Riot.
When she learned that Union survivors of First Bull Run
were short on medical supplies, she began working with relief agencies and lobbying Washington to improve battlefield
medicine. In 1862 the U.S. surgeon general gave her permission to distribute medical supplies directly to field hospitals
and to nurse the sick and wounded. For the next three years
she risked her life distributing medical supplies and caring
for the sick and injured at the battles of Antietam, Second
Bull Run, Cedar Creek, Fredericksburg, and the Wilderness
and during the Bermuda Hundred Campaign. As the war
wound down she assisted the sick and wounded during
Grant's 1864 offensive in Virginia and in the Carolinas Campaign. Earlier she was appointed superintendent of nurses

with the Army of the James, led by Major General Benjamin F. Butler, and cooked meals for the troops, assisted army surgeons, and comforted the injured. The war was in its final weeks when, at President Lincoln's request, she undertook a new element of soldier aid, organizing a program to list the Union Army and Navy's sick and injured, identify the dead buried in mass graves at Andersonville and at other Confederate prisons, and notify families about the fate of their loved ones. In 1881 she founded the American Red Cross, and she served as head of the organization until 1904, when she retired to her home outside Washington, D.C. (See: Andersonville Prison; and Baltimore Riot.)

Barton, General Seth Maxwell, CS
Born in Fredericksburg, Virginia, Barton entered West Point when he was 15 and after graduation was assigned to frontier duty. In 1861 Captain Barton resigned his U.S. Army commission and was appointed a lieutenant colonel of the Confederacy's 3d Arkansas Infantry. Under the command of General Robert E. Lee, Barton fought at Cheat Mountain and at Greenbrier River, and he served General Stonewall Jackson as chief engineer during the 1862 Shenandoah Valley Campaign. Promoted to brigadier general in 1862, Barton served briefly as a brigade commander in East Tennessee, before being shifted to the Vicksburg operation, where he was taken prisoner. After exchange, he returned east, where he commanded a brigade under Major General George Pickett, who filed a complaint leading to Barton's censure for lack of cooperation. When he was reassigned under General Robert Ransom's command at Drewry's Bluff, the senior officer added his criticism to that of Pickett, and Barton was temporarily relieved of duty. Returned to duty after other officers intervened on his behalf, Barton was named to command of a brigade charged with the defense of Richmond. He was preparing to join the fighting at Sayler's Creek while Lee was arranging the surrender at Appomattox.

Bartow, Brigadier General Francis Stebbins, CS

A planter and slave owner, Bartow was a delegate to the Georgia Secession Convention and was elected to the Provisional Confederate Congress. He was a captain in Savannah's home guard Oglethorpe Light Infantry when the Confederate Congress voted to forbid anyone from simultaneously holding political and military office, so he resigned his congressional position. Bartow participated in the seizure of Fort Pulaski before he was transferred to the 8th Georgia Infantry. Promoted to brigadier general, he was leading his troops in a charge down Henry Hill at First Bull Run on July 21, 1861, when he was mortally wounded.

Bate, Brigadier General William Brimage, CS

Bate left his Tennessee home at 16 to work on a steamboat, then enlisted as a private in the Mexican War. He was mustered out as a lieutenant and worked at several civilian jobs before enlisting in the Confederate Army as a private. He was quickly elected colonel of the 2d Tennessee Infantry and led the regiment at Shiloh, where he suffered a serious leg wound. It was the first of three wounds he would suffer as a soldier. Returning to duty, Bate was promoted to brigadier general and fought with the Army of Tennessee in battles from Tullahoma to Chattanooga. Rejecting a nomination for governor of Tennessee, he was advanced to the rank of major general and fought at Dalton, Georgia, and at Atlanta. Bate also fought at Franklin and Nashville, Tennessee, and was in North Carolina when the Confederate Army of Tennessee surrendered. After the war he served two terms as Tennessee governor and was a U.S. senator when he died in 1905. (See: Horses and Mules.)

Bates, Edward

A St. Louis lawyer and U.S. congressman, Bates was appointed U.S. attorney general in the Lincoln cabinet. Bates, who had freed his own slaves, opposed the war and was against recruitment of black regiments. He favored universal amnesty and restoration of property rights to the Confederates and resigned his office because of disagreement with Lincoln's reconstruction policies.

Battery
The basic unit of artillery in both armies, each battery consisted of four to six guns.

Battle Above the Clouds
General Joseph "Fighting Joe" Hooker's seasoned Army of the Potomac veterans were only expected to make a feint on Lookout Mountain to take pressure off other Union troops during the Battle of Chattanooga, but they ran the Confederates off and captured it instead. The surprise Union victory became known as "the Battle above the Clouds" because much of the fighting occurred high in the clouds, the fog, the mists, and the rain atop the towering mountain and natural fortress that overlooked Chattanooga and the Tennessee River. The battle opened early on the morning of November 24, 1863. The Confederates had constructed strong entrenchments under Lookout Point and it was obvious to Hooker that a frontal attack would badly chew up his men, so he devised an alternative plan to move in from the south, along the side of the mountain. Taking advantage of heavy early-morning fog, about 3,800 men led by Brigadier General John White Geary crossed Lookout Creek at Light's Mill and surprised 42 Confederate pickets. The pickets were captured without firing a shot. Then Geary's troops began scaling the 1,500-foot western slope of the mountain and by about 9:30 A.M. were moving north, climbing over boulders and crossing deep ravines. The main defensive force of about 1,500 men was crouched behind breastworks in a thin defensive line and was still unaware of the approaching Bluecoats. At 11:00 A.M., Geary's men attacked while another 3,400 Union troops splashed across Lookout Creek and struck a line of breastworks just below. The entrenchments were constructed to defend from a frontal assault, and the attack along the side of the mountain took the Rebels totally by sur-

prise. After only a few minutes of fighting, 850 Confederates were taken prisoner and the other defenders were retreating to the Craven house and farm. The Confederates had two cannon there, but the heavy cloud cover and the steep angle of fire severely hindered their effectiveness. The artillerymen were also reluctant to fire because of danger to their own troops, and at the conclusion of a fierce firefight the cannon were captured by the Yankees. By 4:00 P.M. it was raining heavily, and fighting died down while troops on both sides concentrated on warding off the dampness and the cold during the long night. Before daylight the next morning, Yankee volunteers shinnied up the sheer rock face of the palisades to see if the enemy was still there. The Rebels had pulled back, and the fight was over. The victorious Federals hoisted the Stars and Stripes on the heights, where it was visible to the rest of the Union troops in the valley. In an official report, Union quartermaster general Montgomery C. Meigs later gave the bruising conflict its nickname. He wrote that the battle was fought "above the clouds." (See: Bragg, General Braxton, CS; and Chattanooga, Battle of.)

Battle Flag, Confederate

The best-known flag flown or carried during the Civil War was known by the nickname the Red Cross Banner. It neither had anything to do with the Red Cross nor was even an official flag, but it continues even today to be the best-known symbol of the Confederacy. It was designed by General Pierre G. T. Beauregard after the Stars and Bars was mistaken at First Bull Run for the U.S. flag. The familiar flag features a square red field crossed diagonally by two blue bars. Thirteen white stars appear on the blue bars. (See: Cary Sisters; and Stars and Bars.)

"Battle Hymn of the Republic"

This stirring tune became the North's unofficial anthem shortly after the Battle of Gettysburg when it was sung to an audience of dignitaries including Abraham Lincoln, by an army chaplain who had been a Confederate prisoner. The president was so touched by the inspiring lyrics and music that he stood and asked to hear it again. The music was borrowed from a hymn sung in the 1850s at Southern camp meetings and was later popularized when it was incorporated into the marching song "John Brown's Body." Poet Julia Ward Howe, whose husband, Samuel Gridley Howe, published the antislavery newspaper *The Abolitionist,* wrote the lyrics. Julia was in Washington, D.C., when she heard soldiers marching under her hotel window and singing "John Brown's Body." She immediately sat down and composed the song that was to become the North's answer to "Dixie." (See: Brown, John; "Dixie"; and "John Brown's Body.")

Beall, Colonel Lloyd J., CS

A former U.S. Army paymaster, Beall was named commandant of the Confederate Marine Corps even though he had no experience as a marine.

Beauregard, General
Pierre Gustave Toutant, CS

The son of a wealthy Creole Louisiana planter, Beauregard was one of the brightest early stars of the Confederacy. As commander of the Rebel troops that captured Fort Sumter, he became one of the South's first heroes of the war. Beauregard was an excellent student who studied at a French military academy in New York City before he was appointed to West Point. He began his military career as an army engineer and served as a staff officer in the Mexican War before returning to West Point early in 1861 to serve as superintendent. He held the job only five days before he was sacked because of his outspoken secessionist views; then he resigned his commission and returned to Louisiana to fight for the South. When the temperamental officer learned that Braxton Bragg had already been appointed commander of Louisiana's armed forces, he enlisted as a private in the Orleans Guards. But Beauregard's military training, experience, and knowledge were too critically needed to overlook, and he was appointed brigadier general in the Confederate Army. After leading Confederate troops against the Union garrison at Fort Sumter in Charleston Harbor, Beauregard played a key role in achieving the South's first major victory at Bull Run. But like many of his contemporaries in the South's new officer corps, he didn't get along with Jefferson Davis, and the Confederate president loudly criticized Beauregard for failing to pursue the enemy in their panicked retreat to Washington. Davis added more criticism after Beauregard took command following General Albert Johnston's death at the Battle of Shiloh, then lost at Corinth. Banished to Charleston, where he had first gained fame, Beauregard put up a spirited, stubborn defense against numerically superior Union forces intent on retaking Sumter and the valuable harbor. In April 1864 he returned to Virginia, where he commanded the defenses of Richmond and Petersburg. Beauregard turned back a Union advance on the Confederate capital in May, and in June, while commanding only 2,500 men, held off a Union attack on Petersburg until Robert E. Lee was able to come to his aid with reinforcements. Instead of rewarding Beauregard for his stellar performances at Richmond and Petersburg, Davis exiled him once more, this time with an administrative assignment in the West. In 1865, Beauregard once more returned to the East as second-in-command to General Joseph E. Johnston, in the Confederacy's doomed effort to hold back Union general William T. Sherman's march through the Carolinas. At the end of the war, Beauregard turned down military commissions from Romania and Egypt to return to his beloved Louisiana and go into the railroad business.

Beaver Creek, Battle of
An alternate name for the Battle of Mechanicsville. Other names include Beaver Creek Dam and Ellerson's Mill. (See: Mechanicsville, Battle of.)

Bee, Brigadier General Barnard Elliott, CS

Killed at First Bull Run, the first great battle of the war, Bee
is best remembered for his last words, which bestowed a famous nickname on another general. As Bee was attempting
to rally his troops, who were beginning to wilt under a strong
Union assault, he pointed toward General Thomas J. Jackson
and shouted, "Look! There stands Jackson like a stone wall.
Rally behind the Virginians!" (Some military historians say
the correct quote is, "Look at Jackson's brigade! It stands
like a stone wall.") The words were barely out of Bee's mouth
before he was mortally wounded, and he died the next day.
Bee was a seasoned military officer who had served on frontier duty and in the Mexican War, and his experience, ability,
and courage might have made him one of the leading generals of the conflict if he had not been killed so early. (See:
First Bull Run, Battle of; and Jackson, Lieutenant General
Thomas Jonathan "Stonewall," CS.)

Beecher's Bibles

When New England abolitionists grubstaked Free-Soilers
so they could spread out over the Kansas prairie and help
bring the territory into the Union as a free state by packing
the polls, the easterners quickly ran into trouble with proslavery neighbors. The town of Lawrence, established by the
Free-Soilers, was sacked by proslavery forces, and the Free
Staters were badly in need of weapons to protect themselves.
So they were disappointed when a big shipment marked
"Bibles" was sent to them by a prominent preacher and abolitionist leader, the Reverend Henry Ward Beecher. But they
felt better when they pried the boxes open and found not
Bibles but shiny new Sharps rifles. Thereafter, the firearms
were known locally as "Beecher's Bibles." (See: Kansas-
Nebraska Act; and Stowe, Harriet Beecher.)

Beefsteak Raid

Rebel soldiers had been chronically hungry and underfed for
years when Major General Wade Hampton led his cavalry on
a raid behind enemy lines on September 16, 1864, that re-

sulted in the capture of nearly 2 million pounds of beef. The raiders lost only ten men, while capturing 2,468 head of cattle and taking 304 prisoners. (See: Hampton, Lieutenant General Wade III, CS.)

Bell, Mary and Molly, CS
These patriotic Southern sisters served two years with Confederate general Jubal Early's cavalry before they were unmasked as women in October 1864 and sent home. The sisters dressed as men and used the names Tom Parker and Bob Martin.

Benavides, Colonel Santos, CS
The great-great-grandson of the founder of Laredo, Benavides was offered a commission as a Union general early in the war but turned it down to fight for the Confederacy after Texas seceded. After putting down revolts against the Confederacy, he was authorized to organize his own partisan rangers. The highest-ranking Mexican-American in the Confederate Army, Benavides and only 42 soldiers successfully defended Laredo against 200 troops of the Union's First Texas Cavalry. (See: Mexican-Americans, Union.)

Berdan, Major General Hiram, U.S.
A talented gunsmith who invented a musket ball, a repeating rifle, and other weapons of war, Berdan was an expert marksman who trained snipers for the Union Army. The patriotic New York inventor recruited 18 companies of sharpshooters from eight states, which were formed into two regiments at the beginning of the war. He was commissioned as colonel of the 1st United States Sharpshooters, and his snipers dressed in green uniforms to blend in with foliage and brush. They were issued the most up-to-date long-range rifles, all equipped with telescopic sights. Their most commonly used weapon was the .52-caliber breech-loading Sharps, which led to their description as "sharpshooters." But they also used other types of meticulously manufactured weapons, such as the

James target rifle, which an expert marksman could use to
consistently place 12-inch groups in targets at a range of
880 yards. Training was rigorous and Berdan's sharpshooters
were widely used as skirmishers and for special assignments. Berdan held several commands in the Army of the
Potomac, fought in the Seven Days Battles and at Second
Bull Run, and commanded brigades at Chancellorsville and
Gettysburg. Despite his talent and courage, he was considered by many of his peers to be so unfit for command that he
resigned his commission as a major general on January 2,
1864. The patriotic New Yorker then returned to his inventions, developing new weapons of war.

Bethel Church, Battle of

Also known as Big Bethel and Great Bethel, the clash during
the blockade of the Chesapeake Bay was the first land battle
fought in Virginia. On June 10, 1861, Major General Benjamin F. Butler ordered columns from Hampton and Newport News to converge on Rebel outposts at Little Bethel and
Big Bethel. Abandoning Little Bethel, the Confederates fell
back to strong entrenchments at Brick Kiln Creek near Big
Bethel Church. The Union launched a frontal attack and was
repulsed with heavy casualties. The 5th New York Zouaves
then attempted to turn the Rebel left flank after crossing the
creek downstream but were thrown back, and their commander was killed. The badly beaten Union troops returned to
Hampton and Newport News after suffering 87 casualties,
including 79 dead. The Confederates had one man killed and
seven wounded. (See: Butler, Major General Benjamin Freeman, U.S.)

Bible

The life of Sam Houston, Jr., was saved when a Bible in his
breast pocket was struck by a bullet. The bullet stopped exactly at the Seventieth Psalm, which states: "O God: Thou art
my help and deliverer." (See: Houston, Sam, Jr., CS.)

Bivouac

A temporary military encampment or the act of camping out at night.

Black Confederates

The number of blacks who fought or served in other capacities with the Confederacy's armed forces is controversial and ranges from estimates of as few as 13,000 who may have actually seen combat to 95,000 or more in all capacities. Both slaves and free blacks, often of mixed race, took up arms for the South. Cavalry general Nathan Bedford Forrest, who was once a slave trader, had both slaves and free blacks serving under his command. Stonewall Jackson is also known to have had 3,000 blacks in various corps at Antietam. As the Confederacy became increasingly hard-pressed to find fighting men, pressure to allow blacks to serve increased. Major General Patrick Cleburne is believed to have torpedoed his chances for further advancement when he presented a plan to utilize black troops at a meeting of most of the ranking generals in the Confederate Army of Tennessee on the night of January 2, 1864. The proposal was firmly rejected. It was early in 1865, as the war was winding down, before President Jefferson Davis finally granted permission to officially organize black troops to fight for the Confederacy. Long before that time, blacks in Mobile, New Orleans, and other major Southern cities formed into local and state militia units in support of the Lost Cause. They included the Louisiana Native Guards in New Orleans, which was also described in French as the Corps d'Afrique, and the mixed-race Creole Fire Department in Mobile, Alabama. Many individuals and some entire black units reportedly defected to the Union Army.

Black Enlistment, Union

Hesitant to upset the applecart in proslavery border states such as Kentucky and Missouri, President Lincoln waited until late 1862 to authorize full-scale recruitment of black soldiers. After black troops were formed as regiments by in dividual states, the Federal government began to organize and muster United States Colored Troops directly into the Union Army. By the summer of 1863, 14 black regiments were serving in the Union Army and 24 more were being formed. Except for a few junior officers, their commanders were white. Although they were generally resented by their white counterparts and the Confederates refused to recognize them as legitimate soldiers, eventually 176,895 blacks took up arms for the North. More than one-third of those in uniform, 68,100, died, most from disease. Black troops fought in 33 major battles and acquitted themselves bravely. Prior to Lincoln's act authorizing their enlistment, many blacks accompanied the Union Army but worked only as personal servants or ditchdiggers and in other menial tasks. (See: Fort Pillow Massacre.)

Blair, Major General Francis Preston, Jr., U.S.

A rarity among political generals appointed to command because of their powerful connections, when Blair moved from Congress to the battlefield he performed superbly as a division and corps leader. Although Blair had no formal military training, his performance at Chickasaw Bluffs during the Vicksburg Campaign was so impressive that he was publicly praised by Major General William T. Sherman. Both Sherman and General Ulysses S. Grant, who were outspokenly critical of most political generals, later rated Blair as one of the most competent military leaders on either side of the conflict. The brother of Lincoln's first postmaster general, Montgomery Blair, Francis began fighting to preserve the Union long before the war began and played a major role in blocking Missouri's shift to the Confederacy. As a Missouri congressman in May 1861, Blair joined Brigadier General Nathaniel Lyon to wrest the St. Louis Arsenal from the Confederates. Blair may be best remembered for promoting the doomed high-level peace conference between North and South at Hampton Roads, Virginia, in February 1860. (See: Hampton Roads Conference; and Lyon, Brigadier General Nathaniel, U.S.)

Blazer's Scouts

Informally named after their commander, Captain Richard Blazer, these Union raiders were assembled by Major General George Crook to forage, steal enemy horses, tear up enemy rail routes, disrupt communications, and bushwhack and generally harass Confederate cavalry in West Virginia and the Shenandoah Valley. A former coal-barge hauler, Blazer was typical of the other men in his command, a collection of southern Ohio and western Virginia farmers, coal miners, and other laborers who responded to Crook's call for men who were "experienced woodsmen and good shots." The audaciously brave, hard-riding Yankees gave the Rebels fits while playing their own game of guerrilla warfare, until November 18, 1864, when Blazer's Scouts bit off more than they could chew. His Scouts reduced through illness and combat to only 82 men, Blazer attacked a far larger unit led by Confederate raider John Singleton Mosby near Kabletown, West Virginia. At last 20 of the Scouts were killed, and Blazer and the others were captured. (See: Crook, Major General John, U.S.; and Mosby, Colonel John Singleton, CS.)

Blood Tubs

Gangs of hoodlums who roamed the streets plotting to abduct or assassinate President-Elect Abraham Lincoln when he visited Baltimore were called blood tubs because of the bloody oaths they took.

Bloodiest Day

The one-day Battle of Antietam was the bloodiest 14 hours of the Civil War. A total of more than 26,000 casualties were suffered by the two sides. (See: Antietam, Battle of.)

Bloody Kansas, also Bleeding Kansas

While Kansas was preparing for statehood in the mid-1800s, it became the first battleground between proslavery forces in the South and abolitionists in the North. The Kansas-Nebraska Act of 1854 provided for "popular sovereignty"—

vote by the people in the territory preparing for statehood—
to determine if the new state would come into the Union as
slave or free. So Northern abolitionists began sponsoring
settlers they trusted to vote against slavery to move into the
new territories. New England abolitionists also shipped rifles, handguns, and ammunition into the territories to arm
antislavery paramilitary groups. Proslavers in Kansas and in
the neighboring state of Missouri responded by organizing
and arming their own militias. When abolitionists led by
John Brown slaughtered five of their neighbors because they
were believed to be proslavery, they weren't even arrested.
After conducting an investigation, Congress also refused to
act. Southerners and proslavers in the territories were outraged, and Kansas was swept by violence and anarchy before
and after it was admitted to the Union as a free state on
January 29, 1861. (See: Anderson, William T. "Bloody Bill";
Border Ruffians; Brown, John; Centralia Massacre; Kansas-
Nebraska Act; Lawrence Massacre; and Quantrill, Colonel
William Clarke, CS.)

Blue Water Navy
Heavy ships with deep drafts composed the blue water navy,
which included most of the larger ships maintaining the blockade of Southern seaports. Ships of the Union's and Confederacy's blue water navies also sailed the oceans.

Blunt, Major General James Kilpatrick, U.S.
An antislavery physician in Kansas before the war, Blunt
was elected lieutenant colonel of a regiment he raised right
after First Bull Run. Placed in charge of Fort Scott, with 200
men of the 6th Kansas Regiment, he pursued and killed a
guerrilla leader named Matthews who terrorized the southern part of the state. Blunt later commanded troops at Fort
Leavenworth.

Boa Constrictor Plan
The name was selected for General in Chief Winfield Scott's
scheme to squeeze the South to death by blockading its ports,

cutting off trade with foreign countries, ruining its economy
and destroying its ability to supply its troops and feed its
people. The name was later changed to the Anaconda Plan
(See: Anaconda Plan.)

Bonnie Blue Flag
Designed with a white star in the center of a rectangular field
of dark blue, this flag was the first banner of secession and
flew over Montgomery, Alabama, during the first Confederate Congress. A song called "The Bonnie Blue Flag" was
sung for the first time in a New Orleans theater in 1861 for
an audience of Texas volunteers. Borrowed from an old Irish
tune, "The Jaunting Car," it became the second most popular
Southern marching song, after "Dixie." (See: "Dixie.")

Booth, John Wilkes
A member of a prominent acting family and the only Confederate sympathizer among them, Booth fatally shot President Lincoln with a single-shot derringer, then broke a leg
during his escape. Nearly two weeks later, the injured killer
was tracked down and trapped with coconspirator David
Herold in a tobacco barn at a farm near Bowling Green, Virginia. Herold surrendered, but Booth refused and after the
barn was set ablaze the presidential assassin was found dead
inside of a single gunshot wound. (See: Corbett, Boston;
Lincoln Assassination; and Rathbone, Major Henry, U.S.)

Border Ruffians
When the struggle over the issue of slavery began in Kansas,
proslavers called Border Ruffians streamed into the state
from Missouri to stuff ballot boxes and terrorize anyone
believed to favor entering the Union as a free state. (See:
Anderson, William T. "Bloody Bill"; Bloody Kansas; and
Kansas-Nebraska Act.)

Border States
Four slave-owning states, all outside the Deep South, hesitated to declare themselves while the nation was being split

up and were strongly courted by both sides. Ownership of slaves was legal in Delaware, Kentucky, Maryland, and Missouri, but slaves were far less important to local economies than in those of the eleven secessionist states. If the border states decided to stand with the South, the Confederacy stood to gain about 45 percent more white population, translating to millions more men of fighting age and condition. There were other important advantages, as well.

Delaware

Tiny Delaware was the first to declare itself a Union state. It had tremendous strategic value to both sides because it was only a heartbeat away from the national capital in Washington, D.C., and close to Philadelphia and other Northern population centers.

Kentucky

Typical of the divided loyalties in the Bluegrass State, Abraham Lincoln and Jefferson Davis, presidents of the USA and the CSA, were both native Kentuckians. Kentucky eventually provided 100,000 fighting men to the North and 40,000 to the South. Like Missouri, Kentucky was bordered by three free states and three slave states, and like Maryland, its legislature attempted to stay out of the approaching maelstrom by voting to remain neutral. But neutrality was difficult to defend politically, because it depended on states' sovereignty, which was at the core of the South's decision to split with the North. Lincoln didn't push the issue, and his patience paid off when Confederate major general Leonidas Polk and Union brigadier general Ulysses S. Grant met in battle in Kentucky. After almost a year of conflicts, the Rebels were firmly pushed out of the state and back into Tennessee. Kentucky remained under firm Union control throughout the rest of the war.

Maryland

Maryland could have been an even juicier prize for the South than Delaware or Kentucky, and it teetered dangerously on the edge of declaring for the Confederacy. As a Confederate state it would not only add greatly to the South's troops and other resources, but because it surrounded Washington, D.C., on three sides—secessionist Virginia was just across the Potomac River on the other side—Maryland would also have tremendous strategic value. Delaware was also only a heartbeat away from Washington, D.C., Philadelphia, and other Northern population centers. Kentucky and Missouri also offered attractive strategic prizes, as pathways to the lush farmlands and industrial centers of the Midwest and an opportunity to win control of the Mississippi, the Ohio, and other rivers. The first blood of the war was shed in Baltimore when rioters attacked Union troops, even though the Union party won an overwhelming victory in state elections in November 1861 and Maryland rejected secession.

Missouri

When a convention of Missouri legislators voted to stay with the Union, former Border Ruffian and secessionist Governor Claiborne Fox Jackson refused to throw in the towel. He called on Confederate president Jefferson Davis for help capturing the Federal arsenal in St. Louis, which was the biggest of any of those in the slave states. Once the guns and munitions in the arsenal were in the hands of pro-secessionist Missourians, there would be more than enough firepower to overcome pro-Union forces and bring Missouri into the Confederacy, Jackson reasoned. But he hadn't figured on U.S. Army captain Nathaniel Lyon, who teamed up with a large number of German-Americans who wanted nothing to do with secession or with slavery and handily beat back the assault on the armory. Captured Confederates were paraded through the street, setting off a riot that left two soldiers and 28 civilians dead. The stubbornly persistent governor responded by appointing a commander of secessionist troops. Captain Lyon, who later became a brigadier general, rode to the rescue again and kicked the secessionists out of Jefferson City and Boonville. So Jackson moved the state capital from Jefferson City to Neosho and established his own government, declaring Missouri a Confederate state. Pro-Northern forces responded by creating their own government in Jefferson City, and Missouri remained in the Union. Missouri continued to be wracked by violence between its own citizens throughout the war, and eventually sent 100,000 men to fight with the Union, while another 40,000 fought for the Confederacy. (See: Baltimore Riot; Confederate States of America; and Secession.)

Bounty
The Union's conscription law of 1863 provided handy escape hatches for draft dodgers who had the cash to pay their way out of military service. For a while they could simply pay the government $300, and about 86,000 men exercised that option before it was closed in 1864, roughly a year after the draft was initiated. The law also made provisions for paying a substitute, and during the approximate two years of the draft 118,000 men took advantage of that opportunity. Predictably, the Enrollment Act's built-in escape hatches led to bitterness among families whose men couldn't afford to buy their way out of the war, and the anger was especially acute among recent immigrants who suddenly found themselves in uniform after coming to the United States seeking new lives of opportunity. The draft law and its special provisions to protect the wealthy led to criticism that the conflict was "a rich man's war and a poor man's fight." (See: Bounty Jumpers; Draft Riots; and Enrollment Act.)

Bounty Jumpers
Provisions in the Union's conscription codes permitting the hiring of substitutes were frequently abused by bounty jumpers who accepted cash to serve for someone else, then quickly deserted and repeated the routine.

Bowie Knives
Billy Yanks and Johnny Rebs sometimes fought with fists, clubs, stones, sabers, and bayonets in hand-to-hand combat, but one of the most feared weapons for close-up fighting was

the bowie knife carried by many Southern soldiers. Named
after James Bowie, one of the heroes of the Alamo, who is
said to have been the designer, the knife was formed with
large, wide blades ranging from 6 to 18 inches long and was
capable of slashing off an arm with a single vicious swipe.

Boy Soldiers
U.S. military records show that between 10 and 20 percent of
Union soldiers who served in the Civil War were boys under
the legal age of 18 set for recruits. At least 127 were only 13,
and a few managed to slip in who were even younger. Records
of the South's boy soldiers either were not kept or were destroyed, but it is believed that those who took up arms for the
Confederacy at least equaled or exceeded the number of
those who fought for the North. (See: Clem, Major General
John Lincoln, U.S.)

Boyd, Belle
This young Virginia teenager used her beauty and feminine
wiles to coax military intelligence from Union officers at her
father's Front Royal Hotel, then boldly rode through enemy
lines at night to deliver the information to Stonewall Jackson
and other Confederate commanders. Belle became a spy
when she was 17 and shot a Yankee sergeant who tried to
force his way inside her home while her mother was slam-
ming the door in his face. She was arrested six times before
one of her lovers turned on her and she was finally locked in
a Washington jail. Even then, she tossed rubber balls with
notes inside out the jail windows to collaborators. After four
weeks she was released in a prisoner exchange, but two months
later she was behind bars again. After falling ill with typhoid
fever, she was released and used the excuse of needing to recuperate from her illness to travel to Britain with secret communications from Jefferson Davis. She was returning aboard
a blockade runner when it was stopped by a Union ship and
the captain, Samuel Hardringe, fell in love with her. Hardringe
helped her escape to Canada and resigned his commission in
the navy before marrying her in England.

Brady, Mathew
See Photography, Battlefield.

Bragg, General Braxton, CS
Considered by many historians one of the South's most in-
nately capable military tacticians, Bragg was long in natural
ability and talent. But serious flaws in his makeup prevented
him from achieving the battlefield and political success he
might otherwise have acquired. At the beginning of the War
between the States, Bragg was in charge of protecting the
Gulf Coast between Pensacola and Mobile. In September
1861, he was promoted to major general; then he served as
chief of staff under General Albert Sidney Johnston. Bragg
fought at Shiloh and in June 1862 succeeded General Beauregard as commander of the Confederate Army of Mississippi.
Bragg had early success in Kentucky but wasted valuable
time unsuccessfully attempting to establish a secessionist
government in Frankfort. He later won at Chickamauga, lost
at Chattanooga, and fought at Murfreesboro. Although he
was known for brilliantly crafted battle plans, he never lived
up to his potential, because he lacked self-confidence and
tended to lose his nerve on the eve of combat. Consequently
his carefully thought-out plans often were never carried
through, and battles deteriorated into disorganized brawls.
He was nearly universally disliked or outright hated by his
officers and men. (See: Hill, Lieutenant General Daniel Har-
vey, CS; and Mexican War.)

Brandy Station
Some 10,000 Union horsemen under the command of Major
General Alfred Pleasanton and a Confederate force led by
J. E. B. "Jeb" Stuart fought at the rail crossing a few miles
northeast of Fredericksburg, Maryland, with sabers and pistols. It was almost sundown before Stuart's men carried the
day, following a series of bloody charges by both sides up and
down the same hill. The June 9, 1863, clash was the biggest
battle of the war fought solely between mounted troops and

the first serious blooding for the Union's five-month-old Cavalry Corps.

Breastwork
Temporary fortifications over which a soldier can fire, breastworks were usually constructed of earth and/or logs. They extended to shoulder height.

Breckinridge, Major General John Cabell, CS
The multitalented Kentuckian was a busy man. He served in the Kentucky state legislature, fought in the Mexican War, and was a U.S. senator, the vice president of the United States, a major general for the South, and for a few weeks the Confederate secretary of war. Although Breckinridge didn't advocate secession, he was also nominated in 1860 by the Southern faction of the Democratic Party to run for president, and carried eleven states in a losing effort. Breckinridge was vice president under James Buchanan. (See: Camp Breckinridge; and Murfreesboro, Battle of.)

Brigades
Commanded by brigadier generals, brigades in both the North and South were composed of four infantry regiments totaling 4,000 men at full strength.

British Recognition
With cotton mills closing because of a lack of raw material, Britain was wavering on the edge of announcing official recognition for the Confederacy if the South managed one more major battlefield victory when the Rebels and the Yanks fought the Battle of Antietam to a virtual draw. A tie wasn't good enough for the cautious British, and the Confederacy lost its last chance to win recognition from European superpowers, break the blockade of Southern ports, and win independence.

Brown, John

This wild-eyed abolitionist harbored such an obsessive hatred of slavery that he committed multiple murder and treason, and did his best to foment a bloody slave rebellion. The son of poor Calvinist parents in Torrington, Connecticut, Brown was humorless and self-taught but developed into a firebrand speaker and one of New England's leading abolitionists. In 1855, he followed five of his sons—Brown fathered 20 children with two wives—to the Kansas Territory to aid antislavery Free-Soilers against proslavery factions. Less than a year after his arrival, God's self-appointed holy warrior and four of his sons took a leading role in the Pottawatomie Creek Massacre. Brown was head of the Free State volunteers on the night of May 24, 1856, when the guerrilla band slaughtered five prominent members of the proslavery Law and Order Party who lived along the creek in southeastern Kansas. Settler James Doyle and his sons, William and Drury, were the first to die when they were dragged outside their cabin and hacked to death with sabers. Then the killers moved on to other isolated prairie cabins and executed Allen Wilkinson, a member of the proslavery territorial legislature, and Bill Sherman, another proslavery settler. Brown and other members of the bloodthirsty band of irregulars went on the lam in Canada and were never brought to justice for the slaughter. But three years later Brown's luck would run out at Harpers Ferry, Virginia. (See: John Brown's Raid on Harpers Ferry; and Surrender at Harpers Ferry.)

Brown Water Navy

Gunboats and other vessels with shallow drafts that could navigate inland waterways were part of the Civil War's brown-water navies. Many ships served in two capacities, sailing the brown water of rivers and estuaries and when needed joining larger ships offshore in deeper gulfs and bays or the open ocean.

Buchanan, Admiral Franklin, CSN

Initially a staunch Union supporter, "Old Buck" Buchanan was commander of the Washington Navy Yard at the beginning of the Civil War when he resigned his commission to fight for the Confederacy. Although he believed in the preservation of the Union, Buchanan considered Lincoln's handling of the crisis between North and South too heavy-handed, and wrongly believed his home state of Maryland would secede. Buchanan commanded the CSS *Merrimac* at the Battle of Hampton Roads, where he was wounded, and was in charge of the Confederate naval defenses at the Battle of Mobile Bay. One of his legs was crushed while his flagship, the CSS *Tennessee,* was being battered by almost every vessel in Union admiral David G. Farragut's fleet during the fight. Buchanan was promoted to admiral after the battle, and earlier in the war he commanded a small fleet assembled to defend Norfolk, Virginia, and the James River. After joining the navy as a midshipman when he was 14, Buchanan served in the Mexican War, was the first superintendent at the U.S. Naval Academy at Annapolis, and was flag captain of Commodore Perry's squadron when Japan was forced to open its ports to Western sailors and commerce. (See: Hampton Roads, Battle of; Mobile Bay, Battle of; and *Tennessee,* CSS.)

Buchanan, President James

Although the last straw in the minds of secession-minded Southerners was the election of Abraham Lincoln, the stage was set for the Civil War before the nation's fifteenth president stepped aside. Buchanan didn't want to become known as the president on whose watch the war was started, and played a delaying game during the final weeks of his administration, following Lincoln's election. Although Buchanan conceded that secession was not provided for by the Constitution or other Federal codes, he claimed he had no authority to prevent it. He finally called for a national referendum to determine if force should be used to preserve the Union, thereby giving himself plenty of time to complete his term of office and leaving the matter for his successor to decide.

Buckner, Lieutenant General Simon Bolivar, CS

With a name like his, it may seem that this Kentuckian had no choice but to grow up to be a general. A West Pointer, Buckner was wounded at Churubusco during the war with Mexico. After leaving the army, he served as adjutant general of the Illinois Militia and directed the reorganization of the Kentucky State Guard. When the Civil War broke out, sentiments in Kentucky were bitterly split between North and South, and Buckner briefly attempted to maintain the neutrality of the state's military. But when Federal supporters on Kentucky's military board ordered the strongly prosecessionist state guard to turn in their arms, most of the rest of the militia joined the Confederacy. When Buckner turned down a commission in the Union Army he was accused of being a traitor and fled south, where he was commissioned as a brigadier general on September 14, 1861. Buckner was placed in command in central Kentucky and teamed up his ground forces with the Confederate Navy to secure the Tennessee and Cumberland Rivers. But when his division launched an ill-fated attempt to relieve besieged Rebels at Fort Donelson, he was forced to surrender the garrison to Brigadier General Ulysses S. Grant and taken prisoner. Released in a prisoner exchange, Buckner was promoted to major general and joined General Braxton Bragg's invasion of Kentucky. Buckner led his division at the Battle of Perryville. By 1863 he fought during Bragg's victory at Chickamauga but was critical of the general's faltering leadership, and joined with other officers seeking his removal from command. In September 1864, Buckner was promoted to lieutenant general and assigned to the Trans-Mississippi Department as chief of staff for General Edmund Kirby Smith. Buckner served in that capacity until the end of the war. He later served a four-year term as governor of Kentucky. (See: Bragg, General Braxton, CS; Fort Donelson, Battle of; and Unconditional Surrender Grant.)

Bucktails

The nickname of the 150th Pennsylvania Infantry Regiment was selected because of the deer tail badges worn on their caps. The 150th was a regiment composed of backwoodsman Pennsylvanians.

Buell, Major General Don Carlos, U.S.

This Mexican War veteran and West Pointer was sacked from command for failure to pursue retreating Confederates after the Battle of Perryville, but enemies in the military and Washington establishments were more responsible for Buell's disgrace than his performance in the field. Buell was at his best as an organizer, and early in the war he helped General McClellan shape the Army of the Potomac into a formidable fighting force, then briefly commanded a division. From November 15, 1861, until October 24, 1862, he led the Army of Ohio. Then he successfully wrested control of the army from the governor of his home state of Indiana, making a powerful enemy in the process. Operating in East Tennessee, Buell led Union troops into Nashville with only minimal opposition, then moved to support General Grant at Pittsburg Landing on the Tennessee River. After arriving and leading his divisions at Shiloh late on the first day of battle, Buell again ruffled feathers by taking credit for saving General Grant from defeat. By late 1862 Buell was leading troops opposing Confederate general Braxton Bragg's thrust into Kentucky and on October 8 fought the Battle of Perryville. Although the battle ended the Confederate invasion and saved Kentucky for the Union, Buell was relieved of command on October 24 and replaced by Major General William Starke Rosecrans. Buell claimed he did not pursue the retreating enemy because he was out of supplies and a military commission investigated, but the findings were not publicly revealed. When Grant became general in chief of Union Armies in 1864 he asked the secretary of war to restore Buell to duty and command. But Grant's recommendation was not acted on, and Buell sat out the rest of the war in Indianapolis awaiting orders. (See: Perryville, Battle of.)

Buford, Brigadier General John, U.S.

A West Pointer who fought Indians while stationed at Fort Laramie, this native Kentuckian was mistakenly reported as killed in action when he was wounded at the Second Battle of Bull Run. But he was back in fighting shape in time to become a Union hero when he called on tactics learned while pursuing Sioux Indians and ordered one of his brigades to dismount and block General A. P. Hill's advancing Confederate corps during the Battle of Gettysburg. The action stalled the Rebels long enough for the Union to reorganize its lines. Buford was in command of the two Union brigades whose engagement with Confederate foragers just north of the town ignited the momentous battle. The gallant Union horse soldier clashed frequently with the Confederacy's J. E. B. "Jeb" Stuart, and their rivalry climaxed when they met at Brandy Station in the biggest cavalry battle ever fought in the Northern Hemisphere. Buford died in the fall of 1863 after contracting typhoid fever. (See: Brandy Station.)

Buford, Major General
Napoleon Bonaparte, U.S.

A half brother of John Buford, N. B. Buford fought with General Grant at Belmont and directed brigades under General Pope at Island Number 10 and under Rosecrans at Corinth. A member of Kentucky plantation society, Buford also served the Union as a brigade commander with the Army of the Mississippi; in eastern Arkansas; and in the Vicksburg Campaign. He served only a few months as an active major general, and his appointment expired on March 4, 1863, because it was never confirmed by the U.S. Senate. He was brevetted back to the rank while on leave at the end of the war.

Bull Run, First Battle of

Bull Run was the first major battle of the war and also marked the first military victory for the Confederacy. The Union was so confident of victory as Bluecoats prepared for the approaching clash on the hot summer day of July 21, 1861, that picnickers rode horses and buggies from nearby

Washington, D.C., to watch the action from nearby hills. A few hours later the holiday mood had disappeared and the picnickers were fleeing back to the nation's capital in terror, ahead of the badly bloodied Yankees. Union general Irvin McDowell, leading 30,000 Union troops, used an artillery barrage to open the assault on the Confederate force of 22,000 men in the Army of the Potomac under the temporary command of General Pierre G. T. Beauregard at the road and rail junction of Manassas. Brigadier General Joseph E. Johnston was nearby with another 18,000 troops at Winchester, Virginia, the gateway to the lush Shenandoah Valley. Although Johnston was commander of the Army of the Shenandoah and in overall command of Confederate forces, he wisely turned over strategic planning to Beauregard because he was at the scene of the battle and was a skilled military tactician. Beauregard called on Johnston to move his forces by rail to reinforce the outnumbered Confederates, while fooling the Union's major general Robert Patterson, who was commanding another 18,000 troops near Winchester, into believing that he was staying out of the Manassas brawl. The Union general was supposed to keep Johnston pinned down in the valley. But flamboyant 1st Virginia general J. E. B. "Jeb" Stuart led his cavalry in a series of movements that made Patterson mistakenly believe he was about to be attacked, and the bulk of Johnston's troops were able to move out on foot, on horseback, and by rail, unnoticed and unmolested. At Manassas, Beauregard spread his forces out along Bull Run, a high-banked stream that was a tributary of the Potomac River, to await the Bluecoat attack. At 7:00 A.M., McDowell opened the battle with an artillery barrage at the stone bridge crossing and a movement aimed at turning the Confederates' left flank. The Rebels were wavering and beginning to break when they rallied behind General Thomas J. Jackson's brigade to defend Henry House Hill, one of the most strategically valuable pieces of terrain at Bull Run. The Confederates held, and as more reinforcements arrived from Winchester, the fresh troops routed the slowly disintegrating Bluecoats. By 4:00 P.M., Union officers were losing control

of their men, and the exhausted soldiers were walking across
the old stone bridge over Bull Run, heading back to Washington. Less than an hour later, Union soldiers were fighting
one another to get over the bridge. The Confederates made a
halfhearted effort to pursue their enemy but were exhausted
and quickly gave up the chase. They had lost a golden opportunity to pursue the retreating Yanks all the way to Washington and place the capital city under siege. The battle cost the
Union 2,900 dead, wounded, and missing; the Confederate
casualty toll was about 2,000. (See: McDowell, General Irvin,
U.S.)

Bull Run, Second Battle of

Major General John A. Pope had all the confidence and
bravado of a John Wayne when President Lincoln put him in
charge of the recently created Union Army of Virginia. Pope
was told to run down General Lee and put the Confederates
out of the war. Lee gave Pope an opportunity to show what
he could do after the Union general took up defensive positions behind the Rappahannock River while waiting for
reinforcements from Washington. Even though for once the
Southerners temporarily outnumbered their enemy, Lee wisely
refused to be lured into attacking across a river. Instead, he
ordered General Stonewall Jackson to make a wide swing behind Pope and capture the Union rail center and supply depot
at Manassas Junction. Jackson's troops marched 60 miles in
two days to take the undefended depot on August 26, 1862,
capturing and destroying supplies and cutting Pope off from
his supply and communications lines. Then Jackson waited
for Pope to attack and clear away the impudent Rebel force
standing between his army and the capital city in Washington. The stage was set for the Second Battle of Bull Run,
at almost exactly the same site where First Bull Run was
fought. Three days later Pope and his 62,000-man army attacked. The Confederates reeled under the assault, but the
badly bloodied Rebels held on and were reinforced the next
day by General Lee and General James Longstreet. Pope was
also reinforced by elements of McClellan's army, and or-

dered another attack against Jackson and his exhausted soldiers. The Confederates fought desperately along an unfinished railroad line, and it appeared that they were about to be overrun when Longstreet ordered an attack on Pope's left flank. Caught by surprise, the Union Army suddenly found itself on the defensive, and it was only through a heroic stand at the base of Henry House Hill that they managed to hold on until nightfall. When the humiliated Pope began an orderly retreat to Washington the next day, he had suffered 14,000 to 16,000 casualties (war historians don't always agree), compared to 9,200 for the South. Shortly after the mortifying defeat, Pope was reassigned to Minnesota to fight Indians. (See: Pope, Major General John A., U.S.)

Bummer

The origin of this term is clouded, but it came into prominent usage during Sherman's March to the Sea. A bummer was generally considered to be a man who temporarily deserted his unit to go on an independent foraging expedition. The term also applied to all cooks, orderlies, and servants.

Burnside, Major General Ambrose Everett, U.S.

A man who knew his own limitations, Burnside tried to beg off when President Lincoln named him to command the Army of the Potomac. The general, who is remembered today more for his distinctive sideburns than for his battlefield accomplishments, pointed out that he had neither the background nor the ability to lead a force of so many men. He had already turned down the job once before. Burnside was a kind, trusting man, and it would seem that anyone who knew much about his pre–Civil War debacles would realize that he was born to lose. On his way to fight in Mexico, the newly commissioned officer lost his traveling money to a card shark. Then Burnside was cleaned out of cash after investing heavily in development of a breech-loading rifle that was too expensive for the U.S. Army to buy. Finally, he was left at the altar when his bride got cold feet during the ceremony. When the Civil War began, Burnside's fighting mettle was up, and he was anxious to serve his country. He talked his way into a command in North Carolina, which he used as a springboard to fight under the direct leadership of "Little Mac" McClellan. That's when bad judgment and misfortune began dogging Burnside again and he performed poorly at South Mountain and Antietam. After Lincoln overrode Burnside's objections and put him in charge of the Army of the Potomac, the reluctant commander proved to one and all that he had known what he was talking about. He presided over the Union disaster at the Battle of the Crater and lost a bloody confrontation with Robert E. Lee at Fredericksburg, where the Confederate general was outnumbered almost two-to-one. Convinced at last that Burnside was in way over his head, Lincoln relieved him of command and remarked of the Fredericksburg performance that the general had somehow managed to "snatch defeat from the jaws of victory." Burnside continued to perform poorly during the final days of the war and resigned his commission in 1865. (See: Fredericksburg, Battle of; and Hooker, Major General Joseph "Fighting Joe," U.S.)

Burnside's Invention
As a general the Union's Ambrose Burnside turned in a spotty performance, but his invention of a breech-loading carbine was a solid success. The revolutionary weapon was especially prized by cavalry. (See: Burnside, Major General Ambrose Everett, U.S.; and Carbines, Breech-Loading.)

Buskirk, Captain David, U.S.
After this 27th Indiana officer's capture the Confederates were so amazed at the 6-foot, 11-inch, 380-pound giant that they put him on exhibit as "the biggest Yankee in the world." Even Jefferson Davis stopped by to take a look. The good-natured prisoner advised the CSA president that he had six sisters back home in Bloomington and when he marched off to war "they all walked up, leaned down, and kissed me on top of my head." (See: Thruston, Private Henry C., CS.)

Butler, "Beast"

As the Union's military governor of New Orleans, Major General Benjamin Freeman Butler ruled with such a heavy hand that Confederate president Jefferson Davis declared him a criminal and ordered his immediate execution if captured. Ironically, while Butler was a delegate to the National Democratic Convention in Charleston, South Carolina, in 1860, he voted 57 times to nominate Jefferson Davis as the party's presidential candidate because he believed a moderate Southerner could hold the nation together. The general was given the nickname Beast Butler after issuing General Order Number 28, on May 15, 1862. Better known as the "Woman's Order," the decree made it a crime for women to publicly insult his soldiers. The order was drawn up after a woman emptied the contents of a chamber pot on the head of a Union captain, and the decree stipulated that "when any Female shall by word, gesture, or movement, insult or show contempt for any officer or soldier of the United States, she shall be regarded and held Liable to be treated as a woman of the town, plying her avocation." The shocked ladies of New Orleans behaved themselves after the order was issued, and there wasn't a single arrest for violating the decree. (See: Butler, Major General Benjamin Freeman, U.S.; and Butler, Spoons.)

Butler, Major General
Benjamin Freeman, U.S.

Until Sherman's famous march through Georgia and the destruction of Atlanta, Butler was the most hated Union general in the South. The controversial general also had a lot of enemies in the North, including the military establishment, where he was resented for his political manipulations and less-than-stellar performances as a field commander. A crafty Massachusetts politician and state legislator, Butler rushed to join the Union Army when the war began and helped restore order after the Baltimore Riots. He was named by Lincoln as a major general of volunteers in May 1861 and almost immediately began to prove how inept political appointees with no military training could be when called on to lead troops in battle. He was in command of Fort Monroe during the Peninsular Campaign, and was nearly sacked after his humiliating defeat at Big Bethel. He also became known for acting without higher authorization, and when Southern slaves began fleeing to the North through Fort Monroe he embarrassed Lincoln by announcing on his own that they were contraband of war. As personal property, he said, they could be confiscated. As the war progressed, Butler's name was widely associated with glaring military blunders and disaster. Powerful political friends repeatedly saved his skin, but even Lincoln became so embarrassed by Butler's behavior as military governor of New Orleans that he was removed from the post in December 1862. Butler bounced back early the next year when he was named to command the Army of the James. But after a stinging defeat by forces led by General Pierre G. T. Beauregard at Bermuda Hundred, his command was trimmed and he was sent to New York, where he was told to await a new assignment. When he learned that General Grant planned to move against Fort Fisher, North Carolina, he used his seniority to win command and then bungled the job. Returning to civilian life at the conclusion of hostilities, Butler was elected to Congress and played a leading role in the effort to impeach President Andrew Johnson. (See: Butler, "Beast"; and Butler, Spoons.)

Butler, Spoons
A habit of helping himself to the silverware in Southern homes where he was temporarily headquartered earned the Union's major general Benjamin Freeman Butler a nickname as Spoons Butler. (See: Butler, "Beast"; and Butler, Major General Benjamin Freeman, U.S.)

Butterfield, Major General Daniel, U.S.
A New York businessman when the war started, Butterfield rose rapidly from the ranks as first sergeant of the Clay Guards, District of Columbia Volunteers, to major general in the regular army and chief of staff for "Fighting Joe" Hooker. Butterfield was thoroughly disliked by most of his peers and was

blamed by many officers for joining with Major General
Daniel Sickles and then General in Chief Hooker to turn the
command headquarters into a combination of barroom and
brothel. Although it was true that Butterfield liked to party
with his cronies, he also fought bravely when it was time
to fight, and he was awarded the Congressional Medal of
Honor in 1892 for his performance three decades earlier at
the Battle of Gaines's Mill in the Peninsular Campaign. Butterfield was wounded while carrying the flag of the 3d Pennsylvania. He commanded a brigade at Second Bull Run and
was a corps commander at Fredericksburg before joining
Hooker's staff. He fought at Chancellorsville, and when
General Meade relieved Hooker as general in chief just before Gettysburg he kept Butterfield as chief of staff rather
than replace him on the eve of battle. On the third day of the
fight, Butterfield was struck by a spent piece of shrapnel and
put out of action. After recovery, he rejoined Hooker as chief
of staff at Chattanooga. When the 20th Corps was formed,
Butterfield was placed in command of a division, which he
led during the Atlanta Campaign. He was forced by illness to
leave the field before Atlanta fell, and finished the war at
Vicksburg.

Butterflies

Attached to General Phil Sheridan's Cavalry Corps, the 3d
New Jersey Cavalry Regiment was given this nickname because of the horse soldiers' resplendent appearance. In an effort to attract recruits, New Jersey authorities outfitted the
unit with a handsome uniform that resembled those worn by
the Hussar regiments of European armies. Cavalrymen with
the 3d New Jersey wore forage caps without visors, elaborately braided jackets, and hooded cloaks. Despite their appearance as dandies, members of the 3d New Jersey Cavalry
were rough-and-ready warriors who fought bravely under
Sheridan at Winchester and at Tom's Brook.

C

Caisson
A two-wheeled vehicle with large chests used for carrying artillery ammunition. Caissons were connected to a horse-drawn limber when moved.

Camels
When Union major James Henry Carleton and his 1st Dragoons were ordered from Fort Tejon to Los Angeles to protect a quartermaster depot, they brought 36 camels with them. Although camels were not widely used in the Civil War, a few were utilized in California, Texas, and some of the Western territories. The Confederates were known to have at least 80 camels and two Egyptian handlers—probably captured from the Union.

Camp Breckinridge
The sprawling U.S. Army base in Kentucky is named after former U.S. vice president and Confederate major general John Cabell Breckinridge. (See: Breckinridge, Major General John Cabell, CS.)

Camp Misery
Federal soldiers recovering and resting up from their wounds or illnesses gave the sarcastic nickname Camp Misery to Camp Convalescent in Alexandria, Virginia. Poorly supplied and equipped, Camp Convalescent was the main collection point for patients after their discharge from hospitals in the

Washington, D.C., area, and 15,000 men lived there in deplorable conditions.

Canby, Major General Edward Richard Sprigg, U.S.

An experienced soldier who participated in the Mexican War, Second Seminole War, and Mormon Expedition, Canby began his Civil War service as a colonel with the 19th Infantry Regiment at Fort Defiance, in the New Mexico Territory. He fought at Valverde, Apache Canyon, and Glorieta, turning back an invasion led by General Henry H. Sibley that would have expanded the Confederate presence from Texas into the Southwest. By early 1864 Canby was a major general in command of the Military Division of West Mississippi. In November 1864 he was wounded by partisans at White River, Arkansas, and after recovering commanded the land assault in the final days of the war that led to the capture of Mobile, Alabama. After the war he was a brigadier general stationed in the Pacific Northwest when he was killed by Modoc Indian chief Captain Jack and others. Canby was unarmed and was attending a peace parley.

Canister

This deadly scattershot was contained in iron can-shaped casements and was deadly when fired by artillery against an enemy at 250 yards or less. When the cannon fired, the casements fell away and dozens of iron balls scattered like shotgun spray, ripping into the flesh and bone of an advancing enemy. Canister was used primarily in defense.

Carbines, Breech-Loading

The breech-loading carbine was the favorite weapon of horse soldiers. These guns were short, lightweight, easy to load, and quick to fire, marking a huge improvement over the old muzzle loaders. Thousands of the weapons were produced for the Union cavalry, but Southerners were generally confined to a few poor copies of the real thing, old-fashioned muzzle loaders, sawed-off shotguns, and whatever breech-loading carbines they could liberate from the battlefield.

Carleton, Major General James Henry, U.S.

A hard man who lived in hard times, Carleton was merciless against his enemies and a strict disciplinarian who demanded the best from his men. After serving as a lieutenant in the Maine Militia during a boundary dispute with Canada known as the Aristook War, he entered the regular army and was assigned to the frontier, where he became an ardent Indian fighter. He was with the 1st Dragoons as commander of Fort Tejon in California when he was sent to Salt Lake City to investigate the massacre of 120 Arkansas emigrants at Mountain Meadows in 1857. Carleton concluded that Mormons dressed as Indians had carried out the slaughter. When the Civil War began he was appointed colonel of the 1st Infantry, California Volunteers, and a short time later was advanced to brigadier general. He may be best remembered today for leading the California Column with 2,350 men, dressed in wool uniforms and fully armed and equipped in the midsummer heat, on a grueling march from Wilmington, California, to El Paso, Texas. It is still considered the longest march in the history of the United States infantry, and not a man was lost to heatstroke or other noncombat causes. After relieving General Edward R. S. Canby as commander of the Department of New Mexico, Carleton restored his predecessor's order establishing martial law. Carleton also sent Colonel Kit Carson with a strong force of soldiers to kill all adult male Mescalero Apaches they could find, then declared war on the Navajos while continuing to guard against Confederate efforts to make inroads in the territory.

Carnine, Levy S.

A slave, Carnine served as a valet and cook for his master in the Pelican Rifles. After his owner was killed, Carnine performed the same duties for the colonel until he was also killed, then fought alongside other members of the infantry company. When the Eastern Theater was cut off from the West, Carnine pretended to defect to the North so he could move through Union lines and carry letters and cash home to Mansfield, Louisiana, for his Confederate companions.

Carpetbaggers
Thousands of slick and/or politically connected Northerners, sometimes carrying only what they could stuff into large bags made of carpeting, flooded the South during Reconstruction to grab cash, property, and positions of power. (See: Reconstruction.)

Carson, Brigadier General Christopher "Kit"
The legendary frontiersman who won fame for guiding explorer John Frémont in the West joined the Union Army with the rank of colonel when the Civil War broke out. Carson, who had been an Indian agent in Taos, New Mexico, was given command of the New Mexico Volunteers. He was later brevetted to brigadier general. After the war he was named superintendent of Indian affairs in the Colorado Territory. (See: Frémont, Major General John C., U.S.)

Cary Sisters
Three Virginia sisters sewed the first Confederate battle flags, known as the Red Cross Banner, and presented them to three Southern generals, Pierre G. T. Beauregard, Joseph Eggleston Johnston, and Earl Van Dorn, at a ceremony in Centerville in October 1861. The patriotic Southern belles were Constance, Hetty, and Jennie Cary. (See: Battle Flag, Confederate.)

Castle Pinckney
The bloodless seizure on December 27, 1860, by South Carolina state militia of Castle Pinckney, a small fort that was part of the Charleston Harbor defense system, was the first overt act of the Civil War. The militia's occupation preceded the fall of Fort Sumter by less than four months. Castle Pinckney was manned only by a U.S. Army lieutenant from Virginia

and an ordnance sergeant with his wife and daughter, and they did not resist the takeover. (See: Fort Sumter.)

Centralia Massacre

On September 27, 1864, "Bloody Bill" Anderson led 70 cut-throats wearing Confederate uniforms (at other times they wore Union blue) into Centralia, Missouri. Drunk on liberated whiskey, Bloody Bill and his men raped, robbed, and murdered, and finally set fire to the town. Anderson added a final grisly touch to the horror when he forced a train to stop and rounded up all the passengers, including 26 unarmed Union soldiers and their lieutenant. After shooting the lieutenant, Anderson ordered the troopers lined up in an open field and strode up and down the ranks, calmly shooting every man in the head while he pleaded for his life. Later that day, Anderson's killers surprised a dismounted detachment of Bluecoats and slaughtered 124 of them, most as they were surrendering and begging for mercy. Anderson and his men then scalped and decapitated the victims and carried away their heads and hair as trophies. (See: Anderson, William T. "Bloody Bill.")

Chain Shot

This formidable naval weapon consisted of two heavy metal balls linked by a chain that was usually fired into the wooden masts and rigging of enemy ships. When the balls or chain struck wood or canvas, the shot whipped around, tearing down masts and rigging.

Chalmers, Brigadier General James Ronald, CS

General Sheridan was commanding 827 men at a forward post near Booneville, Mississippi, in July 1862 when he outfoxed Chalmers, who was leading more than 5,000 Confederate troops, and won the day. Sheridan's men were armed with repeating rifles and pistols, which helped pull off the feat. But the main factor in the battle was Chalmers's trick of repeatedly loading and unloading the same troops on a train to convince the enemy they were facing a much larger force. Sheridan was 31 when he was promoted to major general for his performance at Booneville. Despite his role as goat to Sheridan, Chalmers was a gallant, determined officer who was wounded at Stones River and at Murfreesboro. (See: Sheridan, General Philip Henry, U.S.)

Chambersburg
This Pennsylvania community was the only town destroyed by Confederate cavalry during the war.

Chancellorsville, Battle of
General Robert E. Lee boldly split his greatly outnumbered forces and routed a Union army led by Major General Joseph "Fighting Joe" Hooker at Chancellorsville to save the Confederate capital of Richmond from a Yankee invasion. But the accidental shooting of corps commander Stonewall Jackson by his own troopers made it a bitter victory for the South. Hooker had just taken over command of the Army of the Potomac after the relief of three consecutive predecessors when he faced off early in 1863 with the Army of Northern Virginia at the country crossroads deep within the area of forests and swamps known as the Wilderness. Bold and confident, Hooker had devised a plan to encircle Lee's troops by sending Major General John Sedgwick with two corps—40,000 men—to cross the Rappahannock River and pin down the bulk of the Confederates in Fredericksburg. Hooker planned to furtively move northwesterly up the river and cross at Kelly's Ford before turning east to pounce on Lee's flank and rear. Hooker's remaining two corps were ordered to hold Bank's Ford and the U.S. Ford, while also remaining available as reserves. The cocksure Federal commander was hopeful of either catching Lee's army in a pincer and destroying it or sending the Confederates reeling in retreat back to Richmond, where they could be pursued and destroyed or forced to surrender to bring an early end to the war. Hooker was so self-confident that he told aides, "May God have mercy on General Lee, for I shall have none." With only 60,000

men and 220 cannon to face Hooker's revitalized and newly confident army of 134,000 backed by 414 big guns, Lee called on a masterful command of maneuver, audacity, and surprise to defeat the swaggering new Union commander. Splitting his forces, Lee attacked from two sides. When Hooker was surprised with a fierce assault by 6,600 infantry-men covering the Rebels' left flank, while moving his forces into the dense forests of the Wilderness, he uncharacteristi-cally lost his nerve because he mistakenly concluded that he was about to be attacked by Lee's entire army. Hooker ordered his men to fall back and take up previously con-structed defensive positions around the crossroads. Lee and Jackson moved quickly to seize the initiative that was so unexpectedly abandoned by "Fighting Joe." That night, Jack-son convinced Lee that the Union's right flank was vulnera-ble and the two generals sat together on a log devising their own turning movement to surprise Hooker. While Jackson was executing the maneuver, Lee would be utilizing his re-maining 13,000 men to keep the attention of the 50,000 Fed-erals in the center busy with small skirmishes. The next day, after a local guide helped lead the Confederate flankers through the dense forests and swamps that Hooker had be-lieved to be impassable, at 5:15 P.M., accompanied by the sound of bugles and the terrifying Rebel yell, Jackson's troops burst out of the trees and brambly scrub. With most of the 10,500 men in the XI Corps either eating or already asleep, the Federals were caught unprepared and sent reeling back. Later that evening, while Jackson was scouting out a route to cut off the Yankee retreat across the Rappahannock at the U.S. Ford, soldiers from the 18th North Carolina mis-took him for the enemy and shot him in the arms and shoul-der. Surprised by the sudden rain of fire, three other officers tumbled from their horses and Jackson's mount veered against a tree, knocking him off. The only other officer be-sides Jackson who knew his plans was General Ambrose Hill, and he was severely wounded and sidelined by artillery fire shortly after his commander was shot. With Jackson and Hill taken so unexpectedly out of the battle, all hope of cutting off the escape route and surrounding the Federals was dashed. Some historians believe that if Jackson had not been shot and had been able to press forward to accomplish a quick and decisive defeat the North may have lost faith in Lincoln's government and granted the South the independence it was fighting for. Union resistance stiffened overnight, and early on May 3 Lee ordered the two wings of his army to reunite in order to prevent a potentially disastrous counterattack. With Jackson sidelined and his next-in-command wounded by artillery, General Jeb Stuart took over the command from Brigadier General Robert E. Rodes and carried out the linkup with Lee's forces. By midmorning the Confederates had taken over Chancellorsville, and the Union Army was rapidly retiring toward the U.S. Ford. Hooker was also put out of the fight when he was knocked senseless by an artillery shell, but he had previously ordered Major General John Sedgwick to capture Fredericksburg and hurry to his support. Sedgwick commanded about 24,000 men and had taken Fredericksburg when he headed west toward Chancellorsville. General Lee was ready for Sedgwick. Splitting his forces again, Lee ordered Stuart to keep an eye on Hooker with 25,000 men, then led his remaining 21,000 men in an attack on Sedgwick. Bloodied by the Confederate attack, Sedgwick retired back toward Fredericksburg, while Lee once more linked his two forces together and prepared to finish off Hooker's army. Sedgwick took the opportunity to evacuate the remainder of his army, minus 4,600 lost in the earlier clashes, and in the quiet predawn hours of May 5 they crossed pontoon bridges set up at Bank's Ford. Hooker had also had enough. The Army of the Potomac retreated across the Rappahannock and joined Sedgwick at Bank's Ford early the next day before Lee could catch up to the Federals. More than 40,000 Union soldiers never fired a shot in the battle. The usually brash and confident Union general later shouldered the blame for the defeat, and when asked why he lost replied, "For once I lost confidence in Joe Hooker, and that is all there is to it." When the opposing forces tallied up after the four-day battle, the Army of the Potomac had suffered

7,000 casualties and the loss of 13 cannon to 13,000 men
and 8 cannon for the Army of Northern Virginia. However,
even though the battle went into the record books as a victory for the Confederacy, the loss of Stonewall Jackson, who
died from his injury, was an irreversible tragedy from which
the South and General Lee would never recover.

Chantilly, Battle of

Both generals in immediate command of Union forces in
this clash, also known as the Battle of Ox Hill, were killed.
The battle was joined during a torrential rain on the afternoon of September 1, 1862, when forces led by Stonewall
Jackson encountered Union troops retreating into Virginia
after the defeat at Second Bull Run. The Confederate line was
pressing forward near the Chantilly plantation when Brigadier
General Isaac Stevens snatched up the flag of the 79th New
York Highlanders to rally his troops and was killed with a
shot through the head. Union general Philip Kearny arrived
with reinforcements and, confused by the torrential rain and
growing darkness of early evening, mistakenly rode alone
into the Confederate lines while trying to find Stevens and
his troops. Kearny didn't realize his error until he found himself surrounded by Confederates. Disregarding their shouts
to surrender, he turned and was spurring his horse to escape
back to his own lines when he was struck in the spine by a
minié ball and killed. After their victory, the Confederates
returned General Kearny's body to Union forces under a flag
of truce. The Union suffered 1,300 casualties and the Confederates, 800.

Chaplains

Regimental chaplains ministered to troops on both sides
of the conflict and were considered officers, although they
could give no commands. They were much better paid than
the members of their flocks, receiving $80 per month in the
South and $100 per month in the North.

Chaplin Hills, Battle of
An alternate name for the Battle of Perryville.

Charleston Arsenal
The U.S. arsenal in the South's second-largest city wa
seized in a bloodless takeover by South Carolina state troop
in late December 1861. The vital facility, with 22,430 weap
ons ranging from cannon to pistols and the capacity to turn
out thousands more, was a valuable resource for arming the
soldiers and sailors of the new Confederacy. (See: Fort Sum
ter.)

Chattanooga, Battle of
When Confederate general Braxton Bragg followed Majo
General William Rosecrans's defeated Union Army of the
Cumberland to Chattanooga after Chickamauga, he was un
able to quickly break through the enemy fortifications, so he
settled down to starve the Yankees out. The 60-mile-long
Federal supply line extending downriver and across moun
tains to Bridgeport, Alabama, was cut in October, and the
Yankees were critically short of food and equipment when
Major General Ulysses S. Grant, newly appointed commander
of the Military Division of the Mississippi, replaced the shaken
Rosecrans with Major General George Henry Thomas
Grant also ordered his own troops, as well as two corps o
20,000 veteran troops from the Army of the Potomac, to
hurry to the relief of the Army of the Cumberland under
siege at Chattanooga. Although the Federals were well dug in
inside the city, critical high ground overlooking the city be
longed to the Confederates. Artillery and troops atop Look
out Mountain and Missionary Ridge seemed to put the Rebel
firmly in the driver's seat. But Grant wasn't about to allow
his trapped army to simply waste away, and devised a break
out plan. First on the menu was establishment of a supply
line along the Tennessee River, with a bridgehead at Brown's
Ferry. After an assault that forced the enemy off Raccoon
Mountain, the Confederates launched a fierce counterattack
on the new Union lines at Wauhatchie. But the night attack

was repulsed by the Army of the Potomac veterans under the command of General Joseph Hooker, and the first Union supply ship arrived safely on November 1, 1863. With the supply line now open from Bridgeport into Chattanooga and more reinforcements on the way from Memphis and Vicksburg, Grant went to work forming a strategy for chasing the enemy off Missionary Ridge and Lookout Mountain. Grant got some unexpected help from Bragg, who lost three generals under his command when they were granted transfers because of unhappiness with his reticence to fight at Chattanooga. Bragg also sent about 12,000 men and 35 cannon under Lieutenant General James Longstreet to Knoxville to get rid of another of his most troublesome critics. While Bragg was weakening his position on Missionary Ridge with the loss of Longstreet, General William T. Sherman had arrived with fresh troops from the Union Army of Tennessee. On November 23, Grant opened the battle for Orchard Knob in the center of the Confederate line along Missionary Ridge by demonstrating just how imaginative he could be. He had his divisions dressed in their very best and marched at the foot of the hill, just like they were in a military parade. When the puzzled Confederates moved down to take a closer look, the parading Bluecoats attacked and after savage fighting took control of the critical hill. Grant quickly established his headquarters at the top. He ordered Sherman to cross the Tennessee River and assault the Confederate right. Hooker was sent to make a feint against Lookout Mountain on the Confederate left to take pressure off of Sherman. Early on November 24 Hooker ordered an opening assault, and after several hours of hard fighting in what came to be known as "the Battle above the Clouds." Lookout Mountain was in Union hands. It was afternoon before Sherman, who was delayed by heavy rain, finally showed up on Bragg's right. The Battle of Missionary Ridge began the next morning, but Sherman's artillery-supported forces were driven off after repeatedly battering at the strongly dug in Confederates. In a move to draw enemy troops away from Sherman's front, Grant ordered Thomas to launch a frontal attack at the base of the ridge. Many of the Confederates immediately withdrew up the slopes, leaving their undermanned companions to be overrun by the advancing Yankees. Once the Confederate line was broken, and without orders to do so, the victorious Bluecoats continued the assault, racing up the mountain and completely routing the enemy. The Siege and Battle of Chattanooga were over, and the road to Atlanta and the Southern heartland lay ahead. (See: Battle Above the Clouds.)

1st. Cherokee Mounted Rifles, CSA

The best known of at least fifteen American Indian regiments and battalions enlisted in the Confederate Army, the 1st. Cherokee Mounted Rifles were commanded by a Georgia Cherokee, Stand Watie. The so-called "five civilized tribes" of Cherokee, Chickasaw, Chocktaw, Creek, and Seminole, along with the Osage, took up arms in large numbers for the South. (See: Watie, Brigadier General Stand, CS.)

Chevaux-De-Frise

One of the big advantages of the obstructions built with a long crossbeam supporting a series of lancelike pointed stakes was their portability. They took time and skill to make, but they could be picked up and moved around. They weren't much help against infantry but could be quite frightening for cavalry, whose mounts were likely to spear themselves with the sharp stakes.

Chickamauga, Battle of

Chickamauga is the Cherokee word for River of Death, and after the terrible battle fought there between the Blue and the Gray on September 18–20, 1863, no one could say that the name of the creek in the far northwest corner of Georgia wasn't appropriate. The Confederate victory struck a body blow to the Union war effort in the Western Theater that could have been disastrous if the Rebels had pursued their defeated foe, and if the Yankees hadn't quickly bounced back at the Battle of Chattanooga. Major General William S. Rosecrans was in command of the Union's 57,000-man Army of the Cum

berland when he responded to bad intelligence indicating
that the Confederates were retreating in nearby North Georgia. Rosecrans ordered his troops out of their heavily fortified
positions in Chattanooga to pursue General Braxton Bragg's
67,000-man Confederate Army of Tennessee. Rosecrans had
ambitious plans to destroy Bragg's army, then march south to
take Atlanta and end the war by Christmas, and his initial
maneuvering was solid. Then his leadership began to fall
apart. Rosecrans split his army into three columns, setting
the divided forces up for disaster if Bragg attacked the corps
piecemeal. But the Confederates dithered, and after a few
skirmishes Rosecrans began regrouping his forces on the
west bank of Chickamauga Creek on September 13. On September 18 the battle began with a series of bloody clashes up
and down the lines that ended with neither side gaining any
substantial advantages or territory. During the fighting both
sides received reinforcements, with Rosecrans's third and
final column arriving to reunite his complete army and the
last remaining brigades led by Lieutenant General James
Longstreet shoring up the Confederates. That night Bragg
split his army into two wings, one under Longstreet and the
other under Lieutenant General Leonidas Polk, who were to
attack at dawn and turn the enemy's flank, leading the Union
away from Chattanooga. But orders were lost, confusion
reigned among Bragg's command, and Polk's wing didn't attack until well after 9:00 A.M. Union forces led by General
George Thomas were desperately holding on when Rosecrans mistakenly thought he detected a gap in the center of
the Union line and pulled a critical division from its spot in
the line to fill the nonexistent hole. That created a real hole
left by the divisional shift, which Longstreet quickly moved
to exploit. In minutes the charging Rebels were smashing
through the undefended Union line and drove almost a mile to
the enemy's rear. Rosecrans's right flank collapsed and Bluecoats began fleeing for their lives. The panic was so complete
that Rosecrans and his staff were swept up in the retreat to
Chattanooga. The rout would have been complete if not for
he heroics of General Thomas, who led the remaining Fed-

erals in forming a horseshoe-shaped defensive line around a
strategic high point named Snodgrass Hill. Bragg neglected
to order Polk to join Longstreet in the attack, and Thomas
stubbornly held on until darkness fell and the fighting ended.
Under cover of darkness, Thomas pulled his troops back to
Chattanooga that night. Bragg stubbornly refused the urging
of Longstreet and other generals under his command to pursue and finish off the demoralized enemy. Cavalry general
Nathan Bedford Forrest was one of those most insistent on a
fast follow-up and told Bragg that "every hour is worth a
thousand men." But like Bragg's other officers, Forrest was
ignored. The battle ended as a Confederate victory, but with
golden opportunities lost by both sides. The Army of the
Cumberland suffered 16,200 casualties. The Confederates
had 8,500 fighting men put out of action. (See: Hood, Lieutenant General John Bell, CS; Howard, Major General Oliver
Otis, U.S.; Rock of Chickamauga; and Rosecrans, Major
General William Starke, U.S.)

Chimborazo Hospital
More than 76,000 patients passed through the Confederacy's
main medical complex, constructed on a hill just outside
Richmond.

Citadel Cannoneers
The first artillery shots of the war were fired by cadets from
the South Carolina Military Academy, better known as the
Citadel. And they weren't fired at Fort Sumter but at the *Star
of the West,* an unarmed paddle-wheel steamer sailing from
New York to Charleston Harbor to reinforce the Union garrison with supplies and 200 men from the 9th U.S. Infantry. It
was just after daybreak on January 9, 1861, when the steamer
was spotted in the ship channel and Cadet George Haynes-
worth pulled a lanyard, sending a shot over its bow. Before
the *Star of the West* turned back, the cadets fired 17 shots
from their batteries on Morris Island.

Civil War, Other Names
The bitter conflict fought between the North and South from 1861 to 1865 has been known by many names. They include: The War between the States, the Brothers' War, the War against Slavery, the War for Abolition, the War for the Union, the War of the Sixties, the War for States' Rights, the War of Secession, the War for Southern Independence, the War against Northern Aggression, the Southern Rebellion, the War for Southern Rights, the War for Southern Nationality, the War for Constitutional Liberty, Mr. Lincoln's War, the Great Rebellion, the War of the Rebellion, the Yankee Invasion, and the War to Suppress Yankee Arrogance. Some historians call it America's First Modern War.

Clalin, Private Frances, U.S.
A woman, Clalin posed as a man, dressed in the uniform of a state militia cavalryman, and fought with the Union in Missouri.

Clancy, Sergeant Charles, CS
The standard-bearer for the 1st Louisiana was carrying the regimental colors during the Confederate assault on Culp's Hill at the Battle of Gettysburg when he realized he had outdistanced his comrades. Surrounded by Yankees, Clancy removed the flag from its staff, wrapped it around his body, and kept it there during six months as a prisoner of war before he was exchanged. Then he proudly returned the flag to his regiment.

Clark, Edward
As lieutenant governor of Texas when Sam Houston was forced by the delegates to the State Secession Convention to step down as governor, Clark was named to take his place. (See: Houston, Sam.)

Cleburne, Major General Patrick, CS
Born in Ireland, Cleburne was one of only two foreign-born officers to achieve the rank of major general in the Confed-

erate Army. He was known as the Stonewall Jackson of the West.

Clem, Major General John Lincoln, U.S.

Johnny Clem was nine years old when he ran away from his Ohio home to join the army. He was rejected by one regiment, so he joined another as a drummer boy. Clem became famous after newspaper reporters learned that his drum was blown out of his arms during the Battle of Shiloh. That led to his nickname, Johnny Shiloh, and to a popular song and a stage play written about him. At the Battle of Chickamauga, he shot and killed a Confederate colonel who attempted to take him prisoner. That led to a new nickname, the Drummer Boy of Chickamauga, and promotion to lance sergeant. By the time he was twelve he had been wounded twice, captured once, and released in a prisoner exchange. A few years later, after he was refused an appointment to West Point because of a lack of formal education and his small stature, President Grant arranged for Clem to be commissioned as a second lieutenant in command of a company of black soldiers. Clem retired from the army in 1915 as a major general shortly before the United States entered World War I.

Coal Bombs

The invention of two brilliant brothers who loved to tinker with explosives, these small bombs were enclosed in heavy black iron casings and looked just like lumps of coal. But when they were planted in a coal barge, then unknowingly shoveled into the boiler of a ship—like the captured blockade runner *Greyhound*—they exploded with devastating effect. Union general Benjamin Butler and Admiral David Porter were aboard the bad-luck ship when it blew up and sank in the James River in 1864 but escaped uninjured. (See: Raines Brothers.)

Cockpit Point, Battle of

This fight on January 3, 1862, was bloodless, but two Union gunboats fought furiously in a failed effort to end a three month blockade of the Potomac River by Confederates who had 37 heavy guns in batteries at four locations. The Union ships withdrew with the river still closed but returned on March 9 to fight it out again with the batteries at Cockpit Point, Evansport, Freestone Point, and Shipping Point, only to discover that the Confederates had withdrawn from their positions.

Coffee Cooler

A slang term for malingerers or shirkers. They were considered soldiers who would only begin work when the coffee cooled.

Cold Harbor, Battle of

If there was anything to be learned from the costly Union disaster at Cold Harbor, it was that frontal attacks are a shameful waste of troops ordered to assault an enemy that is well dug in and backed by artillery. Before General Ulysses S. Grant digested this bitter pill, it cost his 108,000-man Army of the Potomac a staggering 7,000 casualties. Confederate general Robert E. Lee, who was in overall command of the 59,000-man Army of Northern Virginia, suffered fewer than 1,500 casualties. On May 26, 1864, during the Virginia Campaign, Grant began an effort to outflank General Lee by taking the little road junction of Old Cold Harbor a bare ten miles northeast of the Confederate capital at Richmond. Anxious to keep his army between the advancing enemy and Richmond, on June 1 Lee ordered General Richard Anderson's I Corps forward to seize the crossroads. At that time it was held by two cavalry divisions under command of General Philip Sheridan, and the outnumbered Bluecoats put up a ferocious defense that enabled them to hold out until the arrival of reinforcements by General Horatio Wright's VI Corps. The reinforced Federals finally repulsed the assault, and both sides moved into positions facing each other along a seven-mile front. At about dusk, the VI Corps, along with General William Smith's XVIII Corps, counterattacked the firmly entrenched enemy with a frontal assault. The attack was a disaster and cost the Federals 2,200 casualties before the survivors fell back. Before daybreak on June 3, Grant ordered another assault, this time with three corps against the Confederate lines now held by Anderson's I Corps and General Ambrose Hill's III Corps. The assault lasted for about an hour before General George Meade, the field commander, called off the disastrous attack. Union survivors of the slaughter dug in about one hundred yards from their enemy, and for the next eight days Billy Yanks and Johnny Rebs fought each other from their trenches. At last, on the night of June 12, a severely chastened Grant ordered the Federals to move out. The Battle of Cold Harbor was over, and Grant expressed lifelong regret over the waste of the lives of so many of his men in the futile frontal assaults. (See: Anderson, Lieutenant General Richard Heron, CS; Hill, Lieutenant General Ambrose Powell, CS; Meade, Major General George G., U.S.; Sheridan, General Philip Henry, U.S.)

Colt Army Revolver

Widely used by Union cavalry, this .44-caliber revolver took either loose powder and ball or cartridges of paper, foil, or skin and was loaded by half-cocking the hammer to free the cylinder. Ammunition was then dropped into each chamber and tamped down with the rammer attached under the barrel.

Colt Revolving Rifle

This Union arm was a rifle-sized version of the Colt revolver. Although highly prized for its rapid action, the .56-caliber breech-loader could be capricious. It was known for sometimes discharging all five chambers at once and severing a few of the shooter's fingers from his forward hand.

Commissioned Officers

More than 125,000 men served in the Union's volunteer army as commissioned officers.

Confederate States of America

Formation of the Confederate States of America was formally announced on February 8, 1861, by delegates to the convention assembled in Montgomery, Alabama, to organize a new government. Delegates from six of the original seven states to secede, minus Texas, whose delegates were still en route, were present. The new confederation, with a population of a mere 9 million, was only about a quarter of the size of the Union. And that included 4 million slaves. Predictably, the CSA's new constitution was strong on states' rights, provided individual states with the right to create their own armies, and allowed the different states to enter into separate agreements with one another. Addressing the touchy issue of slavery, which was at the core of much of the quarreling that had led to secession, the central government was prohibited from passing laws forbidding the ownership of slaves. But it would be illegal to import slaves from outside the CSA. (See: Cradle of the Confederacy; Davis, Jefferson Finis; and Secession.)

Confederate Territory of Arizona

The Civil War was barely under way before Texans led by Lieutenant Colonel John Baylor captured the southern halves of the Arizona and New Mexico territories for the South in July 1861. Baylor named the huge land area the Confederate Territory of Arizona.

Conscription, Confederacy

The first military draft in America's history was authorized on April 16, 1862, by the government of the Confederacy. It was eleven months before the Union passed the Enrollment Act of 1863. Months of tinkering with the Confederacy's compulsory service law filled it with loopholes and amendments that allowed civil servants, certain other professionals, large slave owners, and the wealthy to avoid the draft. Other draft dodgers arranged to have their names falsely added to civil service rolls or joined state militias. The special treat-

ment, including a provision that permitted wealthy draftees
to pay substitutes to take their place, led to bitter complaints
by less-privileged Southerners that they were involved in "a
rich man's war and a poor man's fight." The storm of criticism over hiring of substitutes led to abolishment of the provision in December 1863. Slaves were also exempted by the
Southerners, who were wary of providing them with firearms
and training, as well as doubtful of their reliability to perform under fire. The Confederacy's Conscription Act of 1862
made healthy white males between the ages of 18 and 35
who were not covered by the exceptions liable for a three-
year term of service. Enlistments for one-year recruits were
also extended to three years. The act was amended in September, hiking the age limit to 45, and in February 1864 it
was changed again to permit conscription of men between
the ages of 17 and 50. Railroaders, river workers, telegraph
operators, miners, druggists, and teachers were included with
civil servants among those with exempted occupations. In
October 1864 the act was again changed to exempt men who
owned 20 or more slaves. (See: Enrollment Act.)

Conscription, Union
See Draft Riots; and Enrollment Act.

Contraband
Before Lincoln delivered his historic Emancipation Proclamation, slaves who had crossed Union lines or fled from their
owners were considered and described in the North as contraband. According to a confiscation law passed by the Congress, the Federal government was authorized to seize slaves,
farm animals, and other property owned by anyone who
joined the Confederacy.

Cooper, Major General Joseph Alexander, U.S.
A veteran of the Mexican War, Cooper worked fervently to
keep his home state of Tennessee from seceding. When the
Volunteer State left the Union anyway, Cooper secretly re

cruited like-minded men and traveled with them to Kentucky, where they were sworn into the Union Army, forming the 1st Tennessee Infantry Regiment. He became one of the captains. After fighting at Mill Springs in Kentucky and in several clashes in his home state, Cooper was promoted to colonel of the 6th Tennessee. He served at Stones River, Chickamauga, and Chattanooga before joining Major General William T. Sherman for the remaining Tennessee campaigns and the march on Atlanta. On July 30, 1864, he was promoted to brigadier general. He was placed in command of a brigade, but after the Battle of Jonesboro he held a divisional command at Franklin, Nashville, and Bentonville. At the conclusion of the war he was brevetted major general of volunteers for his service and for his actions during the Battle of Nashville.

Copperhead Regiment
An alternate nickname for the 20th Massachusetts Volunteers Infantry Regiment, the hard-fighting unit associated with the Copperheads because of the antiabolitionist sentiments of many of its officers. Two companies composed of German immigrants also harbored strong antiabolitionist sentiments. The 20th Massachusetts was more commonly known as the Harvard Regiment. (See: Copperheads; and Harvard Regiment.)

Copperheads
Members of a Northern faction of the Democratic Party known as Peace Democrats, who opposed abolitionists and supported the South because they believed the Civil War was unconstitutional, were also called Copperheads. Their political enemies coined the name because they considered Northerners who sympathized with the South as deadly to the Union as the colorful pit vipers were to people. (See: Copperhead Regiment.)

Corbett, Boston, U.S.

Corbett claimed to be the man who shot and killed John Wilkes Booth after the president's assassin was cornered by Federal troops while he was hiding in a rural Virginia tobacco barn. Most historians discount Corbett's claim and point to forensic evidence that indicates Booth took his own life. (See: Lincoln Assassination.)

Corydon, Battle of

See Morgan's Great Raid.

Cotton

Cotton was king in the South, and the Confederacy counted heavily on its exports of raw cotton and tobacco to finance the war and, in a best possible scenario from the Southern point of view, to bring England and perhaps France to its assistance. Almost one-quarter of England's population worked in or otherwise profited from the textile industry, and the Confederacy was hopeful that the need for a continued supply of the raw product would lead the powerful European nations to keep the shipments coming with loans, war matériel, and diplomatic recognition. And many in the South believed that if Federal warships prevented cotton from leaving their ports, England might even declare the blockade illegal under international law and send its own fleet to break the blockade. Early in the war, some Confederate government officials and cotton brokers declared a voluntary embargo in hopes of creating a shortage and speeding up foreign reaction against the Union. The effort at cotton diplomacy turned out to be a costly mistake, because British and French warehouses were bulging with cotton due to a recent bumper crop. There was such an oversupply that in fact Britain sold some to mills in New England, where there was a real shortage, at jacked-up prices. And when the oversupply finally began to dwindle after more than a year, Britain simply turned to other sources in Egypt and India, which at that time were both part of the British Empire.

Cotton-Clads

Gunboats and Confederate warships were sometimes outfitted with tightly pressed bales of cotton as armor in place of
iron, which was in short supply in the South. Cotton was
plentiful, because of the Union blockade of Southern ports
that prevented its sale to foreign buyers. Two cotton-clads
that saw action during the Battle of Galveston were the CSS
Bayou City and the CSS *Neptune*. (See: Galveston, Battle of.)

Cradle of the Confederacy

Montgomery, Alabama, earned its historic nickname when it
was selected for the convention in February 1861 that led to
formation of the Confederate States of America. Jefferson
Davis was inaugurated as the provisional president in a ceremony on the capitol steps, and Montgomery became the
Confederate capital. The small town just below the conflu-
ence of the Coosa and Tallapoosa Rivers held that distinction
for less than three months, before the capital was moved northeast to Richmond, Virginia. (See: Davis, Jefferson Finis; Republic of Alabama; and Richmond, Virginia.)

Crater, Battle of the

Fed up with his inability to take Petersburg, Virginia, in 1864
General Grant agreed to the scheme of a lieutenant colonel
who was a mining engineer in civilian life to dig a hole under
the Confederate positions and blow them up with four tons
of black powder. The colonel, a man named Pleasants, commanded a regiment from the Pennsylvania coal-mining country, and his experienced men dug a 511-foot tunnel and
carried out the dirt in cracker boxes before putting the black
powder in place. The imaginative plan called for four divisions of Bluecoats, including one division of black troops, to
charge into the gap as soon as the explosion was set off. At
dawn on July 30, the explosion ripped a hole 30 feet deep,
80 feet wide, and 170 feet long in the Confederate defenses.
Chunks of two cannon and 278 Confederates who had manned
the fort ceased to exist, except for body parts and a few
chunks of twisted metal. The Bluecoats rushed in, then halted,

milling around and staring at the destruction. More troops joined them to gawk as Lee and his Confederates rallied and attacked. Thousands of Federals were trapped in the crater, unable to climb the 30-foot sides of slippery, shifting loose dirt. They were helpless when the Southerners opened up on the packed mass inside the crater with artillery and followed up with infantry to mop up the Bluecoats hanging around the rim. Lee lost 1,500 men. The Union lost 4,400, and Grant called the event "the saddest affair I have ever witnessed in the war."

Crittenden, Major General George B., CS

Crittenden was a brigadier general commanding Confederate forces in East Tennessee when the Southerners were routed after three hours of fierce fighting at the Battle of Fishing Creek in Kentucky. Crittenden had 4,000 men in two brigades when they attacked the Yankees on January 19 after a grueling nine-mile march in a steady rain. Field formations prevented the Rebels from using their artillery, and the rain made the flintlock muskets most of the infantry were armed with useless. After one of the brigade leaders, Brigadier General Felix Zollicoffer was killed, General Crittenden ordered his demoralized troops to fall back, abandoning artillery and other equipment. Crittenden's brother, Thomas, was a Union Army general. (See: Crittenden, Major General Thomas L. U.S.; and Zollicoffer, Brigadier General Felix Kirk, CS.)

Crittenden, Major General Thomas L., U.S.

The son of U.S. senator John J. Crittenden and the brother of a Confederate general, Thomas fought in the Mexican War with Zachary Taylor. When the conflict between the states broke out the Kentuckian remained loyal to the Union, like his father. He was appointed as a brigadier general in September 1861 and promoted to major general in July 1862.

Crook, Major General George, U.S.

Considered by historians the U.S. Army's greatest Indian fighter for his performances both before and after the Civil

War, Crook was summoned from duty on the Pacific Northwest in 1861 and appointed colonel of the 36th Ohio Infantry. He quickly took advantage of his experience in the territories to direct guerrilla attacks against Confederates in West Virginia. He also fought at the Second Battle of Bull Run and at Chickamauga before he was brevetted major general of volunteers and named to command the Army of Virginia. After the conflict, Crook returned to the Pacific Northwest to pacify warring Paiute Indians. (See: Army of West Virginia; Blazer's Scouts; and Poltroonery.)

Cross Keys, Battle of

A strong Union force of 11,500 men led by Major General John C. Frémont was pursuing Stonewall Jackson's army through the Shenandoah Valley on June 8, 1862, when the Bluecoats clashed with a Confederate division led by Major General Richard S. Ewell at Cross Keys. The battle began with a two-hour artillery duel before Brigadier General Julius Stahel led a brigade against the enemy's right flank. The attackers fell back in confusion after they were badly shot up by Rebels under Brigadier General Isaac R. Trimble dug in on a ridge. Frémont appeared confused after the setback, and when he failed to order either a retreat or an advance Trimble took the initiative. He ordered an attack on a Union battery, which fell back while the Confederates advanced so far that they were cut off from Ewell's troops. Even though the Rebels were outnumbered nearly three to one, Frémont still failed to order an attack. Frémont at last ordered a withdrawal under the protection of Union artillery, and the battle was over. Union casualties were 951 men. The Confederates, who were outnumbered, lost 287 men. (See: Frémont, Major General John C., U.S.; Port Republic, Battle of; and Trimble, Brigadier General Isaac R., CS.)

Crump, Private Pleasant Riggs, CS

A former private with the 10th Alabama Regiment, Crump died on New Year's Eve, 1951, and is believed to have been the last living Confederate soldier. He was outlived by three

other claimants, now believed to have been impostors. There
is no dispute over Crump's place in history as the last surviving Civil War soldier to have been present at Appomattox
Courthouse when General Robert E. Lee surrendered to the
Union's Ulysses S. Grant. Crump was born in Crawford's
Cove, Alabama, on December 23, 1847, and was 16 when he
and a buddy made their way to Petersburg, Virginia, to enlist
in the Confederate Army. Private Crump was assigned to
Company A, 10th Alabama Infantry, and fought at Hatcher's
Run, then during the Siege and Battle of Petersburg before
witnessing the surrender. After walking home to Alabama,
he became a farmer and was eventually given the honorary
title of colonel by the United Confederate Veterans. (See:
Williams, Walter Washington, CS.)

Culpeper Court House, Battle of
General George Custer played a leading role in the Union
victory at the Battle of Culpeper Court House in Virginia on
September 13, 1863, that chased the Confederates from a
vital train depot.

Cumberland Pontoons
Union general George H. Thomas was commander of the
Army of the Cumberland when he spearheaded development
of revolutionary new folding pontoons to help his troops and
equipment ford rivers and streams. They were called Cumberland pontoons, after his army. (See: Thomas, Major General George Henry, U.S.)

Curry, Lieutenant Colonel
Jabez Lamar Monroe, CS
Georgia-born Curry made his mark serving the Confederacy
after moving to Alabama, serving in the state legislature,
then being elected to Congress, where he became an outspoken proponent of secession. When Alabama seceded, Curry
left Washington and was named to the Provisional Confederate Congress, then was formally elected to the seat. Curry
strongly supported the war and urged Confederate president

Davis to take a military command. After Curry was defeated in a reelection bid, then also lost a race for the Senate, he was appointed lieutenant colonel with the 5th Alabama Cavalry. A Mexican War veteran, Curry commanded the regiment in Alabama during the final stages of the war. After the Confederate surrender, he played a leading role in establishing a public school system in the Southern states and accepted diplomatic appointments.

Cushman, Pauline
This lionhearted actress toasted the South from the stage after a performance in Kentucky to gain the confidence of Confederates before she was unmasked as a Union spy. She was arrested and condemned to be shot by a firing squad, but she was freed when the Union Army overran Confederate positions before the sentence could be carried out.

Custer, Lieutenant Colonel Thomas Ward, U.S.
A younger brother of General George A. Custer, Tom was the only soldier ever to win two Medals of Honor during the Civil War. Joining the army as a private in Company H, 21st Ohio, when he was still a teenager, Custer fought at Stones River, Chickamauga, and Chattanooga and in the Atlanta Campaign before being mustered out on October 10, 1864, after completing his three-year enlistment. Less than a month later he was appointed second lieutenant in the 6th Michigan Cavalry and joined the staff of his brother, who was fighting in the Shenandoah Valley. After the division was sent to participate in the Siege of Petersburg, Tom Custer earned his first Medal of Honor for capturing a Rebel flag in a skirmish at Namozine Church on April 3, 1863. Three days later he earned his second award at Sayler's Creek, where he leaped his horse over enemy defenses and captured the Rebel colors despite being shot in the face. Tom Custer turned the colors over to his brother, who placed him under arrest to prevent him from returning to the fight, so he could be given medical attention. Lieutenant Custer was brevetted to major of volunteers, then to lieutenant colonel in the regular army for his

heroism and later died with his brother at Little Big Horn. (See: Namozine Church.)

Custer, Major General George Armstrong, U.S.

Graduating at the bottom of his class at West Point in the year the Civil War started, Custer was appointed a second lieutenant with the 5th Cavalry. The young officer was a better soldier than student and moved quickly up the ranks while serving with the Army of the Potomac, Army of West Virginia, and Army of Shenandoah. At the age of 23 on June 29, 1863, he was promoted to brigadier general, becoming the youngest general in the Union Army. Supremely self-confident and courageous, he was noted for his gallantry during the second day of the Battle of Gettysburg when he led a series of frontal assaults while commanding a Michigan cavalry brigade. Custer also fought at Antietam, Chancellorsville, Bristoe, Mine Run, Yellow Tavern, and Five Forks and in the Peninsular and Appomattox campaigns. He was promoted to major general of volunteers on April 15, 1865. The dashing war hero was later named a regular army lieutenant colonel of the new 7th Cavalry and in 1876 was killed with 265 other officers and men while fighting Indians at the Battle of the Little Bighorn.

Cuvier, Major General Grover, U.S.

A West Pointer, Cuvier served in the West, where he was promoted to captain, before the Civil War began, when he went east to participate in the defense of Washington. Promoted to brigadier general of volunteers, he was given command of the 1st Brigade, 2d Division, 3d Army Corps, Army of the Potomac. Brevetted lieutenant colonel, U.S., for gallantry at Williamsburg and colonel for his performance at Fair Oaks, he was transferred with his brigade to General John Pope's army. After leading his men in a valiant bayonet charge against heavily entrenched enemy, Cuvier was transferred to the Department of the Gulf. There he led the 4th Division of the 19th Corps during the capture of Baton Rouge and fought in the Siege of Port Hudson. Cuvier also fought valiantly at Winchester, Fisher's Hill, and Cedar Creek, where he was wounded and brevetted major general of volunteers. On March 13, 1865, he was brevetted to the rank of major general in the regular army. After the war he served on frontier and garrison duty with the cavalry. (See: Mosby, Colonel John Singleton, CS.)

D

Dahlgren Gun

A naval cannon designed by Union admiral John A. Dahlgren, who commanded the South Atlantic Blockading Squadron. The 11-inch gun could hurl a 170-pound shell at the enemy and was especially useful against ironclads. (See: Dahlgren, Rear Admiral John A., USN.)

Dahlgren, Rear Admiral John A., USN

Dahlgren was chief of the Bureau of Ordnance when he was shifted from shore duty to a combat assignment so he could prove himself as a shipboard and fleet commander. He assumed command of the Union fleet during the blockade of Charleston and the combined army and navy assault on Fort Sumter and other coastal defenses. Charleston was still holding out in January 1865 when Dahlgren met with General Sherman to coordinate army and navy operations for the march through the Carolinas. A few weeks later the admiral's flagship, the USS *Harvest Moon,* was sailing in Wynyah Bay when it struck a torpedo. The ship sank in minutes, but Dahlgren escaped with the loss of only a single crewman. (See: Dahlgren Gun.)

Davis, Brigadier General Jefferson Columbus

This U.S. Volunteers brigadier general was the Civil War's "other Jeff Davis," and the Clark County, Indiana, native fought for the Union. But the arrogant boaster who enlisted as a private in the 3d Indiana Regiment and fought at Buena Vista during the Mexican War in 1847 served as an officer at

Fort Moultrie, and was at Fort Sumter during the siege that opened the Civil War isn't remembered for his heroics. Davis made the history books when he fatally shot his superior officer, army major general William Nelson, 37. The fatal encounter occurred after Davis was ordered to assist Nelson setting up defenses at Louisville and the senior officer ordered the younger man to organize a home guard detachment of local citizens. The cocky Davis considered the task beneath him, leading to a confrontation that ended with Nelson angrily ordering Davis back across the Ohio River to Cincinnati. Davis returned to Louisville with General Don Carlos Buell at the head of his own division of U.S. Volunteers, and when on Sept. 29, 1862, he demanded an apology from Nelson the burly major general slapped him across the face with the back of his hand, then stalked away. Outraged, Davis borrowed a pistol from a companion. A few minutes later when the two enemies confronted each other in a hallway, and without uttering a word, Davis raised the pistol and fired a single shot into Nelson's heart. Although Davis was immediately placed under arrest, fate intervened and two generals who vowed to see justice done were killed in battle. Davis also had powerful friends, and the dead man had made bitter enemies. Between them, they saw to it that Davis was never court-martialed or tried in a civilian court for the murder of General Nelson. Davis returned to duty and participated in several Civil War battles before he mustered out in 1866, then fought in the Modoc Indian War. He died in Chicago of pneumonia in 1879. (See: Buell, Major General Don Carlos, U.S.; and Nelson, Major General William.)

Davis, Jefferson Finis

Sworn in as provisional president of the Confederacy on February 8, 1861, Davis was formally elected to a six-year term in November and inaugurated on February 22, 1862—George Washington's birthday. Davis respected and got along well with General Lee but quarreled with just about everyone else in his administration and the military over strategy and tactics. Like most of the generals who fought for him,

including former classmate Robert E. Lee, Davis was a West
Point graduate. But unlike his generals, he graduated in the
lower third of his class and had just enough knowledge of
military strategy and tactics to consider himself an expert.
After graduation, the young officer was assigned to posts in
Illinois and Wisconsin and briefly fought Indians during the
Blackhawk Wars. He also fell in love with Sarah Taylor, the
daughter of one of his post commandants, Colonel Zachary
Taylor, and eventually married her against her father's wishes
after resigning from the army. The lovers were married less
than three months before they both caught malaria and Sarah
died. Although Davis was born in Christian County, Kentucky, he owned a plantation in Mississippi, and after his
wife's death he worked there ten years before the outbreak
of the war. During that decade he had become an ardent
proslaver and outspoken defender of states' rights. In 1845
he was elected to Congress and married for the second time.
Davis had barely been sworn into his new job when he resigned to fight inflated confidence in his own military knowledge. After the Mexican War, Davis returned to Washington,
this time as a U.S. senator from Mississippi. In 1853 he
moved from the Senate to the cabinet of President Franklin
Pierce, where he served three years as secretary of war. Then
he returned to the sharply divided Senate, where he sought a
political compromise that would preserve the Union, until
the election of Abraham Lincoln as the new president. Re-
acting to Lincoln's statement that he would not tolerate slavery in any of the territories, Davis resigned from the Senate
on January 21, 1861, and returned to the South, where he
hoped to be named military commander of the Confederate
armies. Instead, he became the president of the Confederate States of America. (See: Cradle of the Confederacy; and
Davis, Jefferson, Capture of.)

Davis, Jefferson, Capture of

With the defeat of his ragtag armies and the South devastated, General Robert E. Lee notified CSA president Davi‹

that the Confederate capital at Richmond could no longer be defended and it was time for the government to flee. Davis was still hopeful that he and his cabinet could fall back to Danville on the North Carolina border and the South could continue the war. So he gathered the $500,000 in gold that remained in the Confederate treasury, a chest full of jewels, Confederate banknotes, and negotiable bonds, then boarded a train for Danville. Federal troops entered Richmond and Petersburg the next day. A week after Davis and his cabinet fled the capital, General Lee surrendered to Grant. The Confederacy was dead, and Davis and members of his cabinet split up to make their escape. Several of the dispossessed bureaucrats, including Davis, hoped to find refuge in Texas or Mexico. Davis had been reunited with his wife and family in Georgia when the already-determined Bluecoats stepped up their manhunt with a vengeance following the death of President Lincoln. President Andrew Johnson had mistakenly—and wrongly—named Davis as a conspirator in the assassination. On May 10, a month and a day after Lee's surrender, a detachment of the 4th Michigan Cavalry captured the fugitive near Irvinville, Georgia. As he and his family were transported to nearby Macon, Union soldiers taunted him by chanting, "We'll hang Jeff Davis from a sour apple tree." Davis wasn't hanged but was shackled and locked up in Fort Monroe, Virginia. He remained there without trial for two years before the national press stirred up world opinion sufficiently to obtain his release on $100,000 bail. Newspaper giant Horace Greeley and another abolitionist put up the bail. The Federal government dismissed all charges against Davis in 1869, and he lived another 20 years before his death on December 9, 1889. The man who served as the only president of the CSA never sought restoration of his American citizenship. But more than a century after Davis's death, his citizenship was at last restored by a former Georgia governor, President Jimmy Carter. (See: Davis, Jefferson Finis.)

D.C. Emancipation Bill

After a long and difficult campaign by Abraham Lincoln to end slavery in the District of Columbia, the D.C. Emancipation Bill was signed into law by the president on April 16, 1862. The Senate passed the bill by a 29–14 vote on April 3, and the House approved it by a 92–36 margin on April 12. The new law freed 3,100 slaves living in the district. Former slave owners were compensated with nearly $1 million, at a rate averaging about three hundred dollars per slave. (See: Thirteenth Amendment.)

Denbeigh, CSS

This Confederate blockade runner slipped past Federal gunboats off Mobile Bay so regularly that people in the Alabama port city began calling the swift little ship the packet. It at first appeared the *Denbeigh* was off to a poor start when on its first run from Havana it ran aground in heavy fog near the entrance to Mobile Bay. Federal gunboats put a shot through the stricken ship's wheelhouse and continued their target practice until the *Denbeigh* unloaded enough cargo to refloat her and escape. On July 26, 1864, on the *Denbeigh*'s seventh and last run to the port, the ship became the last Confederate vessel to slip through the blockade to open sea before Mobile fell to the Union. The *Denbeigh* then made seven successful runs through the blockade into Galveston, the last major port still held by the Confederacy on the Gulf of Mexico. The war ended for the *Denbeigh* on the night of May 23, 1865—six weeks after General Lee's surrender at Appomattox—when she ran aground on Bird Key while trying to enter Galveston Harbor. After the crew escaped to the shore, boarding parties from Federal gunboats burned the stranded vessel. (See: *Lark,* CSS.)

Devil's Coffee Mill

See Machine Gun.

Devil's Den (Gettysburg)

A clump of boulders at the foot of a hill known as Little Round Top where some of the fiercest fighting of the Battle of Gettysburg occurred.

Devil's Den (Mississippi)

The name given to a cave by a band of Union sympathizers and Confederate deserters in eastern Mississippi who used it as a hideout from which they launched raids. The guerrillas left their refuge on an island in the Leaf River in Jones County to ambush Rebel soldiers, assassinate tax collectors and other Confederate supporters, burn bridges, sink ferryboats, and provide food to local families left destitute because of their Union sympathies and the war. (See: Knight, Newton; and Maury, Colonel Henry, CS.)

Dictator, the

See Rail Gun.

Divine Retribution

When Charleston, South Carolina, was ravaged by a fire on December 11 and 12, 1861, which raced across 540 acres, leaving little except brick and stone chimneys in its path, Northerners pronounced the calamity divine retribution wreaked on the city where the war began. Institute Hall, where South Carolina's Ordinance of Secession was signed, was among the casualties. (See: Fort Sumter; Secession; and Stone Fleet.)

Dix, Dorothea

Shortly after the war began, Dorothea Dix was appointed the Union's superintendent of women nurses. During the course of the war she had responsibility for recruiting, training, and assignment of 2,000 female nurses tending to the Union's sick and injured. She turned down thousands of young women volunteers for being too young, too pretty, or perceived husband hunters.

"Dixie"

The unofficial anthem of the Confederacy, "Dixie" was actually popular with troops on both sides of the conflict, and it was even played at the inaugurations of Abraham Lincoln and Jefferson Davis. It wasn't even composed by a Southerner but by New Yorker Daniel Decater Emmett. The original title of the song, written in 1859, was "Dixie's Land," but the Rebels and Yankees who sang it while marching into battle or sitting around campfires knew it as simply "Dixie." Historians disagree on the genesis of the song. Some link it to the Mason-Dixon Line, but others trace it to the ten-dollar notes issued by Louisiana that were known as "Dixies." Louisiana's French influence was recognized on the note with the word *ten* printed as *dix*. (See: "Battle Hymn of the Republic"; and Mason-Dixon Line.)

Dog Tags

There were no dog tags in the Civil War, so soldiers bought IDs from sutlers, fashioned their own from flattened bullets and other scrap metal, or simply wrote out their names and other information on scraps of paper to carry with them into battle. At least 10 different types of ID tags are known to have been peddled by sutlers and were made from various materials, including coins, brass, pewter, and lead.

Dog Tent

Both the North and the South suffered from lack of proper equipment, and Yankee soldiers were almost a full year into the war before they were issued the two-man shelters quickly nicknamed dog tents. That was because the tents were said to be barely big enough to cover a dog. Tent mates each carried half a canvas, which they buttoned together at night to make a crude shelter that had no flaps at either end and left their heads and feet open to the elements.

Doubleday, General Abner, U.S.

The Union officer who is generally credited with inventing the sport of baseball was a captain and second in command at Fort Sumter when he ordered the first shots fired at Southern forces. By the opening day of the Battle of Gettysburg, Doubleday had advanced to the rank of general and took over command of the Union I Corps after the death of General John F. Reynolds. (See: Fort Sumter; Gettysburg, Battle of; and Reynolds, Major General John F., U.S.)

Douglass, Frederick

Born Frederick Augustus Washington Bailey to a slave mother and an unknown white father in 1817, this abolitionist firebrand was taught to read and write by the mistress of a home in Baltimore where he was sent at age eight to work as a house servant. After moving on to New Bedford, Massachusetts, and changing his last name to Douglass to make it more difficult for slave catchers to find him and return him to his owner, he became a full-time lecturer for the Anti-Slavery Society. When the Civil War began, Douglass encouraged blacks to enlist in the Union Army to help achieve emancipation and all the rights of full citizenship. (See: Abolition.)

Draft Riots

Opposition to conscription and loopholes that favored the wealthy led to draft riots in Northern cities and towns that culminated with four days of arson, lynching, and looting in New York City from July 13 to 16, 1863. The riot broke out at a draft office at Third Avenue and 46th Street while names were being drawn from a lottery wheel, and the building was burned. Then the mob marched to other areas of the city, looting an armory of more than 1,000 rifles, burning the Negro Orphan Asylum, and setting fire to other buildings. Blacks were especially singled out for lynching and beatings by the overwhelmingly Irish rioters, who blamed them for taking jobs and causing the war. Riots also occurred in other cities and towns around the country, including Port Washington, Wisconsin, near Milwaukee, where immigrant farmers from Luxembourg believed the draft commissioner was unfairly exempting Republican and Masonic friends. The draft commissioner was beaten up and thrown down the courthouse steps and fled to Milwaukee to summon government troops. The rioters chased down and beat Masons, tore up the Masonic Hall, and loaded the town's single cannon with the only available cannonball before six companies of the 28th Wisconsin Regiment arrived and put down the rebellion. One hundred and fifty rioters were arrested and imprisoned for a year.

Dranesville, Battle of

Brigadier General J. E. B. Stuart was at the head of a mixed force of Confederate cavalry, infantry, and artillery on December 20, 1861, protecting a foraging expedition in Fairfax County, Virginia, when he clashed with a Union brigade near Dranesville. The Bluecoats were led by Brigadier General E. O. C. Ord. After ensuring that his supply wagons were safely out of danger, Stuart broke off the firefight and withdrew. The Confederates suffered 230 casualties; the Union, 71.

Dred Scott Decision

The U.S. Supreme Court's 7–2 decision of 1857 in *Dred Scott vs. John F. A. Sandford* seemed be a blessing for the South, but it stoked Northern antagonism to slavery, widened sectional differences, and helped set the stage for the Civil War. The court ruled against Scott, who had sued for his freedom in Missouri claiming that because he had lived with his master in free states he was no longer a slave.

Drewry's Bluff, Battle of

When the Confederate ironclad CSS *Virginia* (*Merrimac*) was scuttled at the Gosport Navy Yards in 1862 to prevent its capture during the Peninsular Campaign, the James River was open to Federal gunboats. Five Union gunboats, including the ironclads USS *Monitor* and USS *Galena,* steaming up the river to test the Richmond defenses were blocked by underwater obstacles, then targeted by a bombardment from batteries on Drewry's Bluff. The *Galena* was badly damaged, and the ships withdrew, ending the battle, known variously as Drewry's Bluff, Fort Drewry, and Fort Darling. (See: *Mer-rimac*, CSS; *Merrimac*, CSS, Sinking of; and *Monitor*, USS.)

Droop Mountain, Battle of
Two Union brigades were on a raid in southwestern Virginia to disrupt movement on the Virginia & Tennessee Railroad on November 6, 1863, when the force led by Brigadier General W. W. Averell encountered Confederates at Droop Mountain. After a short but fierce clash with the Rebels led by Brigadier General John Echols, Averell rode away with a victory and rejoined the other Union column, commanded by Brigadier General Alfred Napoleon Alexander Duffie, in Lewisburg the next day. Total casualties on both sides in the battle were 526 men. (See: Echols, Brigadier General John, CS.)

Drummer Boy of Chickamauga
See Clem, Major General John Lincoln, U.S.

Drums
Drums weren't used merely to inspire troops with martial music while marching but were also important tools for signaling maneuvers and tactical movements on the battlefield.

Duke, Brigadier General Basil Wilson, CS
A former Kentucky lawyer, Duke enlisted in the Lexington Rifles, commanded by his brother-in-law, John Hunt Morgan. Duke followed the brigadier general into the cavalry and on the famous raid into Indiana and Ohio, and after capture in Ohio he was exchanged in 1864. He was fighting in Virginia when he was promoted to brigadier general and took over his brother-in-law's old command after Morgan was killed. Duke provided protection for Jefferson Davis and the Confederate cabinet when they fled Richmond as the Confederacy fell, and led the last organized command responsible to the South's War Department.

Duryee's Zouaves

Abraham Duryee, a wealthy New York merchant who was active in the prewar state militia, raised his own regiment, the 5th New York Volunteers, on April 25, 1861. The 5th New York was better known as Duryee's Zouaves. Considered the most smartly dressed of all Zouave regiments, the 5th New York was outfitted with fezzes and white turbans, baggy red trousers, and blue Chasser jackets. The fez was sometimes replaced by a more practical red stocking cap in the field. Duryee's Zouaves was one of the most famous of all the volunteer regiments and was praised for its gallantry and discipline while engaging in combat at Gaines's Mill, Bull Run, Fredericksburg, Big Bethel, Chancellorsville, and the Siege of Yorktown. (See: Zouaves.)

D'Utassey, Frederick George, U.S.

The first commander of the Garibaldi Guard, D'Utassey was sent to prison after he was convicted of fraud and cashiered.

Dwight, Brigadier General William, U.S.

Dwight was a lieutenant colonel of the 70th New York Volunteers when he was wounded twice at the Battle of Williamsburg, where his regiment lost half its men. After being left for dead on the field, he was taken prisoner, then released in an exchange. On November 29, 1862, he was promoted to brigadier general of volunteers as reward for his gallantry on the field. Dwight was reassigned to the Western Theater and in 1863 led his brigade in the attack on Port Hudson on the Mississippi River. In the spring of 1864 he served as chief of staff to Major General Nathaniel P. Banks during the Red River Campaign, and that July Dwight was sent east again and assigned to the 1st Battalion of the 19th Army Corps. He served with General Philip H. Sheridan during the Shenandoah Valley Campaign and fought at Winchester, Fisher's Hill, and Cedar Creek. After the war, the Massachusetts native went into business in Cincinnati.

Dysentery

Poor food preservation and preparation, along with poor sanitation, led to devastating outbreaks of diarrhea, the symptom, and dysentery, the disease, which killed thousands of men, crippled entire regiments, and may have even affected the outcome of the Battle of Gettysburg. General Lee was suffering from a serious attack of the ailment on the critical third day of the battle, which most Civil War historians credit with turning the tide of the war in the Union's favor.

E

Early, Lieutenant General Jubal Anderson, CS

A West Point graduate and Virginia aristocrat, Early was pro-
fane and nasty-tempered but was a good general who was respected by his men. After serving in the Mexican War and
the Seminole Wars, he retired to practice law and go into poli-
tics. As war clouds prepared to burst over the nation in 1861
he attended the Virginia secession convention and voted to
remain in the Union. But the overall vote favored secession,
and Early joined the Confederate Army to defend Virginia
from invasion. He fought at First Bull Run in the first major
engagement of the war. Promoted to brigadier general after
the battle, he commanded a brigade during the Peninsular
Campaign in Virginia in the spring of 1862 and suffered a
shoulder wound at Williamsburg. Recovering quickly, he led
his division at Antietam, Chancellorsville, Fredericksburg,
Gettysburg, and the Wilderness. Advanced to lieutenant general, Early was put in charge of the new 1,400-man Army
of the Valley and ordered to move up through the Shenandoah Valley to throw a scare into Washington while foraging
for supplies to send back to Lee's forces at Petersburg.
Early's army marched into Maryland, and near the Monocacy River he routed a force of Yankees attempting to slow
down his advance toward Washington until reinforcements
could arrive. Two days later Early was only five miles outside
Washington. A strong troop of Federal reinforcements arrived just in time to prevent Early from capturing or burning
the city. Greatly outnumbered, Early was forced to withdraw
back into the Shenandoah but he was soon back to his old

tricks. This time he led his forces into Pennsylvania and burned Chambersburg after the residents refused to pay a $500,000 ransom. His earlier raid into Hagerstown and Frederick produced more than $200,000 in ransom money to save these cities. General Ulysses S. Grant finally put a stop to Early's marauding by ordering General Philip H. Sheridan to chase him down on his own ground in the Shenandoah Valley. Sheridan tore into his enemy with a vengeance, inflicting tremendous casualties. Early's forces were chewed up and shattered in three quickly successive battles from mid-September to mid-October 1864 at Winchester, Fisher's Hill, and Cedar Creek. After Sheridan had retaken the valley, he gave one more licking to Early at the Battle of Waynesboro. The spanking was so bad that General Lee relieved his fighting general of his command and sent him west to serve in Texas. The war ended before Early arrived to take on his new assignment. (See: Army of the Valley.)

Echelon
A staggered stair-step-like formation of parallel units of troops.

Echols, Brigadier General John, CS
A bear of a man who towered 6 feet, 4 inches tall and weighed 260 pounds, this former state legislator and commonwealth attorney recruited volunteers from western Virginia when the war began. Echols was appointed lieutenant colonel of the 27th Virginia and led the regiment during the First Battle of Bull Run. The 27th joined with four other regiments to earn a fighting reputation as the "Stonewall Brigade." Echols fought during the Shenandoah Valley Campaign and was wounded at Kernstown. He was still recuperating a few weeks later when he was promoted to brigadier general. After returning to duty, he assumed command of a brigade with the Army of Western Virginia, then was assigned as commander of the Army of Southwest Virginia. Echols's troops were defeated at the Battle of Droop Mountain, and he fought at the Battle of New Market and at Cold Harbor

before he was named to command the District of Southwest Virginia. Late in the war, he replaced Lieutenant General Jubal A. Early as commander of the Department of Western Virginia and was on his way to join Robert E. Lee's Army of Northern Virginia when he learned of the surrender at Appomattox. Echols turned his troops around and marched them to North Carolina, where they joined General Joseph E. Johnston's holdouts before surrendering in Augusta, Georgia.

Edmonds, Sarah Emma

A nurse from Canada, Sarah Emma was a mistress of disguise who crossed over from Union to Southern lines in Virginia 11 times on intelligence-collecting forays. The first time, she dyed her face brown and posed as a black man working on fortifications at Yorktown. When the dye began to fade and someone noticed her blue eyes she claimed to be a mulatto and hurried back to Union lines with the fortification plans. At other times she disguised herself as a washerwoman. When the Confederates began circulating her description, her Union collaborators kept her on their side of the lines as a counterespionage agent. Prior to becoming a spy, she used her amazing abilities of disguise to serve two years as a Yankee soldier while dressed as a man. (See: Women Soldiers.)

Ellerson's Mill, Battle of

Another name for the Battle of Mechanicsville, also sometimes known as the Battle of Beaver Creek or Beaver Dam Creek. (See: Mechanicsville, Battle of.)

Ellsworth, Colonel Ephraim Elmer, U.S.

Commander of the Volunteer 11th New York Fire Zouaves, Ellsworth, 24, became the first officer killed in the war after ripping a Confederate flag off the roof of the Marshall House hotel in Alexandria, Virginia, on May 24, 1861. As Ellsworth carried the flag downstairs, innkeeper James W. Jackson blasted him with a double-barreled shotgun. Moments later, Corporal Francis E. Brownell shot Jackson in the face, then bayoneted him. Ellsworth was a close friend of the president and worked in Lincoln's law firm before the war.

Elmira Prison

Confederate inmates called the prison at Elmira, the Union's notorious counterpart to Andersonville, in upstate New York "Hellmira." There was good reason for their bitterness, because conditions at the camp were appallingly brutal. The camp at Elmira wasn't open as long as Andersonville, but during its single year of existence, 1864–65, 3,000 of just more than 12,000 inmates died. That was a mortality rate of 24.4 percent, more than twice the 11.7 percent average for other Union camps. It was also higher than the average 15.3 percent death rate for all Southern prison camps and close to the ghastly 28 percent mortality for inmates at Andersonville. Unlike Andersonville, where the camp commandant appeared to thrive on brutal treatment of prisoners, the prison at Elmira was run by a humanitarian, Benjamin F. Tracy, who did his best to provide decent care for the inmates. But Tracy's best efforts were often blocked by Secretary of War Edwin Stanton's hatred for Confederates. As a result, the Southerners, housed in small tents and drafty barracks, sweltered in the summer, froze in the snowy, fierce winter, and suffered from lack of proper sanitation, medical care, and food. Smallpox, dysentery, pneumonia, and other dreadful diseases swept through the 30-acre camp. In October 1864, just when it was needed most, Stanton canceled delivery of beef to the prison and it was sold locally instead. Tracy's efforts to buy vegetables for inmates were also stopped by Stanton. Prisoners supplemented their meager diet of bread and a thin gruel that was mostly water by cooking rats. In one instance, a small dog belonging to a prison guard was captured and cooked. Hellmira closed after the last sick prisoner was repatriated in September 1865. (See: Andersonville Prison; and Tracy, Benjamin F.)

Elmore, Edward C.

The treasurer of the Confederacy, Elmore fought a duel with a newspaper editor who couldn't use his right arm because it was shattered at the Battle of Gaines's Mill. Elmore was upset because John Moncure Daniel printed a story in the Richmond *Examiner* claiming a high official in the treasury department had spent government money in faro parlors and on a bribe. The two men squared off in the uneven duel on August 16, 1864, with the right-handed Daniel shooting with his left hand. Daniel missed, but Elmore's single shot struck him in the right leg. Daniel was still recuperating a month later when Elmore was indicted for playing faro, paid a $500 fine, and resigned his cabinet position.

Elzey, Major General Arnold, CS

After graduating from West Point, Elzey dropped Jones as his last name and replaced it with his middle name, which was the family name of his paternal grandmother. With that out of the way, the Maryland native fought gallantly in the Mexican War and Seminole Wars. When the Civil War began, Elzey was in charge of the arsenal at Augusta, Georgia, and surrendered it to the South. Then he resigned his captain's commission in the U.S. Army and offered his services to the Confederacy. Commissioned as a colonel of the 1st Maryland Infantry Regiment, he fought at the First Battle of Bull Run, where he assumed command of his brigade after the temporary commander was wounded. Elzey's performance won him promotion to brigadier general, and he led a brigade under General Stonewall Jackson during the Shenandoah Campaign. A horse was shot out from under Elzey while he fought at Port Republic, and during the Seven Days Campaign Elzey was severely wounded in the face at Gaines's Mill. After recovery, he was promoted to major general and placed in charge of the defense of the Confederate capital as commander of the Department of Richmond. After being relieved of that command, he organized government clerks into a Local Defense Brigade, then served for a short time as chief of artillery of the Army of Tennessee. After the war he returned to Maryland and became a farmer.

Emancipation Proclamation

Union armies essentially became armies of liberation when Lincoln issued his historic Emancipation Proclamation on September 22, 1862. The commander in chief established a deadline in the proclamation, giving the breakaway states until January 1, 1863, to return to the Union. If the Confederates refused to comply and meet the deadline, all the slaves in those states would be "thenceforward and forever free." Of course, the rebellious slave states at that time were under control of the Confederacy, and before the decree could be enforced they would have to be occupied by Union forces. The proclamation nevertheless delivered a body blow to Southern morale, extended an olive branch to European powers that might be considering entering the war on the Confederate side, and encouraged support among the president's own political party at home, especially among the abolitionists. But like all elected officials, Lincoln was a politician, and the proclamation wasn't everything that it might have seemed to be. While it offered freedom to slaves in the South, there was no mention of slaves in neutral or loyal Union states. That was an important exclusion, especially for border states like Maryland and Kentucky, where Southern sympathies were strong, and provided the North with insurance against their possible bolting to the Confederacy. Slaves in territories that were not yet states were still slaves, and the proclamation made no provision for their emancipation. The president also offered financial compensation for the loss of slave property in states that were not in rebellion and recommended repatriating slaves to Africa or somewhere else outside the United States. (See: Hamlin, Hannibal.)

Emory, Major General William H., U.S.

Early in 1861, Emory's troops captured a contingent of Texans, the first Confederate prisoners of war taken in the four-year conflict. An 1831 West Point graduate and veteran army officer, Emory delivered his captives to Fort Leavenworth. Named a lieutenant colonel with the 6th Cavalry in May 1861, he fought in the Peninsular Campaign under General George B. McClellan and was commissioned brigadier general of volunteers on March 17, 1863. As commander of the 19th Corps under General Nathaniel Banks, Emory participated in the Red River Campaign and fought at Sabine Crossroads, Pleasant Hill, and Cane River. Transferred back to Virginia, he defeated Confederate lieutenant general Jubal Early at Opequan Creek and fought at Fisher's Hill and Cedar Creek. In 1865 Emory was named commander of the Department of West Virginia. He remained in the regular army after the war and retired in 1876 with the rank of brigadier general.

Enfield Rifle Musket
The most popular shoulder arm with Confederate troops was the British .577-caliber Enfield. The closest to a standard firearm of any of the varied weapons used by Confederate troops, the Enfield weighed more than nine pounds and was 55 inches long. It was reasonably accurate up to 1,000 yards. The Confederacy imported 400,000 Enfields from Britain.

Enfilade
A form of gunfire that rakes an enemy formation lengthwise or a formation that allows for such a tactic.

Enlistment, South
Of an estimated 1,140,000 men of combat age at the beginning of the war, more than 850,000 enlisted. Overall, including enlistment and the draft, through four years of war the Confederacy mobilized 1,250,000 men.

Enrollment Act
In March 1863 the Federal government adopted the Enrollment Act, allowing for conscription for three years of mili-

tary service of able-bodied men between the ages of 20 and 45. The new draft law marked the first time in history that compulsory military service was instituted by the U.S. government, although the Confederacy had initiated the draft almost a year earlier. At the beginning of the war, the North had about 4 million men who were the right age and physically fit for the draft. Before war's end, 2 million men had served in the Union military. That included 46,000 men who were drafted and 118,000 paid substitutes, as well as volunteers who served for various lengths of time. New immigrants, including many from Ireland, swelled the North's reservoir of military recruits throughout the war. (See: Bounty; Bounty Jumpers; and Draft Riots.)

Evans, Brigadier General Nathan G. "Shanks," CS

This native South Carolinian and West Pointer first distinguished himself at First Bull Run when his minibrigade faced off with numerically superior forces during the opening Federal attack and delayed a vital turning movement until the Confederates could organize a better defense. The Union was still smarting from the shocking defeat at Bull Run when the former Indian fighter, commanding a brigade of seasoned troops, administered a humiliating beating at Ball's Bluff, Virginia. Promoted from colonel to brigadier general after his showing at Ball's Bluff, the hard-drinking warrior led his troops at Second Bull Run and Antietam and fought with General Joseph Johnston at Vicksburg. A heavy drinker and obstinately mule-headed, Evans often clashed with his peers and superiors and at the Battle of Gettysburg ordered the arrest of fellow general John B. Hood during a dispute over captured ambulances. Evans's heavy drinking and mule-headed contrariness eventually led to two court-martials, both resulting in acquittals. Evans was eventually relieved of command by General Pierre Beauregard. (See: Baker, Colonel Edward D., U.S.; and Ball's Bluff, Battle of.)

Ewell, Lieutenant General Richard Stoddert, CS

Loss of a leg at Groveton while leading a division at Second Bull Run has been blamed for squeezing much of the fight out of the pop-eyed general called Old Bald Head by his troops. A West Point graduate who served during the Mexican War and on the frontier, Ewell had already led a distinguished military career before joining the Confederate Army as a cavalry instructor, then moving to command of an infantry brigade. He was a major general when his leg was shattered, and after returning to duty he seemed to have lost much of his grit, and his formerly aggressive command decisions became tentative and confused. Ewell lost the confidence of General Robert E. Lee after refusing to press the attack late on the first day of the Battle of Gettysburg. After more disappointing leadership performances in the Wilderness and at Spotsylvania, Ewell was relieved of command of his corps by Lee and replaced by General Jubal Early. Ewell was later put in charge of the defenses of Richmond, and captured while the city was being evacuated. (See: Hallucinations.)

Executions

Not all of the more than 360,000 soldiers and sailors who died during the Civil War were killed in combat or by accidents or disease. A total of 267 were executed by Federal military authorities, led by 147 put to death for desertion. Another 120 were executed for mutiny, murder, or rape.

Ezra Church, Battle of

During the Siege of Atlanta an assault against a strongly entrenched Union force ordered by newly arrived lieutenant general Stephen Dill Lee without orders to do so led to the most lopsided Union victory of the war. While Confederates were fiercely defending the city known as the Gateway to the South, Union general William T. Sherman ordered General Oliver O. Howard to attack from the west and cut the enemy's last railroad supply line between East Point and Atlanta.

Confederate general John Bell Hood sent four corps, two under Lee and two under Lieutenant General Alexander P. Stewart, to meet the Union attack, leading to the battle on July 28, 1864. After Lee's initial assault was beaten back, Stewart arrived with his column and joined in more attacks that were also repulsed. The Confederates prevented Howard from destroying the railroad supply line but suffered 3,000 casualties in the attack. The Union counted up 562 casualties, and after the intense three-hour battle Confederate general William S. Hardee sadly advised Hood that the fight had broken the proud spirit of the Confederate Army of Tennessee. (See: Atlanta, Battle of; and Atlanta, Siege of.)

F

Fair Oaks, Battle of
See Seven Pines, Battle of.

Farragut, Admiral David Glasgow, USN
One of the U.S. Navy's greatest heroes, Farragut is less well known for his role in forging Union victories than he is for his famous statement during the Battle of Mobile Bay: "Damn the torpedoes—full speed ahead!" Although Farragut was born in landlocked Tennessee, he was adopted by an earlier navy hero, Commodore David Porter, and took readily to seagoing life. Farragut was a 50-year navy veteran who fought in the War of 1812, served in the Mediterranean, and was assigned to the Norfolk Navy Yard in Virginia when the conflict between the states broke out. In January 1862 Farragut was named commander of a squadron ordered to capture New Orleans, and when the Queen City was subdued with a minimum of Federal casualties he became one of the Union's most celebrated heroes. Promoted to the new rank of rear admiral, Farragut fought at the successful battles of Vicksburg, Port Hudson, and finally Mobile Bay. He was rewarded for his success at Mobile Bay with promotion to vice admiral, a new three-star rank created just for him. The aging Farragut's health began to fail after Mobile Bay, and he played only a marginal role in navy activities through the rest of the war. By an act of Congress on July 25, 1866, Farragut became the navy's first full admiral and was given his fourth star. (See: Mobile Bay, Battle of; New Orleans; Port Hudson, Siege of; and Vicksburg, Battle of.)

Federal Military Telegraph System

U.S. secretary of war Edwin Stanton was a former executive with the Atlantic and Ohio Telegraph Company and spearheaded and supervised the early use of the new communication system on the battlefield. With the cooperation of Northern companies, Stanton created the Federal Military Telegraph System to work jointly with the U.S. Signal Corps. In late 1863, responsibility for strategic and tactical use of the telegaph became the sole responsibility of civilian MTS operators. (See: Signal Corps, U.S.; and Telegraph.)

Ferguson, J. B.

In September 1862 this Confederate quartermaster purchasing agent slipped through the Union blockade and sailed to England to buy shoes, bulk wool cloth, and other desperately needed items to clothe and equip the South's fighting men. (See: Uniforms, South.)

Fessenden, Major General Francis, U.S.

A Maine lawyer, Fessenden was commissioned as a captain in the 19th Infantry at the beginning of the war. While commanding a company with the Army of the Cumberland early in 1862, he was wounded at Shiloh. After recovery he was promoted to colonel of the 25th Maine Volunteers and commanded a brigade defending Washington. Later he was commissioned colonel with the 30th Maine Infantry and was promoted to brigadier general in the volunteer army on May 10, 1864. During the Red River Campaign he fought at Sabine Crossroads, Pleasant Hill, and Monett's Bluff. While leading a charge by his brigade at Monett's Bluff he suffered such a severe leg injury that the limb was amputated. Despite the loss of his leg, he was commissioned major general of volunteers in November 1865 and placed in command of the 1st Infantry Division, Department of West Virginia. He was later assigned to the 1st Veteran Corps and after the war served as assistant commander of the Bureau of Refugees, Freedmen and Abandoned Lands. After retirement from the army with the rank of brigadier general and brevetted major general in the regular army, he was elected mayor of his hometown, Portland, Maine.

Fifty-Sixth Illinois Infantry
The 205 men in this ill-fated regiment lost in the sinking of the SS *General Lyon* during a fierce storm off Cape Hatteras were more than its total number of casualties during the entire war. (See: SS *General Lyon.*)

First Minnesota Infantry
These midwesterners won a reputation for hard fighting, and suffered the highest casualty rate of any Union regiment in a single battle when 215 of their 262 men were killed, wounded, or captured at Gettysburg. Earlier, the 1st Minnesota suffered the most casualties of any regiment engaged in the First Battle of Bull Run while stubbornly holding the line against a Confederate assault until other units had pulled safely back.

Five Forks, Battle of
After joining his forces with those of Grant during the Siege of Petersburg in March 1865, General Thomas Sherman launched a surprise attack on Confederate troops led by Major General George Pickett at Five Forks. Pickett had left his command to make a social call without telling his subordinates where he would be, and the leaderless Southerners were routed, with the loss of 5,200 men. After General Lee learned of the disaster, he ordered the evacuation of Petersburg and Richmond. (See: Pickett, Major General George, CS.)

Flag of Truce
After the gallant Union general Philip Kearny was killed at the Battle of Chantilly on September 1, 1862, Robert E. Lee returned his body to Federal lines under a flag of truce. Lee also sent Kearny's horse and equipment to the fallen warrior's widow. (See: Chantilly, Battle of; and Kearny, Major General Philip, U.S.)

Flags, Confederate
Three national flags and a battle flag were authorized by the Confederacy. Many other flags were carried during the war, identifying individual states and units.

Flags, Marking
During the winter of 1861–62 Union troops started marking their national and regimental flags with the names of battles they participated in. The practice, which dated to the 1830s in the regular army, was officially sanctioned by the War Department on February 22, 1862.

Flags, Union
The flag that flew over Fort Sumter when the Confederates opened fire to begin the war had 33 stars, one for every state in the Union as it existed before secession. Eleven of those stars represented states that would join the Confederacy. Later in the war, the number of stars on the U.S. flag was increased to 34 when Kansas was admitted to the Union, then 35 when West Virginia was recognized as a state.

Flank
The right or left end of a military formation. Troops flanking an enemy must go around the far end, either on the right or left, of the enemy's position.

Florida, CSS
Under two successive masters, the CSS *Florida* was second only to the CSS *Alabama* as a successful commerce raider, seizing or burning 40 Union merchantmen. Under the command of Captain John Newland Maffitt, the *Florida* captured or destroyed 23 ships during a seven-month cruise and created panic when he once sailed it to within 50 miles of New York Harbor. Maffitt also reoutfitted some of his captured vessels and sent them back to sea as Confederate raiders. One of Maffitt's miniraiders, the CSS *Tacony,* captured 15 ships in just two weeks. The *Florida* destroyed another 13 vessels under its second master, Captain Charles Morris, be-

fore it was rammed just off the neutral harbor of Bahia, Brazil, by the USS *Wachusett* and seized. The *Florida* sank a few weeks later after colliding with a U.S. Army transport as diplomats were arranging for its return to Brazil. (See: Maffitt, Captain John Newland, CSN; and *Wachusett,* USS.)

Food Riots

Critical shortages of food and other necessities on the home front led to destructive riots in Richmond and other cities of the South. On April 2, 1863, a huge mob of women and boys formed and marched into the retail district of Richmond, smashing windows and doors, then carrying off flour and other food and clothes. Then the looters turned to luxuries such as jewelry and fine clothes and finally banks before the mayor appeared and threatened to order troops to open fire if they didn't leave. Finally Jefferson Davis climbed onto a wagon and the mob broke up after listening to his pleas to disperse. Less than a month earlier more than 75 women, including the wives of soldiers, took up axes and clubs, then forced their way into warehouses and stores where they suspected that speculators were hoarding food.

Foragers

As the war progressed, it became increasingly difficult to obtain and deliver supplies to feed the armies of the North and the South, and the Confederates especially found themselves forced to forage, or live off the land. Most of the fighting occurred in Southern states, and Confederates asked for food from local farmers and others but were sometimes forced to simply help themselves and take it by force.

Ford, Antonia

A delicate Southern belle, Antonia Ford was arrested as a spy after providing information to John Singleton Mosby that helped him carry out a bloodless raid on Fairfax Court House leading to the capture of a Union general. The Virginia beauty wheedled information from Union officers billeted in and around her father's home and passed the intelligence on to Colonel Mosby. After the Fairfax Court House raid, Antonia was tricked by a female Secret Service agent into showing off a document signed by General J. E. B. "Jeb" Stuart identifying her as an "honorary aide-de-camp in the provisional army of the Confederate States of America." Although Stuart had given Antonia the document as a joke, it was enough to have the 24-year-old spy locked up in the Old Capitol Prison in nearby Washington, D.C. Union major Joseph Willard, who was provost marshal at Fairfax Court House, arranged to have her freed, then married her. But the months of imprisonment in a dank cell, combined with poor food, had broken her already-delicate health, and she died when she was only 33. (See: Greenhow, Rose O'Neal; and Old Capitol Prison.)

Foreign-Born Soldiers, Confederacy

Although the South lagged far behind the North in attracting foreign-born soldiers to its colors, thousands of immigrants and mercenaries fought for the Stars and Bars. Irish made up one complete Rebel brigade, several regiments were all German, a Polish legion fought in several battles, and thousands of native Mexicans fought alongside their former enemies in Texas. A European brigade of soldiers from various countries was formed in Louisiana and commanded by the flashy French count Camille Armand Jules Marie, Prince de Polignac. (See: Prince de Polignac, Major General Camille Armand Jules Marie, CS.)

Foreign-Born Soldiers, Union

The Union far outstripped the Confederacy in attracting foreign-born soldiers to its colors. Irish and Germans made up the largest contingents of Union foreign troops, but thousands of others also fought for the North. More than 60,000 Canadians and Englishmen fought under the Union banner. The 79th New York Infantry Highlanders, formed in the 1850s, were 100 percent Scots immigrants but at the beginning of the war began taking in Irish, English, and a few other foreign-born troops. French, Hungarians, Scandinavians, Mexicans, and other foreign immigrants and soldiers of fortune, even a handful of soldiers from the Orient, fought for the Union. (See: Sigel, Major General Franz, U.S.)

Forrest, Lieutenant General Nathan Bedford, CS

This dashing cavalry leader once stated his philosophy of warfare as "Get there first with the most men." The credo served him well and helped him to repeatedly frustrate the enemy while becoming one of the most enduring heroes of the South. Forrest was a plantation owner and slave trader who estimated his fortune at about $1.5 million and had no military training when he enlisted as a private in Josiah H. White's cavalry company on June 14, 1861. Forrest had barely pulled on his boots before he was asked by the governor of his home state of Tennessee to raise a mounted battalion at his own expense. The former private became lieutenant colonel of Forrest's Tennessee Cavalry Battalion, then colonel of the 3d Tennessee Cavalry, and held other commands while moving up the ranks as a brigadier general, major general, and finally lieutenant general on February 28, 1865. Forrest fought through the entire war in his native Tennessee and elsewhere in the Western Theater. He led his cavalry and other Rebel troops through Union lines after failure of the breakout attempt at Fort Donelson, then directed the rear guard. He was also in charge of the rear guard during the retreat from Nashville and at Shiloh. He was wounded the day after the Battle of Shiloh ended but recovered and served during the Siege of Corinth. Promoted to brigadier general after Corinth, he raised a brigade that captured Murfreesboro along with its garrison and a valuable store of supplies. Forrest's forte was as a raider, and his swift hit-and-run strikes in West Tennessee played an important role in the decision by the Union's General Ulysses S. Grant to abandon his campaign in central Mississippi. Forrest commanded a corps at Chickamauga but, like many other officers, was critical of and frequently quarreled with General Braxton Bragg, commander of the Confederate Army of Tennessee. At his own request, Forrest was transferred to West Tennessee with a deliberately small number of men, but through a diligent recruiting effort he rapidly rebuilt and reshaped his command into a formidable raiding force that created so much trouble for the Federals that General Sherman repeatedly ordered his commanders to bring him in. Forrest escaped capture and led his cavalry in the capture of Fort Pillow at Jackson in West Tennessee and slaughter of most of the Union garrison, including more than 200 black soldiers. Forrest followed up Fort Pillow with a victory at Brice's Crossroads, fought at Tupelo, and led his cavalry during General Hood's invasion of central Tennessee. In the final months of the war, Forrest's depleted command fought in Alabama and Georgia. Financially ruined, he went back to work as a planter, became president of the Selma, Marion & Memphis Railroad, and helped found the Ku Klux Klan during Reconstruction. (See: Fort Pillow Massacre; and Gould, Lieutenant Andrew Wills, CS.)

Fort Blakely and Spanish Fort, Battle of

Mobile, Alabama, was said by some to be the most heavily fortified city in the Confederacy when the Union belatedly moved in the spring of 1865 to capture it. Despite the Union victory in the Battle of Mobile Bay, which closed one of the South's last remaining seaports to blockade runners, the town itself had never surrendered. Water approaches to Mobile were heavily mined, and the west side was guarded by three lines of fortifications and 300 artillery pieces. The city and its fortifications were defended by a 10,000-man garrison. So a battle plan to attack from the east was proposed to the commanding Union general, E. R. S. Canby, by General Thomas Sherman and kicked off with a two-pronged attack against Fort Blakely and Spanish Fort on the east side of the Tensaw River. Backed by a small fleet of ironclads, a Union column of 32,000 men began a siege of Spanish Fort on March 27. Federals breached the Confederate lines on April 8, and the defenders retreated into Mobile on riverboats. After several days of skirmishing, the second Union force, of 13,000, was joined by about 3,000 of the victors from Spanish Fort in an all-out attack on Fort Blakely. The garrison of 4,000 men was quickly overwhelmed, and the fort fell on April 9, the same day that General Lee was surrendering the Army of Northern Virginia at Appomattox. Major General Dabney H. Maury, the Confederate commander in Mobile, ordered the city evacuated. It was declared an open city on April 12. Only 200 of the defenders at Fort Blakely escaped; 250 were killed and 3,400 were taken prisoner. (See: Mobile Bay, Battle of.)

Fort Donelson, Battle of

Less than one week after the capture of Fort Henry in February 1862, Union forces under Brigadier General Ulysses S. Grant and navy flag officer Andrew H. Foote moved across country and by river to launch a joint assault on Fort Donelson in Kentucky. Efforts by Confederate forces under General Simon B. Buckner to reinforce the fort and break a nearly weeklong siege ended on February 16 with the unconditional surrender of the survivors of the 12,000-man garrison. Buckner's troops were among the captured Confederates, but cavalry led by Brigadier General Nathan Bedford Forrest rode and marched safely through the Union lines prior to the surrender without a shot being fired. Forrest had stormed angrily out of a meeting when Buckner and other officers decided to accept Grant's surrender demand. The twin losses of Fort Donelson and Fort Henry broke the back of the South in Kentucky and ensured that it would remain with the Union, while opening the way for Federal attacks along the Tennessee and Cumberland Rivers. (See Buckner, Lieutenant General Simon Bolivar, CS; Forrest, Major General Nathan Bedford, CS; and Unconditional Surrender Grant.)

Fort Fisher, Battle of

A Union victory during the three-day battle of Fort Fisher on January 13–15, 1865, left the South's last Atlantic Coast seaport open to capture by Federal forces. Union major general Benjamin Butler was relieved of command after his failure the previous December to subdue the fort protecting the port at Wilmington, N. C. The new assault was a land and sea operation led by Major General Alfred Terry and Rear Admiral David D. Porter. General Braxton Bragg was in overall command for the Confederates. In command of nearly sixty ships and gunboats, Porter opened the battle with a fierce bombardment just ahead of a landing by a large Union force. On the third day of fighting an elite force of Federal troops attacked the fort from the rear and carried the parapet, forcing surrender of the garrison. The defenders were weakened after repelling an earlier afternoon attack by a landing party of sailors and marines. Total casualties on both sides were estimated at about 2,000 men. (See: Hero of Fort Fisher; Pennypacker, Major General Galusha, U.S.; and Porter, Rear Admiral David Dixon, USN.)

Fort Henry, Battle of

This old earthen fort on the Tennessee River was already partly flooded by the Tennessee River on February 6, 1862, when the Union's brigadier general Ulysses S. Grant landed two divisions nearby and opened an assault. Seven gunboats under command of Flag Officer Andrew H. Foote bombarded the crumbling old fort from the river while Grant's forces moved up to block off escape routes for the Confederate defenders. Despite the efforts of the Union ground forces, the Confederate commander, Brigadier General Lloyd Tilghman, ordered his outdated artillery batteries to hold off the gunboats while he led most of the defenders outside the fort. After sending his men on to Fort Donelson, ten miles away, Tilghman returned to Fort James and negotiated its surrender along with the remaining defenders. (See: Fort Donelson, Battle of.)

Fort Jefferson

This old fort in the Dry Tortugas off the southern tip of Florida was converted into a military prison in 1861 for Union Army men convicted of serious crimes, and the oppressive heat, insanitary conditions, and overwork killed many inmates. After Lincoln's assassination, Dr. Samuel Mudd, who had treated John Wilkes Booth's broken leg, was locked up in the prison.

Fort Moultrie

The first two forts constructed on Charleston Harbor's Sullivan Island were destroyed by hurricanes, and the third Fort Moultrie played a role in the Civil War. After a small garrison of Federal troops was secretly moved a mile across the harbor entrance from Moultrie to the more defensible Fort Sumter early on the morning of December 28, 1860, the abandoned Sullivan's Island fort was occupied by 225 South Carolina state troops. (See: Anderson, Major General Robert, U.S.; and Fort Sumter.)

Fort Pillow Massacre

When Brigadier General Nathan Bedford Forrest's cavalry rode away with a big haul of Union artillery and other supplies after capturing Fort Pillow at Jackson, Tennessee, only 200 of the 557 defenders were still alive. Northern politicians and the press immediately began calling for a swift and terrible revenge for what they described as "the Fort Pillow Massacre." The garrison, just across the Tennessee border from Columbus, Kentucky, was manned by 295 whites and 262 blacks when it was attacked in April 1864. According to survivors, only a small number of casualties occurred during the fight for the fort, and most of the dead were bayoneted, shot, or cut up with sabers by Forrest's cavalry after the surrender. Almost all the blacks were killed, and many of the whites. Four members of the president's cabinet—Secretary of State William Seward, Secretary of War Edwin M. Stanton, Secretary of the Navy Gideon Wells, and Secretary of the Treasury Salmon Chase—publicly called for an equal number of Southern prisoners to be executed in revenge. Lincoln condemned the atrocity but refused the demands for a tit-for-tat response. Neither Forrest nor any of his men were ever brought before a military tribunal or civilian court to answer the accusations after the war. (See: Forrest, Lieutenant General Nathan Bedford, CS.)

Fort Sumter

At 4:30 A.M. on April 12, 1861, a mortar was fired, signaling 43 Confederate guns surrounding a stubborn Federal garrison at Fort Sumter in Charleston Harbor to begin a bombardment that opened the Civil War. Being outnumbered, low on supplies, and deep within Southern territory weren't the only disadvantages for the small Federal garrison. Although the fort was designed for 146 heavy cannon, it was still under construction on an artificial island in the harbor and only 15 were mounted. Equally troubling was the fact that the fort was designed to protect Charleston from an attack by sea and almost all the guns and embrasures faced in that direction. But the Confederate barrage was coming from land and other islands that were part of the harbor defenses where Confederate troops had assembled under General Pierre G. T. Beauregard. Hot shells ignited Sumter on the second day of bombardment, and the commander, Major Robert Anderson, reluctantly hoisted a white flag. Ironically, no soldiers were killed in the clash, but two Union men suffered fatal injuries when a cannon exploded during a ceremony to salute the Stars and Stripes while the fort was being officially surrendered. The surviving members of the garrison were put aboard the Confederate steamer *Isabel* and turned over to the masters of three Federal ships that had arrived too late with supplies just outside the harbor. (See: Anderson, Major General Robert, U.S.; Beauregard, General Pierre Gustave Toutant, CS; Castle Pinckney; and Fort Moultrie.)

Four Apostles, the

These four six-pound artillery pieces were produced for training of cadets at the Virginia Military Institute and were christened Matthew, Mark, Luke, and John because they "spoke a powerful language." At the beginning of the war the Four Apostles were transferred to the Rockbridge Artillery under the command of William Nelson Pendleton, then moved to the capital city as part of Richmond's defenses. Ironically, they were not used at the Battle of New Market, where teenage

VMI cadets acquitted themselves so gallantly. (See: Virginia Military Institute.)

Fourth of July

Residents of Vicksburg have never forgotten that the Mississippi River city fell to the Yankees on the Fourth of July, and after the siege and battle residents didn't begin celebrating Independence Day again until World War II.

Fractured Families

Thousands of families were irreconcilably split by their differing sympathies for the North and South during the Civil War, and some of the most bitter discord occurred between one of the Union's most gifted generals and his sisters. Major General George H. Thomas was a Virginian and career soldier who married a New York woman, then was disowned by his home state and by his sisters when he chose to remain loyal to the Union. (See: Rock of Chickamauga; and Thomas, Major General George Henry, U.S.)

Frankfort

Near the end of August 1862, Confederates led by General Kirby Edmund Smith swept into the state capital at Frankfort, Kentucky, and chased off the pro-Union legislature. Then the Rebels raised the Confederate flag. (See: Smith, General Edmund Kirby, CS.)

Franklin, Major General William B., U.S.

Franklin fought bravely throughout the Peninsular Campaign and other battles, but a charge of failure to obey orders at Fredericksburg led to his temporary removal from command and the resignation of Major General Ambrose E. Burnside. Burnside was commanding general at the battle, and his accusation against his subordinate led to Franklin's censure by the Congressional Committee on the Conduct of the War and an order for his removal for insubordination. When President Lincoln failed to approve the order of removal, Burnside resigned. After several months, General Franklin was returned to duty and sent to the Western Theater, where he participated in the Red River Campaign and was wounded at Sabine Crossroads. He was an invalid on sick leave riding a Baltimore & Philadelphia train when he was captured by Confederate raiders, but he escaped the same night. Early in his career, Franklin graduated first in his class at West Point, and served in the Mexican War as a topographical engineer on the frontier and in the Washington, D.C., area until the Civil War began. He was promoted to colonel of a volunteer infantry regiment, then commissioned brigadier general of volunteers on May 14, 1861. Three days later he moved up to major general. He commanded a brigade at First Bull Run, then became a division commander with the Army of the Potomac, followed by command of the new 6th Army Corps. During the Peninsular Campaign, he fought at Yorktown, West Point, White Oak Bridge, Savage Station, Malvern Hill, and Harrison's Landing. Later he commanded the army's left wing at Crampton's Gap and fought at South Mountain and at Antietam. On March 13, 1865, he was brevetted major general in the regular army for gallant and meritorious service. (See: Burnside, Major General Ambrose Everett, U.S.)

Fredericksburg, Battle of

A bullheaded, unimaginative general who chose to fight at the wrong place and the wrong time cost a huge Union army a ghastly toll of dead and injured and a humiliating licking at the Battle of Fredericksburg. On November 7, 1862, President Lincoln finally lost patience with General McClellan's reluctance to fight and replaced him with Ambrose E. Burnside as the new commander of the 120,000-man Army of the Potomac. Anxious to show his fighting spirit while throwing a scare into the Confederate capital at Richmond, Burnside began moving his men to the Rappahannock River at Fredericksburg, Virginia. The army arrived on November 17 but couldn't cross the 400-foot-wide river until engineers erected a pontoon bridge. It was December 10 before Burnside's forces were finally able to make the crossing, and by that time Confederate general Lee had cobbled together a defensive force of 70,000 in his Army of Northern Virginia. Marye's Heights was strongly defended on Lee's left flank by the Corps led by General James Longstreet. General Thomas "Stonewall" Jackson's II Corps was spread out on a wooded ridge on the right flank. Despite the critical delay crossing the river that gave the defenders time to assemble and dig on the hills overlooking the city, Burnside continued with his plan to attack. Early on December 13, while partly concealed by heavy fog, General William Franklin's Grand Division led the assault. Despite heavy artillery fire, the Federals managed to penetrate the Confederate line after several hours of savage fighting. But there was no follow-through by reinforcing troops, and after a successful counterattack by Jackson that drove the Yankees back to their original positions the heavy fighting shifted upstream. General Edwin Sumner's Grand Division was ordered to advance across an open field, where the exposed troops were raked by heavy rifle fire and Longstreet's artillery. Stubbornly walking into the curtain of flying metal with their shoulders hunched and their rifles at the ready, row after row of Bluecoats were mowed down. The slaughter continued two hours before they were finally allowed to withdraw out of range. Then it was the turn of Union general Joseph Hooker's III and IV Corps to walk into the devastating barrage of artillery and rifle fire. Late in the afternoon, Burnside ordered Hooker to open an assault and move through Fredericksburg to take Marye's Heights. Hooker committed three divisions to the assault, but they were bloodily repulsed by the well-dug-in Confederates and suffered heavy losses. Blue-coated bodies stacked up like cordwood in front of a four-foot stone wall at the edge of a sunken road at the foot of the high ground. But Burnside, well away from the action, was determined to try again until his commanders, who had begun to disobey his orders, outright refused to prepare for new attacks the next day. Instead, on the night of December 14 Burnside withdrew the Army of the Potomac and recrossed the Rappahannock. The Battle of Fredericksburg was over, but the political fallout from the demoralizing defeat wasn't. Lincoln was roundly criticized in the press and in Congress. And Burnside, Franklin, and Sumner were relieved of their commands. "Fighting Joe" Hooker was named as the new Commander, Army of the Potomac. (See: Burnside, Major General Ambrose Everett, U.S.; and Hooker, Major General Joseph "Fighting Joe," U.S.)

Freedmen's Bureau

This bureau was established by Congress on March 4, 1865, and given one year to help more than 4 million southern blacks who suddenly found themselves free but without jobs, money, homes, or education. Provisions were also made to establish emergency stations to feed, clothe, and provide other assistance to whites who were left destitute after five years of war. Formally named the Bureau of Refugees, Freedmen and Abandoned Lands, the agency was headed by General Oliver Otis Howard, U.S. Army, who worked hard to provide the former slaves with legal and other protection, schools, health care, and land while helping to keep peace between the races. The thousands of acres of land needed for distribution to the former slaves were to come from property confiscated or abandoned during the war. Although the Federal government had promised "Forty Acres and a Mule" to every freed slave family, only about 2,000 freedmen in South Carolina and 1,500 in Georgia actually shared in the distribution. In the summer and fall of 1865, President Andrew Johnson ordered confiscated lands returned to white owners pardoned after the war. (See: Howard, Major General Oliver Otis, U.S.; and Special Field Order #15.)

Freedom's Cost

Historians have estimated that one life was lost for every six slaves freed during the Civil War.

Fremantle, Arthur

This British Guards officer was sent from England as an observer of the war. He traveled with Confederate major general James Longstreet. Fremantle was an admirer of the

Southern cause and described General Lee by remarking that
he was "as near to perfection as a man can be."

Frémont, Major General John C., U.S.

One of many Union generals who never lived up to expecta-
tions, Frémont began his wartime service with dazzling credentials. He was one of the young nation's greatest explorers,
celebrated for mapping most of the Oregon Trail, trekking
through the Great Basin and the Pacific coast, and making a
midwinter crossing of the Sierra Nevada mountains with Kit
Carson. During the Mexican War, Frémont was commissioned as a U.S. Army colonel and helped annex California,
then served as governor of the new state. He became a multi-
millionaire when gold was discovered on his estate during
the California Gold Rush. A fierce opponent of slavery, he
ran as the Republican Party's first presidential candidate, losing to Democrat James Buchanan. Passed over for a cabinet
post by Lincoln, Frémont was appointed as a major general
in the Union Army and assigned to the Western Department,
based in St. Louis. He immediately got into trouble with the
president by pronouncing that all slaves owned by Confederates in Missouri had become free men. Then Frémont compounded his blunder, which Lincoln feared would stampede
border state slave owners into the Confederacy, by refusing
to publicly modify his announcement. So he was replaced by
conservative general Henry Halleck and sent to the Mountain Division, where he performed poorly against Stonewall
Jackson in the Shenandoah Valley. By late June 1862, Lincoln was fed up with Frémont and transferred the hero of the
West and his troops to the command of Major General
John J. Pope. Frémont refused to serve under Pope's command and sat out the remainder of the war in New York.
(See: Cross Keys, Battle of.)

G

Gaines's Mill, Battle of

The third clash in the Seven Days Battles was fought on June 27, 1862, at Gaines's Mill and saved Richmond from the invading army of "Little Mac" McClellan. The Union general had withdrawn his forces to the more easily defensible position after the Union victory at Mechanicsville the previous day. Lee was determined to protect the Confederate capital and ordered an attack against a strong defensive line established by Brigadier General Fitz John Porter's V Corps. The Yankees were well dug in behind Boatswain's Swamp north of the Chickahominy River and inflicted heavy casualties while repulsing repeated Confederate assaults. Just after sunset, General Lee's troops finally broke through the Union lines at Turkey Hill, and the Federals fell back. The V Corps survivors used the cover of darkness to complete an orderly retreat across the river, and the fight—also known as First Cold Harbor—was over. Timid as always, McClellan was convinced by the Union defeat to halt his advance on Richmond and withdraw his forces back down the peninsula to the James River. The vital victory cost the Confederates 8,700 casualties. Union casualties amounted to 6,800 dead, wounded, taken prisoner, and missing. And three more costly scraps lay ahead before the Seven Days Battles were fought out. (See: Seven Days Battles.)

Galveston, Battle of

The first time the Texas seaport at Galveston changed hands in the Civil War, the transfer was bloodless. When Union commodore William B. Renshaw sailed unmolested into the harbor on Christmas Day, 1862, and demanded the island's surrender, the Confederate commander, Colonel James J. Cook, had no defense force and no choice. He surrendered! A few weeks later, Major General John Bankhead Magruder was named Confederate commander of the District of Texas, New Mexico, and Arizona. Immediately he began scheming to return the valuable port to the South and break the Federal blockade. Magruder planned a joint land-sea assault to be headed by a couple of river steamers, the CSS *Bayou City* and the CSS *Neptune,* newly outfitted with guns, and with bales of compressed cotton along the deck to protect the crews from boarding parties trained to overpower the crews of enemy ships. On New Year's Day, 1863, the Confederate ground forces launched their land attack and the pair of cotton-clads steamed into the west end of Galveston Harbor heading straight for the copper-sheathed gunboat USS *Harriet Lane.* While the Federal fleet of eight ships held off the ground attack with heavy bombardments, the *Neptune* was quickly sent to the bottom of the harbor by the *Harriet Lane's* gunners. But the woefully outnumbered *Bayou City* was still in a fighting mood and made a second run at the *Harriet Lane,* boarding and capturing her. The tide of battle changed for good when the Federal flagship *Westfield* ran aground. The crew was unable to refloat her, so a truce was called. During the lull in fighting, Renshaw, the Union commander, rigged up a barrel of gunpowder in an effort to scuttle the *Westfield* so it wouldn't fall into enemy hands, then rowed away. The gunpowder didn't ignite, so the Federal sailors rowed back to the stricken ship to try again. They were still scrambling over the sides after rerigging the gunpowder bomb when it exploded prematurely. Renshaw and 13 members of his crew were killed. The white flags were still flying on the surviving Union ships when they stoked their boilers, hoisted anchors, and headed back unmolested to open sea. The Union garrison fighting at Kuhn's Wharf surrendered when it realized it had been abandoned by the navy. Recapture of Galveston Harbor cost the Confederates one small cotton-clad, 26 dead, and 117 wounded. The Union lost two ships, with the capture of 400 crewmen and almost twice as many dead and wounded as the Rebels. (See: Cotton-Clads.)

Garfield, Major General James Abram, U.S.

Civil War general Garfield and Civil War president Abraham Lincoln had much in common. They were both born in log cabins, opposed slavery, became lawyers, served in their state legislatures and in Congress, became Civil War leaders, were elected president, and were shot to death by assassins. Garfield had served as the nation's twentieth president only four months when he was killed in 1881 by Charles Guiteau.

Garibaldi Guard

The 39th New York Volunteer Infantry Regiment was named after Italian patriot Giuseppe Garibaldi. Uniforms were identical to those worn by crack riflemen of the Bersaglieri Light Infantry. The guard was armed almost exclusively with the Model 1841 .58-caliber Jager, modeled after the German huntsman's design, and the rifles were equipped with a mount for the fearsome 22 ½ inch saber bayonet. The legend on the regimental flag appeared in both English and Italian. Volunteers came from all over the world. They were led by a Hungarian, Colonel Frederick George D'Utassey, and had an Italian lieutenant, a German surgeon, and foot soldiers from Bavaria, England, Switzerland, and India, and a host of other countries. (See: D'Utassey, Frederick George, U.S.)

Garnett, Brigadier General Robert Selden, CS

The first Civil War general killed in action on either side, Garnett died on July 13, 1861, at Corrick's Ford during the Confederate retreat from Laurel Mountain. (See: Rich Mountain, Battle of.)

Gatling Gun

See: Machine Gun.

Geary, Brigadier General John White, U.S.
See: Battle Above the Clouds.

Geary, Major General John White, U.S.
This general was knocked unconscious by the wind of a cannonball that passed within inches of his head and could talk only in whispers for a week. Before the war, Geary was governor of Kansas and mayor of San Francisco, where a major street is named after him. After the war he was a two-term governor of Pennsylvania. (See: Battle Above the Clouds.)

General Lyon, SS
One of the most tragic incidents of the war occurred in the waning days of the conflict when the SS *General Lyon* burned and sank in a raging storm off Cape Hatteras, North Carolina, taking approximately 600 people with her. The old-style screw steamer named after a slain Civil War general was packed with former POWs from Confederate prison camps, Southern civilian refugees fleeing to the North, convalescing soldiers, and the 56th Illinois Regiment. Only 29 confirmed survivors escaped the sinking on April 2, 1865. (See: Fifty-sixth Illinois Infantry; Lyon, Brigadier General Nathaniel, U.S.; Robinson Crusoe of the Civil War; and Ward, Captain Minott.)

General Sedgwick, SS
Named after Union general John Sedgwick, this steamboat rescued survivors from the burning SS *General Lyon* on April 2, 1865. The *Sedgwick* was only about a mile away when the *Lyon* caught fire, leading to the deaths of about 600 passengers and crew. (See: *General Lyon,* SS; and Sedgwick, Major General John, U.S.)

Generals, Confederacy
The South commissioned 425 generals throughout the war. Of those, 77 were killed.

Germans

More than 200,000 native-born Germans served Federal armed forces during the war, including both officers and enlisted men. New York and Ohio each provided ten regiments composed almost entirely of the German-born, and the 9th Wisconsin was 100 percent German. Many Germans announced they were enlisting to "fight *mit* Sigel." Major General Franz Sigel was the Civil War's highest-ranking German-born officer. Commonly referred to by their comrades in arms as "Dutchmen," Germans were disciplined, stubborn soldiers but were often poorly led by their officers, causing them to acquire an unfortunate reputation for breaking and running under pressure. (See: Foreign-Born Soldiers, Union; and Sigel, Major General Franz, U.S.)

Gettysburg, Army of Northern Virginia, Order of Battle

Lee, 75,000 men. I Corps, Longstreet: McLaw's division/ Kershaw's brigade, Semmes's brigade, Barksdale's brigade, Wofford's brigade/Pickett's division, Garnett's brigade, Kemper's brigade, Armistead's brigade/Hood's division/Law's brigade, Robertson's brigade, G. T. Anderson's brigade, Benning's brigade. II Corps, Ewell: Early's division/Hays's brigade, Smith's brigade, Gordon's brigade, Avery's brigade/Johnson's division, Stuart's brigade, Walker's brigade, Williams's brigade, Jones's brigade/Rodes's division, Daniels's brigade, Iverson's brigade, Dole's brigade, Ramseur's brigade, O'Neal's brigade. III Corps, Hill: R. H. Anderson's division/Wilcox's brigade, Wright's brigade, Mahone's brigade, Lang's brigade, Posey's brigade/Heth's division/Pettigrew's brigade, Brokenbrough's brigade, Archer's brigade, Davis's brigade/Pender's division, Perrin's brigade, Lane's brigade, Thomas's brigade, Scales's brigade/cavalry. Stuart: Hampton's brigade, F. Lee's brigade, Robertson's brigade, Jenkin's brigade, Jones's brigade, W. H. F. Lee's brigade.

Gettysburg, Army of the Potomac, Order of Battle

Meade, 85,500 men. I Corps, Reynolds: 1st Division Wadsworth/Meredith's brigade, Cutler's brigade. 2d Division, Robinson/Paul's brigade, Baxter's brigade/3d Division, Rowley/Biddle's brigade, Stone's brigade, Stannard's brigade, Zook's brigade, Brooke's brigade. 2d Division, Gibbon/Harrow's brigade, Webb's brigade, Hall's brigade/3d Division, Hays/Carrol's brigade, Smyth's brigade, Willard's brigade. III Corps, Sickles: 1st Division/Birney/Graham's brigade, Ward's brigade, De Trobriand's brigade. 2d Division, Humphreys/Carr's brigade, Brewster's brigade, Burling's brigade. V Corps, Sykes: 1st Division, Barnes/Tilton's brigade, Sweitzer's brigade, Vincent's brigade/2d Division, Ayres/Day's brigade, Burbank's brigade, Weed's brigade/3d Division, Crawford/McCandless's brigade, Fisher's brigade. VI Corps, Sedgewick: 1st Division, Wright/Torbert's brigade, Bartlett's brigade, Russell's brigade/2d Division, Howe/Grant's brigade, Neill's brigade/3d Division, Newton/Shaler's brigade, Eustis's brigade, Wheaton's brigade. XI Corps, Howard: 1st Division, Barlow/von Gilsa's brigade, Ames's Brigade/2d Division, von Steinwehr/Coster's brigade, Smith's brigade/3d Division, Schurz/Schimmelfenning's brigade, Krzyzanowski's brigade. XIII Corps, Slocum: 1st Division, Williams/McDougall's brigade, Lockwood's brigade, Ruger's brigade/2d Division, Geary/Candy's brigade, Cobham's brigade, Greene's brigade. Cavalry Corps, Pleasonton: 1st Division, Buford/Gimble's brigade, Devin's brigade, Merritt's brigade/2d Division, Gregg/McIntosh's brigade, Huey's brigade, Gregg's brigade/3d Division, Kilpatrick/Farnsworth's brigade, Custer's brigade. Artillery Reserve, Tyler: Ransom's brigade, McGilvery's brigade, Taft's brigade, Huntingon's brigade, Fitzhugh's brigade.

Gettysburg, Battle of

Eight days after Robert E. Lee's victory at Chancellorsville, he convinced the Confederate War Cabinet to approve his long-delayed invasion of Pennsylvania so he could force a final confrontation that would allow him to destroy the Army of the Potomac, shatter Union morale, and win independence for the South. The manpower of Lee's army was at its peak, with nearly 70,000 veteran fighting men. Major General J. E. B. "Jeb" Stuart had another 10,000 cavalry sabers at his command, and the South had assembled nearly 300 cannon. The Southern commander's most glaring weakness was the loss of so many top officers in previous fighting, and the death of Stonewall Jackson at Chancellorsville was especially crippling. Lee and other Confederate leaders were hopeful, nevertheless, that a decisive victory on Northern territory might influence England or France to formally recognize the South. Although the Union commander, Major General Joseph Hooker, favored marching on Richmond, he was overruled by President Lincoln. The president considered the destruction of Lee's army to have priority over any attack on the Confederate capital and ordered Hooker to meet and shatter the enemy. But when Hooker learned that Lee was marching north, he cautiously pulled his army back toward Washington. Hooker waited almost two weeks before finally moving his troops into Maryland to pursue Lee. By that time the Army of Northern Virginia was already crossing into Pennsylvania and Lincoln was fed up with his commander's timidity and shilly-shallying. "Fighting Joe" was removed from command and replaced with George G. Meade, a corps commander known for his fierce temper and a seasoned veteran of all the war's major battles. Meade immediately ordered the Army of the Potomac to cross into Pennsylvania and march toward Harrisburg. A cavalry unit was sent toward Gettysburg, a small college town near the Maryland border. When the two armies began their march north, the Confederates had amassed 75,000 men; the Union, 93,000. Ironically, the epic battle that was to determine, as much as any single engagement, the outcome of the Civil War began almost by accident. General Lee had ordered his always-reliable cavalry commander, Stuart, to make a quick reconnaissance to determine the size and exact location of the Union forces. For once, Stuart uncharacteristically failed his commander and, instead of taking a quick look at the enemy, led his troopers on a wide sweep around the Union Army. In the process, he was pushed so far east that he didn't get back to Lee for almost ten days. With no report from Stuart and left on the eve of battle without his mounted eyes and ears for other scouting missions, Lee not only didn't know the size of the army already facing him, but he also wouldn't learn until July 28 that Major General George G. Meade had replaced Hooker and crossed the Potomac River with fresh troops. The reinforcements were headed in Lee's direction. The Confederate commander ordered his troops to converge west of Gettysburg until Stuart showed up with the missing intelligence. A group of ragged Confederate soldiers was in Gettysburg foraging at a shoe factory when they were spotted by Brigadier General John Buford, a Union cavalry commander. Buford's troops were camped just southwest of the town, and as he called for reinforcements the Rebels clattered back to their lines and spread the alarm. A Confederate attack was ordered on the Union cavalry, and the Battle of Gettysburg was joined. During the first day of fighting, the outnumbered Bluecoats, led by Major General Winfield Scott Hancock, were driven through Gettysburg to Cemetery Ridge. As nightfall approached, Lieutenant General Richard Ewell lost an opportunity to further damage the Union forces and achieve a major victory when he decided against ordering a final assault. The next morning the Union Army was well dug in and their new defensive positions were formed in the shape of a giant fishhook, with the shank centered at Cemetery Ridge. The barb of the fishhook was dug into Cemetery Hill and Culp's Hill. While Lee and his subordinates were considering their plan of attack, Union major general Daniel Sickles moved his corps about a mile forward and occupied a peach orchard and wheat field. The move weakened the Union left, but by the time Union general James Longstreet ordered an attack at about 4:00 P.M. Meade had taken advantage of the delay to reinforce Sickles's position. In the late afternoon and early evening, the two forces fought savagely in the peach orchard and the field and among a clump of huge boulders known as the Devil's Den. Confederate troops made blistering attacks on Cemetery Hill and Culp's Hill, but by the time the sun set on the second day of battle little had changed. On the third day of battle, Lee was faced with retreating or mounting one final desperate assault aimed at turning the tide and routing the Federals. As Lee was preparing to order the attack, Stuart finally showed up with his cavalry. Lee ordered the attack, directing Major General George Pickett to lead 15,000 fresh troops against the center of the Union line at Culp's Hill while Stuart attacked the enemy rear with his cavalry. After a fierce nearly three-hour artillery duel, Pickett's men launched the attack. They were slaughtered, most dying from another barrage of Union artillery. Stuart was equally unsuccessful, and at the end of the day Lee realized that the battle was over and had ended in a Union victory. He began the miserable retreat to Virginia the next day. Nearly 7,000 wounded Rebels were left on the field. Meade's Bluecoats were also bloodied and exhausted and failed to follow through by pursuing the retreating Confederates. Both sides were exhausted by the terrible battle, and for the next three months there was very little fighting in the East. (See: Brandy Station; Devil's Den (Gettysburg); Gettysburg, Army of Northern Virginia, Order of Battle; Gettysburg, Army of the Potomac, Order of Battle; Gettysburg, Casualties; Longstreet, Lieutenant General James, CS; Meade, Major General George G., U.S.; Pickett's Charge; and Sickles, Major General Daniel, U.S.)

Gettysburg, Casualties
By the end of the ghastly three days of carnage at Gettysburg, the Confederates had suffered 20,448 casualties, a crippling loss to the manpower-strapped South. The losses included 2,592 dead, 12,706 wounded, and 5,150 captured or missing. The Union listed 23,001 casualties. That included 3,070 dead, 14,497 wounded, and 5,434 captured or missing in action.

Gibbon, Major General John, U.S.
A Pennsylvanian and captain of artillery prior to the war, Gibbon remained faithful to the Union while three of his

brothers fought for the Confederacy. He had prepared the United States Artillery Manual of 1859, which was still consulted by officers with both the North and the South. But he was best known for his Civil War exploits as leader of the famous Iron Brigade and later commander of the Second Division of Major General Winfield Scott Hancock's II Corps. Gibbon fought at Gettysburg, Second Bull Run, Antietam, Fredricksburg, and Chancellorsville and in the Wilderness Campaign. After the war he fought Indians on the frontier and led the column in 1876 that rescued Seventh Cavalry survivors after General Custer's defeat at Little Big Horn. (See: Ream's Station, Second Battle of.)

Gladstone, William Ewart

England's Chancellor of the Exchequer, Gladstone praised the Confederacy during a speech in Newcastle in October 1862 that drew heavy criticism because it flew in the face of the government's official policy of neutrality. Gladstone later said the speech was one of the great errors of his career.

Glendale, Battle Names

The Battle of Glendale during the Peninsular Campaign is known by at least seven different names. In addition to Glendale, they are Charles City Crossroads, Frayser's Farm, Nelson's Farm, New Market Road, Riddel's Shop, and White Oak Swamp.

Glendale, Battle of

The fighting at Glendale, the fifth of the Seven Days Battles, began on June 30, 1862, when Confederate divisions led by Generals Ambrose Powell Hill, James Longstreet, and Benjamin Huger converged in Henrico County, Virginia, on the retreating Union Army of the Potomac. The divisions led by Longstreet and Hill crashed through the Union defense near Willis Church, routing a Union division and capturing its commanding general, George A. McCall. Huger's advance was halted after sharp fighting on the Charles City Road, and a ferocious counterattack by divisions led by General "Fighting Joe" Hooker and Philip Kearny sealed the gap in the Union lines. Confederate general Thomas J. "Stonewall" Jackson was engaged against Union forces at White Oak Swamp and prevented from shoring up the Southern lines. An effort by Confederate general T. H. Holmes to turn the Union's left flank at Turkey Bridge was stopped by a barrage of cannon fire from Federal gunboats on the James River. The daylong fight ended with General McClellan's army falling back to strong new positions on Malvern Hill. No one had scored a conclusive victory, and casualties for the two armies totaled about 6,500 men. In addition to McCall's capture, two Union generals and three Confederate generals were wounded in the fierce fighting. (See: Glendale, Battle Names; and White Oak Swamp, Battle of.)

Gordon, Brigadier General George Washington, CS

Gordon studied at the Western Military Institute in Nashville and worked as a surveyor before joining the 11th Tennessee Infantry Regiment as a drillmaster. He fought at Stones River, Chickamauga, Chattanooga, Kennesaw Mountain, Atlanta, Nashville, and Franklin. Promoted to brigadier general on August 15, 1864, Gordon was wounded and taken prisoner at Franklin and imprisoned at Fort Warren in Boston. After the war he became the last living Confederate general to serve in Congress. Gordon was first seated in 1906 and was reelected twice.

Gorgas, Josiah

Industrially, the primarily agricultural South was an impoverished cousin of the North, and Gorgas's work was cut out for him when he was named Confederate chief of ordnance. He had to supply Southern armies with rifles, artillery, ammunition, and other ordnance to fight a war with only a handful of factories to produce the critical military equipment. And he had to work fast! Captured Union equipment and blockade runners carrying arms purchased from Great Britain with cotton credits provided a quick initial supply. Confeder-

ate purchasing agents Caleb Huse and Edward Anderson
worked full-time in England and arranged a single deal that
acquired 350,000 Enfield rifles for the South. Other agents
brought in another 150,000 Enfields. The South got a big
shot in the arm when Rebels captured a large Federal arsenal
in South Carolina. While purchasing agents were doing their
bit abroad and troops in the field were scavenging for Union
equipment, Gorgas, a Pennsylvanian, was establishing a series
of arsenals in Richmond, Fayetteville, Augusta, Charleston,
Columbia, Macon, Atlanta, and Selma to manufacture the
Confederacy's own weapons. Ironically, with an agrarian
economy and all the cotton produced in the South, the Confederacy started the war without factories capable of producing clothing or shoes. So factories to produce those necessary
products were also established, but there was such a critical
shortage of leather that many Johnny Rebs marched off to
battle wearing canvas shoes with wooden soles. (See: Cotton; Horses and Mules; and Privateers.)

Gould, Lieutenant Andrew Wills, CS

Colonel Nathan Bedford Forrest and this young lieutenant
wounded each other during a quarrel that erupted after
Gould abandoned two prized artillery pieces during a skirmish at Sand Mountain, Alabama. Both men lost their tem-
pers when the lieutenant confronted Forrest at the Masonic
Building in Columbia, Tennessee, on June 13, 1863, and demanded he rescind an order for Gould's transfer. Gould was
pulling a pistol from his pocket when he shot through his
coat, striking Forrest above the left hip. Forrest grabbed Gould
and, while holding on with one hand, opened a pocketknife
with his teeth and stabbed him in the side. Gould died a few
days later. (See: Forrest, Major General Nathan Bedford, CS.)

Grand Army of the Republic

This organization for Union veterans was founded in
1866 in Springfield, Illinois, by former battlefield surgeon
B. F. Stephenson. Membership peaked in 1890 at just above
490,000, and the GAR officially disbanded in 1949 with only

six surviving members. (See: Memorial Day; United Confederate Veterans; and Woolson, Private Albert H., U.S.)

Grant, General Ulysses Simpson, U.S.

During Grant's childhood and early manhood, the Ohio tanner's son didn't appear to be perfect material for molding a future Civil War hero and American president. He was a good horseman but a poor student, who managed to get into West Point only through the good graces of a local congressman. But the congressman must not have been all that impressed with his protégé, because he didn't even get the young man's name right. The West Point appointee's birth name was Hiram Ulysses Grant, but in his nomination letter to the academy the congressman called him Ulysses Simpson Grant. The youth liked that name and kept it. After graduating twenty-first in a class of 39, Grant was sent to Jefferson Barracks near St. Louis, then assigned to duty on the southwest frontier. During the Mexican War he served under Zachary Taylor and Winfield Scott, who passed on their firsthand knowledge of military strategy and combat. Grant served in several posts following the war, before developing a bad drinking habit while stationed on the West Coast. He resigned his commission after a reprimand from his commanding officer and moved his family to St. Louis, where he eventually took a job as a clerk in a leather store owned by his two brothers. In June 1861, after the Civil War began, he was appointed colonel of a regiment of volunteers from Illinois. Three months later he was promoted to brigadier general. Grant engineered a series of stunning victories in the West, including the capture of Vicksburg, which opened the Mississippi River to the Union and split the Confederacy. The general led his Bluecoats at Missionary Ridge and Lookout Mountain in Tennessee a few months later. His accomplishments didn't go unnoticed in Washington, and Grant was called to the East in 1864. Appointed general in chief of all Union armies, he continued to prove himself to Lincoln as a pugnacious, hard-slugging military leader. The president responded by defending Grant from critics after a near defeat at Shiloh. In complete charge and with the president solidly behind him, Grant devised a plan for a three-pronged assault on the Confederates. General George Meade and the Army of the Potomac would face off against General Lee, General Benjamin Butler would chip away at Lee's support with the Army of the James, and General William Sherman would oppose General Joseph Johnston and his Army of the Tennessee and lead the march to Atlanta and the sea. There was no holding back under Grant, and the North suffered heavy casualties, but it was worse for the South. The Confederate war machine was dismantled chunk by bloody chunk until April 9, 1865, at Appomattox Courthouse, where Grant accepted Robert E. Lee's surrender. (See: Lee, General Robert E., CS; Missionary Ridge; Unconditional Surrender Grant; and Vicksburg, Battle of.)

Grapeshot
Artillery rounds consisting of iron balls, usually nine, bound together were fired from a cannon, and the balls broke apart. The deadly rounds were named for their resemblance to a cluster of grapes.

Gray Ghost
A nickname given to Confederate raider John Singleton Mosby for the daring hit-and-run attacks he launched against Union regulars. Mosby helped expand his reputation as the Gray Ghost of the Confederacy after the war with swashbuckling recollections recounted to biographers. (See: Mosby, Colonel John Singleton, CS.)

Great Britain
Although Britain ultimately decided against open support for the South, it was the last nation in the world to lower the Confederate flag. Britain also constructed and sold ships to the South and provided 700,000 rifles for Rebel soldiers.

Great Escape, the

Like World War II, the Civil War had its own "great escape," which occurred when 109 Yankee POWs tunneled out of the cellar of a three-story former cotton warehouse in Richmond. The former Libby and Son Chandlers and Grocery held almost 1,200 Union officers when Colonel Thomas E. Rose organized the run for freedom. Fifty-nine of the escapees made it safely back to Union lines, two drowned, and the others—including Rose—were recaptured.

Greenhow, Rose O'Neal

Information sent to General Pierre G. T. Beauregard by this Washington, D. C., society leader, friend of powerful Northern politicians, and secret Southern sympathizer was credited by Jefferson Davis with helping the Confederates win the First Battle of Bull Run. Mrs. Greenhow used coded messages, sent by female couriers on horseback, to pass on the intelligence she gathered. Exposed as a spy by Chicago detective Allan Pinkerton who was chief of Union counterespionage, she was placed under house arrest. But while Pinkerton and his men lurked nearby to catch treacherous Union officers who might be consorting with the spy, her eight-year-old daughter had climbed a tree, where she perched and yelled to anyone who came near, "Mother has been arrested!" After a few weeks, Mrs. Greenhow was moved to the Old Capitol Prison, where she continued to smuggle information to the enemy through her female collaborators. Finally banished behind Confederate lines, she was welcomed by President Davis and sent to England and France to talk up the Southern cause. She was aboard the British blockade runner *Condor* when the ship ran aground near Wilmington, North Carolina, and she drowned. She was fleeing on a rowboat when it capsized in the surf and she was dragged down by her heavy skirts, which she had filled with gold sovereigns she had earned for a book about her exploits. (See: Ford, Antonia; Old Capitol Prison; and Pinkerton, Allan.)

Gregg, Brigadier General John, CS

A transplanted Texan, Gregg was a slave owner and delegate to the Provisional Congress of the Confederacy in Montgomery and the Congress in Richmond before resigning to take a combat role. After returning to his home state following the First Battle of Bull Run, he recruited the 7th Texas Cavalry and was appointed colonel. After capture at Fort Donelson and parole, he fought during the Vicksburg Campaign and in other battles before he was wounded at Chickamauga. After recovery he was named commander of Hood's Texas Brigade and fought in northern Virginia until he was killed while leading a counterattack at New Market Road near Richmond on October 7, 1864. (See: Gregg, Mary.)

Gregg, Mary

After General John Gregg was killed, his widow, Mary, traveled by wagon across battle lines to claim his body and arrange for burial. Several other widows from both sides have been credited with similar acts.

Grudge

Old enmities in the South die hard even when "old soldiers" like General Douglas MacArthur are involved. MacArthur and a group of aides walked into an Atlanta church one Sunday morning in the 1920s and were reminded by the congregation that the Civil War hadn't been forgotten or forgiven. It was more than a half-century after the conflict. Arthur MacArthur was one of the Yankee commanders who participated in Sherman's march through Georgia.

H

Halleck, Major General Henry Wagner, U.S.

A man of many talents, Halleck was a West Point graduate, teacher, lawyer, and author before becoming a general. He wrote learnedly about legal issues and military theory and served as secretary of state of California, where he was a respected attorney during the Gold Rush. When the Civil War began he hurried back east and accepted a commission as a major general. By the autumn of 1861 he was in command of the Department of the Missouri. He was so good at training troops and such a gifted administrator that he acquired the nickname Old Brains. But Halleck was less impressive as a field commander and shared the same affliction of many Union generals early in the war—he tended to be too cautious and tentative. He fought at Gettysburg, Chancellorsville, and other battles. Although he performed poorly at Corinth, Mississippi, in May 1862, two months later he was named general in chief of all Union armies by President Lincoln. Once more, Halleck proved himself as an administrator, but his shortcomings in field affairs continued to dog him. When General Grant replaced him as general in chief of all Union armies, Halleck became chief of staff. After Appomattox, he served as commander of the Military Division of the James and was with the Division of the Pacific and the Division of the South. (See: Hooker, Major General Joseph "Fighting Joe," U.S.)

Hallucinations

Lieutenant General Richard S. Ewell's best years were behind him when the Civil War began, and he developed a repu-

tation for periodically losing contact with reality and believing he was a bird. During the bad times, Ewell softly chirped
to himself in his tent and reportedly refused anything at
meals except a few grains of wheat and seeds. (See: Ewell,
Lieutenant General Richard Stoddert, CS.)

Hamlin, Hannibal

Vice president when the Civil War began, Hamlin would
have become the nation's seventeenth president had he not
been replaced during Abraham Lincoln's second term by Andrew Johnson. Hamlin was an influential lawyer and leading
politician in Maine when he was nominated for vice president on the second ballot at the Republican Party convention
in Chicago. He was also an ardent abolitionist, who had
abandoned the Democratic Party in 1856 over the issue of
slavery to become a Republican. Lincoln and his vice president had a close, friendly relationship, although Hamlin was
unable to convince the president to act early in the war to declare emancipation and to permit enlistment in the military
by black soldiers. When the president did finally announce
the Emancipation Proclamation it contained some changes
in wording suggested by Hamlin after Lincoln had shown
him a rough draft. Despite his desire to serve a second term
as vice president, Hamlin was dropped from the ticket by
Republicans who hoped to attract the support of proadminis-
tration Democrats by replacing him with Democrat Andrew
Johnson. Even after Hamlin was shunted aside by Republican comrades, he wasn't done with public service. In 1869
he returned to the U.S. Senate, and he served 12 years before
leaving to accept appointment as U.S. minister to Spain. He
died in 1891.

Hampton, Lieutenant General Wade III, CS

The grandson of a heroic Revolutionary War officer and the
oldest son of one of the wealthiest plantation owners in
the South, Hampton was born in Charleston, South Carolina
with a silver spoon in his mouth. He was a man's man who
balanced a classical education with lone trips through the

forests armed with only a knife to hunt wild bear. In 1859 he argued forcefully in the state legislature against reestablishing the slave trade, which he considered an evil that would lead his state and others to secession. When he was proven to be right about slavery and secession, he remained loyal to the South and accepted an appointment as a colonel in the Confederate Army. Then he organized his own elite 650-man fighting force, of infantry, cavalry, and artillerists, which became known as Hampton's Legion. At his own expense he imported six Blakely cannon and 400 Enfield rifles from England for his troops. Before the end of the war, he spent his entire personal fortune for the Confederacy, was wounded five times, lost a brother and a son in battle, and saw his eldest son critically wounded. Hampton earned a reputation for leading from the front, from the time of his first major battle, First Bull Run. He was a brigadier general when he joined J. E. B. Stuart's cavalry as leader of a brigade and participated in the famous ride that circled General McClellan's Union Army. Hampton fought at Brandy Station, then at Gettysburg, where he fought hand-to-hand, firing his pistol and slashing and stabbing at the enemy with an enormous double-edged 45-inch-long straight sword. Hampton was twice slashed in the head by sabers and was struck in the side by shrapnel during the battle. He was promoted to major general in September 1863, and when General Stuart was mortally wounded on May 12, 1864, Hampton was named by Lee to take over the cavalry command. He led his horse soldiers at Trevilian Station in the biggest all-cavalry battle of the war, routing a Union force that was armed with repeating rifles and outnumbered the Confederates two to one. He was a lieutenant general on March 10, 1865, less than a month before Lee's surrender, when he led a charge with only 5 other cavalrymen against 70 Federals. Hampton killed 3 of the 13 Bluecoats killed in the clash, then captured 12 others before the enemy fled in panic. The Confederates lost only one horse. After the war Hampton was elected governor of South Carolina, then resigned the office to serve in the U.S. Senate. (See: Stuart, Major General James Ewell Brown "Jeb," CS.)

Hampton Roads, Battle of

The massive Confederate ironclad CSS *Virginia*—better known today as the *Merrimac*—started the Battle of Hampton Roads at about 1:00 P.M. on March 8, 1862, when it steamed through Chesapeake Bay and headed straight for several wooden Union ships. The heavy Confederate warship was partly submerged when it rammed and sank a frigate and the USS *Cumberland,* one of the largest of the Union ships on blockade duty at the mouth of the James River. Then the *Virginia* grounded and burned the 50-gun *Congress* and knocked the flagship *Minnesota* out of the battle. The dismayed Union seamen fired salvo after salvo at the metal monster, but shells from even their biggest guns merely bounced off the sides of the enemy vessel. Army batteries at nearby Newport News supported the Union ships, but their shells skidded harmlessly off the enemy's sloping iron plating that had been greased with hot pork fat before the battle. The only damage to the *Merrimac* was a broken ram and a thigh wound to its commander, Franklin Buchanan, who was shot by a sharpshooter. The lumbering USS *Monitor* showed up early the next morning, and at 9:00 A.M. the first battle between two ironclad ships in the history of warfare began. The curious duel lasted for four hours, while the ships smashed into each other and fired repeated salvos that merely bounced off each other's iron-plated sides. The *Monitor* finally broke off the engagement after Captain John Worden was injured by a shell blast. The *Virginia-Merrimac* was taking on water and having engine troubles and also had had enough. The Union suffered terrible losses during the attack by the Confederate ironclad on the wooden warships, including 121 men killed aboard the *Cumberland.* But the Union also claimed a small strategic victory, because the *Virginia-Merrimac* failed to break the blockade of Hampton Roads. Tactically, the battle was a draw. (See: Buchanan, Admiral Franklin, CSN; Ironclads; *Merrimac,* CSS; *Monitor,* USS; Worden, Lieutenant John, USN; and *Zouave,* USS.)

Hampton Roads Conference

On February 3, 1865, barely two months before the Civil War ended, President Lincoln met aboard the Union steamboat *River Queen* at the mouth of the James River with the vice president of the Confederacy in a failed effort to negotiate a peace agreement. The meeting was conceived by newspaper editor Francis P. Blair, Sr., who hoped to convince the feuding parties to bury their differences and join together to chase the French out of Mexico. Blair was the father of Lincoln's first postmaster general and of another son who was a major general in the Union Army. Although neither side appeared to believe there was much of a chance to hammer out a peace treaty at the Virginia conference, Lincoln initially tapped Secretary of State William H. Seward as the Union's chief negotiator. Jefferson Davis dispatched Confederate vice president Alexander Hamilton Stephens, assistant secretary of war John A. Campbell, and Senate president Robert M. T. Hunter to represent the South. At the last minute, Lincoln decided to join the conference. Lincoln's position was inflexible on three main points: (1) restoration of national authority over all the states, North and South; (2) no change in the Union's position on slavery and emancipation; and (3) no armistice short of a permanent end to the war and disbanding of all Confederate forces. Lincoln was more conciliatory when it came to the question of treatment of Southern leaders and promised generous use of his power of pardon. He also suggested that slave owners might be compensated by the government for up to about 15 percent of the 1860 value of their former property. The Southern negotiators were boxed by Davis into their own implacable position, opposing abolition and restoration of the Union, and the talks ended after four hours with no progress. Davis later attempted to capitalize on the failed conference by rallying lagging spirits through printing Lincoln's demands in newspapers and handbills throughout the South. In the North, radical Republicans used Lincoln's offer of mild treatment of a defeated enemy during reconstruction to drum up support more punitive measures.

Hancock, Major General Winfield Scott, U.S.

A West Point graduate, Hancock served on the western frontier, in Mexico, and in the Seminole Wars in Florida and
other conflicts before being posted as chief quartermaster
of the Southern District of California. When the Civil War
began he requested active duty in the East and was made
brigadier general of volunteers. Hancock assisted General
McClellan in organizing the Army of the Potomac and fought
in the Peninsular Campaign. During the Battle of Antietam
he commanded the first division of the army II Corps, and he
fought in the Battle of Fredericksburg. In May 1863, following the Battle of Chancellorsville, he assumed command of
the II Corps and molded it into one of the Union's most highly
respected fighting forces. His star shone brightest during the
terrible bloodletting in the Wilderness Campaign and at the
Battle of Gettysburg. In the Wilderness, his II Corps shattered
Confederate general Richard S. Ewell's corps in a strongly
defended area of breastworks at Spotsylvania called the
Mule Shoe because of its distinctive shape. At Gettysburg, in
the absence of General George G. Meade, the newly appointed
commander of the Army of the Potomac, Hancock stepped in
to lead three Union corps during the first day of fighting. On
the third day, while Hancock and his troops were repelling Pickett's Charge, he was critically wounded. The injury
dogged him the rest of his life. (See: Gettysburg, Battle of.

Handguns

About 370,000 handguns were purchased by the Union during
the Civil War. Colt and Remington .44-caliber and .36-caliber
six-shooters were the most reliable and favored. Most handguns on both sides were issued to cavalry and mounted light
artillery. Confederates also restricted issuance of sidearms
primarily to horse soldiers, and Colt Army revolvers and
Colt Navy revolvers were heavy favorites, although a variety
of handgun types was obtained from private donations, foreign manufacturers, newly developed manufacturers in the
South, and the fallen enemy.

THE COMPLETE HANDBOOK   159

Hardee, General William Joseph, CS

One of the original lieutenant generals authorized by the Confederacy, Hardee fought nobly throughout the conflict between the states, ending his Civil War service at the Battle of Bentonville in North Carolina—several days after Lee's surrender. Hardee's only son was killed there. A West Point graduate, Hardee resigned his commission as a lieutenant colonel of cavalry after serving in the Mexican War and against the Seminoles to join the Confederate Army. Commissioned a colonel of cavalry, he moved quickly up the ranks while commanding troops in Arkansas and at Shiloh, where he was wounded. After recovery he commanded his corps at Corinth, Mississippi, and accompanied General Bragg into Kentucky, where Hardee fought at Perryville. Among a large group of officers who despised Bragg, Hardee arranged to leave the senior general's command to join General Joseph E. Johnston in Mississippi but soon returned to the Army of Tennessee and led a corps at Chattanooga and during the Atlanta Campaign. Hardee felt basically the same about the leadership of his commanding general, John Bell Hood, as he had felt about Bragg and once more arranged a transfer. This time Hardee was given command of the Atlantic coast, where he finished out the war. Hardee and Joseph E. Johnston surrendered their forces on April 26, 1865. (See: Bragg, General Braxton, CS.)

Hardtack

This flour-and-water biscuit was teamed with strong coffee to form staples of the Union soldier's diet. The weevils and maggots that often infested the biscuits after they were stored for a while were either brushed off or consumed. Confederates, who were chronically short of just about everything, seldom had the luxury of coffee made with real coffee beans and had to settle for substitutes brewed from chicory, peanuts, potatoes, or peas. Corn bread, often infested with worms or mold, was another staple of the Southern soldier's diet.

Harpers Ferry

John Brown's raid was just the beginning of trouble for Harpers Ferry and the Federal armory and arsenal there. The strategically located community changed hands eight times during the war. The Battle of Antietam was shaping up when Stonewall Jackson captured the armory and arsenal along with more than 11,000 Federal troops by convincing them that they were outnumbered and faced annihilation if they refused to surrender. Jackson's coup marked the biggest surrender of Federal troops of the war, and in addition to the prisoners the Confederates captured rifles, cannon, wagons, and other precious supplies.

Harriet Lane, USS

Named after President James Buchanan's niece and official White House hostess, this Union gunboat was captured by Confederates at the Battle of Galveston. For several months after returning from a voyage to China, the vessel served as Rear Admiral David Farragut's flagship. (See: Galveston, Battle of.)

Hartford, USS

The flagship of Rear Admiral David G. Farragut at the Battle of Mobile Bay, this 24-gun screw sloop was under the command of Captain Percival Drayton. (See: Mobile Bay, Battle of.)

Harvard Regiment

This nickname for the 20th Massachusetts Volunteers Infantry Regiment was popularized because so many of its young officers were Harvard graduates. The regiment was organized in Reading, Massachusetts, in 1861 and fought most of the major battles in the Eastern Theater of the war until it was mustered out in July 1865. Attached to II Corps, Army of the Potomac, the 20th Massachusetts suffered the fifth highest casualty rate of the 2,000 regiments that fought in the war. (See: Copperhead Regiment; and Holmes, Brevet Colonel Oliver Wendell, Jr.)

Hascall, Brigadier General Milo Smith, U.S.

A former store clerk and teacher in Goshen, Indiana, Hascall graduated from West Point and served one year on garrison duty in Rhode Island before returning to his home and civilian life. When the war began he was named aide-de-camp to the commander of the Indiana Brigade, Thomas A. Morris. After fighting at Philippi in western Virginia, Hascall was commissioned a colonel in command of the 7th Indiana Volunteer Infantry Regiment and in October 1861 led his troops at the Battle of Greenbrier River, also in western Virginia. Shortly after, Hascall was attached to General Don Carlos Buell's Army of the Ohio, joining it the day after the Battle of Shiloh. Promoted to brigadier general, Hascall fought at the Battle of Corinth in Mississippi and at Stones River, and during the Battle of the Round Forest he temporarily assumed command of a division after General Thomas J. Wood was wounded. Following transfer to the command of General Ambrose Burnside, Hascall was assigned to the District of Indiana and tracked down deserters. Late in 1863, he participated in the defense of Knoxville, Tennessee, and commanded a division during the Atlanta Campaign. After a recommendation for promotion to major general was rejected, Hascall resigned his commission and returned to Goshen to become a banker.

Haverlock

This head covering was originally popularized by Sir Henry Haverlock of the British army in 1857 during the Sepoy Rebellion in India. The hat could be of either linen or cotton.

Hawes, Richard

This pro-Southern governor had just been installed at the Kentucky capital in Frankfort by Confederate general Braxton Bragg early in 1862 when his inaugural address was interrupted by the boom of artillery fire. Union general Don Carlos Buell had just moved a division up to the capital city's outskirts as part of a diversionary tactic preceding the Battle of Perryville. A few weeks later the border state of Kentucky was solidly in Union hands. (See Buell, Major General Don Carlos, U.S.; and Perryville, Battle of.)

Hawkins, Colonel Rush Christopher, U.S.

After serving in the Mexican War, Hawkins started a military club and eventually transformed it into a fighting unit. The 9th New York Volunteers, which became widely known as Hawkins's Zouaves, fought in the Maryland Campaign, at South Mountain and Antietam, and in eastern Virginia. Hawkins later married the daughter of the founder of Brown University and became a collector of rare fifteenth-century books, eventually amassing a collection that was said to rival that of the British Museum.

Hayes, Major General Rutherford B., U.S.

The man who would become the nation's nineteenth president in 1877 fought with the 23d Ohio Regiment and was wounded in action.

Heg, Colonel Hans Christian, U.S.

A Norwegian immigrant, Heg was a major in the 4th Wisconsin Militia and a Wisconsin state prison commissioner when he was named by the governor as colonel of the 15th Wisconsin Volunteer Infantry Regiment. Colonel Heg quickly went to work recruiting other immigrants from Norway, with a few from Denmark and Sweden, leading to the 15th's nickname as the Scandinavian Regiment. Heg led the regiment through small skirmishes in the Western Theater of war and in its first big fight at the Battle of Perryville, in Kentucky, which was also known as the Battle of Chaplin Hills. At the Battle of Murfreesboro (also known as the Battle of Stones River) in Tennessee, for the first time the Scandinavian Regiment suffered heavy casualties. General William S. Rosecrans rewarded Heg for his performance by naming him to command the new 3d Brigade of the 1st Division, 20th Army Corps of the Army of the Cumberland. A few months later, he was shot in the stomach at the Battle of Chickamauga and died on September 20, 1863, at the First Division Federal field hospital in Crawfish Springs, Georgia. General Rosecrans later said he had planned to promote Heg to brigadier general, but even as a colonel Heg was the highest-ranking Wisconsin soldier to die in combat. (See: Johnson, Colonel Ole C., U.S.; and Wilson, Major Jurgen, U.S.)

Height and Weight of Soldiers
The average height of Union soldiers was five feet, eight inches. The average weight was 145 pounds. Similar averages for the Confederate Army are unknown because so many official records were destroyed in the final weeks of the war.

Helm, Brigadier General Ben Hardin, CS
Abraham Lincoln's brother-in-law, Helm turned down an offer from the president of a commission in the Union Army to fight for the South. Helm was killed at the Battle of Chickamauga. (See: Lincoln In-Laws.)

Henry Repeating Rifle
Along with its counterpart, the Spencer, this revolutionary firearm devastated Rebel regiments once it was introduced into the Union Army. The .44-caliber Henry was described by some Rebels as the "tarnation Yankee rifle that they load on Sunday and shoot all week." The Henry carried 15 rounds in its magazine, and its lever action simultaneously cocked the rifle and ejected the spent shell while moving a fresh cartridge in the chamber case to provide a rapid rate of fire. The firearm was so popular and at times so scarce that some soldiers privately purchased their own Henrys.

Herbert, Lieutenant Colonel, CS
After capture at the Battle of Fair Oaks, Herbert was a prisoner of war at the Union's Fort Monroe in Virginia when he saw navy ships for the first time. Thirty years later the former Rebel officer began a four-year term as the U.S. secretary of the navy.

Hero of Fort Fisher

A former printer for the *Chester County Times,* Union colonel Galusha Pennypacker was still a teenager when he led the 2d Brigade of Major General Alfred H. Terry's 24th Corps during the Battle of Fort Fisher. Pennypacker was severely wounded during the engagement but was brevetted brigadier general the day after the battle. Dubbed by his admiring troops as "the Hero of Fort Fisher," he was later awarded the Medal of Honor for his courageous leadership during the battle. (See: Fort Fisher, Battle of; and, Pennypacker, Major General Galusha, U.S.)

Heth, Major General Henry, CS

Heth was in charge of Confederate foragers when they were spotted in Gettysburg by Brigadier General John Buford. Hours later, Heth led his division against the Union 1st Corps, under the command of Major John Reynolds, at McPherson's Ridge. One of Reynolds's best fighting units, the Iron Brigade of the West, was shattered and he was killed in the bitterly fought clash as McPherson's Ridge fell to the Gray and the Bluecoats were pushed back to Seminary Ridge. (See: Buford, Brigadier General John, U.S.; Gettysburg, Battle of; Iron Brigade; Reynolds, Major General John F.; and Seminary Ridge.)

Hickok, James Butler "Wild Bill"

This legendary Wild West gunfighter fought alongside Union supporters in Bloody Kansas before the Civil War. After the Confederacy was formed, he served as a Union scout. (See: Bloody Kansas.)

Highlanders

The 79th New York Highland Volunteer Regiment owed its structure and many of its traditions to the British army, in which a number of its officers and men had previously served. Even the regiment's number designation, 79th, was a tribute to an existing Highland regiment, the 79th Cameron Highlanders. The regiment maintained its Scots identity, including the forming of a pipe and drum band, which was an integral part of any Scots regiment. The uniforms mirrored their identity and consisted of the traditional Highland doublet, a blue Glengarry cap, a kilt or plaid trousers called trews, a white-haired sporran, knee-length woolen socks with gaiters, and a fearsome dirk sheathed in the right sock. The Highlanders fought at First Bull Run, Second Bull Run, and 57 other engagements before the unit was mustered out on May 13, 1864.

Hill, Lieutenant General Ambrose Powell, CS

Named by Lee to replace Stonewall Jackson after his death at Chancellorsville, Powell was a West Pointer and an anti-slavery Episcopalian from Virginia who followed his home state into the Confederacy. He was known for being especially solicitous to his troops and was popular with the men of his famous Light Division, who affectionately called him Little Powell. He built a reputation for maintaining high morale, giving credit where credit was due, and got along with his superiors, peers, and subordinates. Powell spearheaded Confederate attacks during the Seven Days Battles. When the Light Division ran out of ammunition at Second Bull Run, the spunky Rebels, with their general among them, lobbed rocks at the enemy. Hill saved the Confederates from disaster at Antietam when he showed up on Union general Ambrose Burnside's flank and turned the tide of battle with his Light Division after a 17-mile forced march from Harpers Ferry. Even Hill had his flaws, however, and he functioned best with divisional command. When he was faced with directing one of Lee's expanded corps, Hill's self-confidence wilted and he was known to beg off that he was sick when he suspected the Army of Northern Virginia commander was expecting too much of him. On April 2, 1865, Hill was trying to hook up with his command after a Union breakthrough on the last morning of the Siege of Petersburg when he was shot and killed by a Union skirmisher. Hill had been temporarily separated from his troops and was trying to

get back to them during the confusion of battle. (See: Antietam, Battle of.)

Hill, Lieutenant General Daniel Harvey, CS

One of Robert E. Lee's fiercest fighting generals, Hill was almost impossible for his superiors, peers, and subordinates to
get along with. The morosely religious writings of the former college professor illustrated his belief that humans were
sinful wretches. He was brutally frank about his dislikes,
which included almost everyone as well as the cavalry and
high command. Like many of his peers while fighting in the
West, Hill had little respect for the abilities of his commanding general, Braxton Bragg, and told him about it to his face.
Bragg responded to the blistering verbal attack by firing Hill,
although he was quickly restored to a command. But his iras-
cible personality was so grating that it was even recognized
by General Lee, who dubbed him with the nickname Old
Croaker. Despite Hill's unpleasantness, his performance on
the battlefield made him a constant candidate for promotion.
An outspoken Christian like his brother-in-law Stonewall
Jackson, Hill was a fatalist and impervious to danger. He in-
sisted on leading from the front and was considered the best
tactician in the Confederate Army. He fought in numerous
battles, including Big Bethel, Malvern Hill, Sharpsburg, and
Chickamauga, surviving all before dying in bed of stomach
cancer more than a decade after the war. (See: Bragg, General Braxton, CS.)

Hodgers, Jennie, U.S.

This young woman left Ireland as a stowaway, then dressed
in masculine clothes to enlist in the 95th Illinois Volunteers
under the alias Albert D. J. Cashier. Described by fellow soldiers as the smallest man in the company, she fought at
Vicksburg, in the Red River Campaign, and at Nashville.
She maintained the disguise after the war and collected a soldier's pension.

Holmes, Brevet Colonel Oliver Wendell, Jr., U.S.

The young Yankee officer who was to become the longest sitting Justice on the U.S. Supreme Court was nearly killed in combat at Ball's Bluff. Newly graduated from Harvard, Holmes was a lieutenant attached to the 20th Massachusetts Infantry Regiment when he was struck in the chest by two musket balls. Holmes was later promoted to captain and eventually served as a brevet colonel and aide-de-camp on the staff of General Horatio Wright and was wounded in two other battles before he was mustered out of service. (See: Ball's Bluff, Battle of; Copperhead Regiment; and Harvard Regiment.)

Home Guard

Throughout the South, planters organized plantation patrols known as home guards to control slaves and prevent them from running away.

Hood, Lieutenant General John Bell, CS

Courageous and totally devoted to the Southern cause, Hood didn't even allow the loss of his right leg at Chickamauga to keep him off the battlefield. But he lacked the ability as a strategist needed for the commander of an army and performed poorly during several campaigns and battles that may have otherwise ended more favorably for the South. Hood was at his best early in the war when he earned his fighting reputation as a brigade and division commander during the Seven Days Battles and at Second Bull Run, Antietam, Gettysburg, where he was also wounded, and Chickamauga. But under his leadership late in the war, the undermanned, underequipped, and exhausted Confederate Army of Tennessee was virtually wiped out in its doomed efforts to defend against Union General William Sherman's devastating sweep through the South.

Hooker, Major General Joseph "Fighting Joe," U.S.

Brevetted three times in the Mexican War, then performing gallantly as a divisional commander in the Civil War, Hooker earned his martial nickname. He performed well on the field and blustered and boasted his way to the affection of his men and an admiring press. The onetime California militia commander fought with the Army of the Potomac in all its major battles. But after helping maneuver Major General Ambrose Burnside out of command and taking over the Army of the Potomac himself in January 1863, he mysteriously lost his nerve. Hooker proved himself a near equal to Robert E. Lee as a master of strategy and maneuver, but when it came down to the job of fighting and carrying through he suddenly became timid and indecisive. About one month after losing to Lee at Chancellorsville in May 1863, Hooker was relieved as commander of the Army of the Potomac on the eve of the Battle of Gettysburg. Through the remainder of the war he fought in the West, under the command of General George Thomas and General William Sherman at the Battle of Chattanooga and the Siege of Atlanta. (See: Butterfield, Major General Daniel, U.S.; Gettysburg, Battle of; and Meade, Major General George G., U.S.)

Horse Artillery

Howitzers and other small cannon capable of being easily taken apart and either packed on or pulled by horses over rough terrain, the artillery was widely used by cavalry.

Horses and Mules

Steady, dependable warhorses and sturdy mules were in short supply on both sides of the conflict, but ironically the problem was most acute in the agrarian South. That was especially true as attrition chipped away at the animals Southern cavalry and mule skinners had started with at the beginning of the war. Animals were often overworked and underfed, and thousands died in artillery barrages or during other combat. Some cavalry officers survived a score or more mounts

killed under them in combat. Confederate cavalry commander
Nathan Bedford Forrest had 30 horses shot from under him,
and his fellow cavalry general "Fighting Joe" Wheeler lost
18 horses during battle. Six horses were killed while being
ridden by Confederate general William B. Bate. The shortage became especially severe for the Rebels when they were
chased out of the Kentucky and Tennessee horse country
early in the war. But the Union also had trouble keeping a
supply of good mounts. Brigadier General William T. Sherman had three horses shot out from under him in a single
battle, Shiloh. (See: Bate, Major General William Brimage,
CS.)

Hospital Railroad Car, U.S.

At the beginning of the war, the North outfitted freight
coaches and boxcars so they could transport the sick and injured in litters over long distances to hospitals. Some ailing
men were even transported on flatcars if they were considered capable of holding on and not falling off the sides. But
the U.S. military railroad and army medical authorities eventually developed a hospital car, with heating stoves, skylight
ventilation, and rows of stretchers or litters inside the com-
partments. Nurses were also assigned to ride with and care
for the injured men.

Hough, Private Daniel, U.S.

Hough became the first casualty of the Civil War when he
was killed in an accidental cannon explosion during a 100-
gun salute marking the lowering of the Stars and Stripes at
the surrender of Fort Sumter. Another member of the Federal
garrison, Sergeant James Galway, was also fatally injured
in the mishap and died in a Charleston hospital. (See: Fort
Sumter.)

Housatonic, USS
See: *Hunley,* CSS.

Houston, Sam

The fabled Texan was removed from his job as governor by members of the Texas Secession Convention after refusing to swear allegiance to the new Confederate States of America. President Lincoln twice offered Federal troops to help Houston keep his job, but he refused. (See: Clark, Edward; and Houston, Sam, Jr., CS.)

Houston, Sam, Jr., CS

Against his father's advice, Sam Houston, Jr., joined the Confederate Army, and he was wounded at the Battle of Shiloh. (See: Bible; and Houston, Sam.)

Howard, Major General Oliver Otis, U.S.

When James B. McPherson, one of the Union's most experienced corps commanders, was killed at the Battle of Atlanta, he was replaced by Howard. The new corps commander was ordered to sever Confederate general John B. Hood's communication lines west of Atlanta, and on July 28 the two forces clashed at the Battle of Ezra Church. Howard remained with Sherman throughout the March to the Sea. As the war wound down to its final days, Howard was named to head the Freedmen's Bureau and oversee 900 agents charged with responsibility for helping indigent Southern blacks and whites and keeping peace between the races. (See: Atlanta, Siege of; Ezra Church, Battle of; and Freedmen's Bureau.)

Huger, General Benjamin, CS

A Mexican War veteran, Huger was superintendent of armories for Virginia, Maryland, and other states in the South when he resigned from the U.S. Army to join the Confederacy. Commissioned as a brigadier general in June 1861, he was promoted to major general in May 1862 and placed in charge of the Department of Norfolk. After deciding that his forces were insufficiently strong to put up an adequate defense, he ordered destruction of the city works and the navy yard and scuttled the CSS *Virginia*. Moved to command of Roanoke Island, he failed to reinforce the garrison, which

Battle of Gettysburg (*Bruce Hall Collection*)

**Typical
ironclad
(*Bruce Hall
Collection*)**

**Union F officer during
Sherman's march (*Bruce
Hall Collection*)**

Union ironclads at Vicksburg (*Bruce Hall Collection*)

Confederate general Robert E. Lee (*Virginia Military Institute Archives*)

General Fitzhugh Lee (*Bruce Hall Collection*)

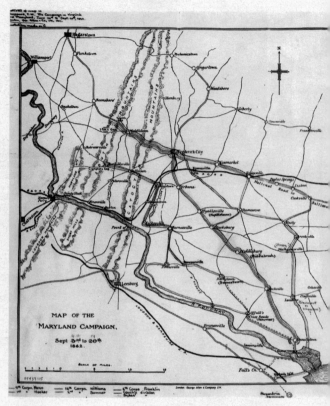

Map of Maryland campaign (*Library of Congress*)

Merrimac engaged with Union fleet off Hampton Roads (*Library of Congress*)

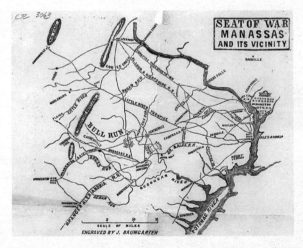

Manassas map (*Hargrett Rare Book and Manuscript Library, University of Georgia Libraries*)

Map of the Mobile Bay campaign (*Bruce Hall Collection*)

USS *Monitor* (*Bruce Hall Collection*)

Battle of Murfreesboro/Stones River (*Bruce Hall Collection*)

Confederate blockade runner

Brady, upon his return from Bull Run (*Library of Congress*)

Railroad gun and crew, Petersburg (*Library of Congress*)

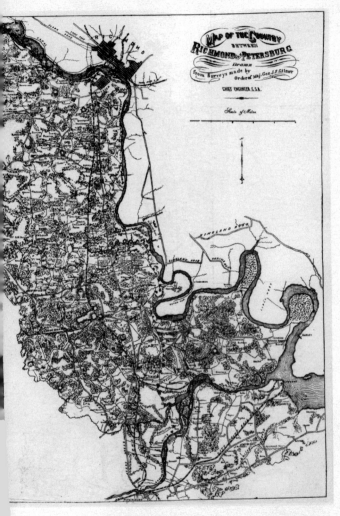

Richmond and Petersburg (*Hargrett Rare Book and Manuscript Library, University of Georgia Libraries*)

**General
Rosecrans
(*Bruce Hall
Collection*)**

**General
Sumner
(*Bruce Hall
Collection*)**

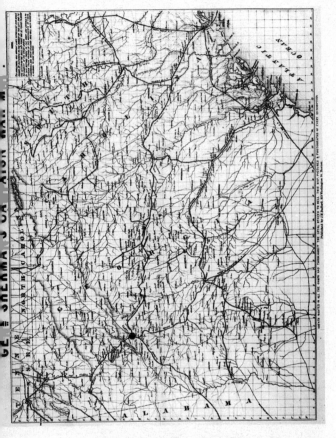

General Sherman's campaign war map (*Hargrett Rare Book and Manuscript Library, University of Georgia Libraries*)

Civil War torpedo (*Bruce Hall Collection*)

Members of the dead at Antietam (*Bruce Hall Collection*

Company F private (*Library of Congress*)

General Joe Wheeler (*Bruce Hall Collection*)

Cavalry engagement at Yellow Tavern (*Bruce Hall Collection*)

Wounded, from the Battle of the Wilderness (*Library of Congress*)

Historical war map (*Hargrett Rare Book and Manuscript Library, University of Georgia Libraries*)

Typical
Zouaves
(*Bruce Ha*
Collection

Federal soldier from New York (*Library of Congress*)

Alabama, Confederate raider (*Bruce Hall Collection*)

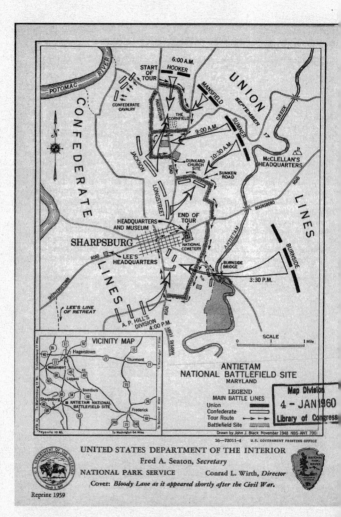

Antietam national battlefield site (*Library of Congress*)

Antietam, Md.: a cavalry orderly (*Library of Congress*)

Federal soldiers and artillery in captured fort, Atlanta (*Library of Congress*)

Battle of Lookout Mountain (*Bruce Hall Collection*)

**Major
General
Blunt**
(*Bruce Hall
Collection*)

General Buford
(*Bruce Hall
Collection*)

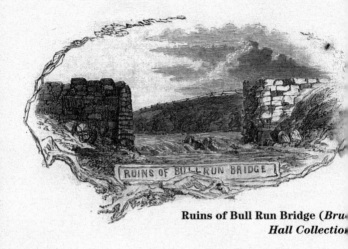

Ruins of Bull Run Bridge (*Bruce Hall Collection*)

Confederate soldier (*Bruce Hall Collection*)

Federal cavalry at Sudley Ford, Bull Run (*Library of Congress*)

**General
Crittenden
(*Bruce Hall
Collection*)**

Chattanooga campaign (*Bruce Hall Collection*)

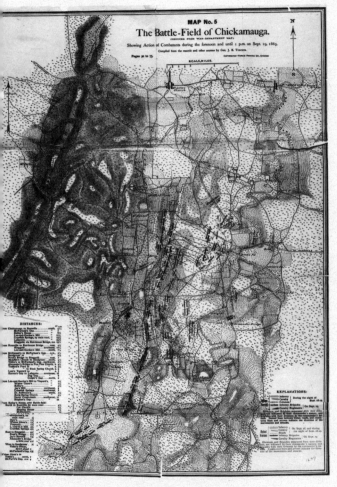

Battlefield of Chickamauga (*Hargrett Rare Book and Manuscript Library, University of Georgia Libraries*)

Stuart and Cuscer engaged at the Culpeper Court House
(*Bruce Hall Collection*)

Devil's Den, Gettysburg (*Bruce Hall Collection*)

The men of Battery M, Culpeper (*Library of Congress*)

Admiral Dahlgren (*Bruce Hall Collection*)

Jefferson Davis (*Virginia Military Institute Archives*)

ead Confederate soldier in Devil's Den, Gettysburg
(*Library of Congress*)

Federal soldier (*Library of Congress*)

Fair Oaks (*Bruce Hall Collection*)

Hauling siege guns (*Bruce Hall Collection*)

Mayre House, Fredericksburg (*Library of Congress*)

Battlefield of Gettysburg (*Hargrett Rare Book and Manuscript Library, University of Georgia Libraries*)

was forced to surrender to the Union. Despite investigation of his poor performance by the Confederate Congress, President Jefferson Davis gave Huger a divisional command under General Joseph Eggleston Johnston. Huger led his division at Seven Pines, White Oak, Malvern Hill, and other battles during the Seven Days Campaign, but he continued to perform poorly and was relieved of command on July 12, 1862. He was reassigned as an artillery and ordnance inspector and exiled to the Western Theater for duty with the Trans-Mississippi Department.

Humphreys, Brigadier General Benjamin Grubb, CS

A Mississippi native, Humphreys entered West Point in 1825, but he was kicked out in the wake of a Christmas Eve riot the following year. Returning to Mississippi, he was elected to both houses of the state legislature, where he strongly opposed secession. But when war broke out, he stayed true to his Southern roots, recruiting an infantry company and accepting a commission as a captain with the 21st Mississippi. He was later promoted to colonel and led the 21st until mid-1863. Attached to General William Barksdale's brigade, Humphreys led the 21st Mississippi during combat at the Seven Days Battles, Antietam, Fredericksburg, and Chancellorsville. When Barksdale was killed at Gettysburg, Humphreys assumed command of the brigade. He was promoted to brigadier general on August 12, 1863, and led his regiment at Chickamauga, Knoxville, the Wilderness, Spotsylvania, and Cold Harbor. The regiment was sent to the Shenandoah Valley in August 1864 to reinforce General Jubal Early, and a month later Humphreys was so severely wounded that he could no longer command in the field. He completed his service as head of a military district in Mississippi and was selected the Magnolia State's first postwar governor but after less than three years was removed from office by Federal military authorities. (See: Barksdale, Brigadier General William, CS.)

Hunley, CSS

Some leaders of the Confederate Navy were counting on the first submarine to become a secret weapon for breaking the Union's blockade of Southern ports. But things didn't go exactly as planned, and even though the CSS *Hunley* became the first submarine ever to sink a large enemy surface ship, it was an unlucky boat. It was basically a 30-foot-long iron boiler powered by a hand crank; it had an open hatch at the top so an officer could stick his head out as the boat skimmed just below the surface of the water and guide it to its target. The bad luck started when the rough submersible sank three times during trials, drowning 20 sailors. And when it blew up the USS *Housatonic* off Charleston Harbor, it either blew itself up along with the Union ship or was dragged down with it, killing the entire nine-man submarine crew.

Hunt, Brigadier General Henry Jackson, U.S.

One of the great Union artillerymen of the war, Hunt was promoted to brigadier general for his gallant performance, which played a crucial role in withstanding Confederate assaults at Malvern Hill. Hunt also directed artillery at Antietam, Fredericksburg, Chancellorsville, and Gettysburg.

I

Income Tax
The nearly universally hated Federal tax was initiated early in the Civil War to pay the crushing expenses of maintaining the Union's fighting forces. Although private loans were used at the beginning of the war, costs were running about $2.5 million a day by early 1862 and the unsettling string of Union defeats on the battlefield was making it difficult to continue attracting private capital. The first income tax was assessed at just 3 percent of earnings. The Confederacy was also forced to begin assessing a demoralizing package of taxes, including an income tax.

Indian Allies of the Confederacy
Fifteen regiments and battalions of American Indians, about 5,500 warriors, enlisted and served with the Confederates. Although the Indians were effective when they felt like fighting, they had a reputation as indifferent soldiers who were troublesome and difficult to lead. At times the Indians tortured and scalped captured and fallen enemy. Most of the Indians were enlisted from the Cherokee, Chickasaw, Choctaw, Creek, Osage, and Seminole tribes and people. (See: Indian State; and Watie, Brigadier General Stand, CS.)

Indian Allies of The Union
Approximately 3,600 to 4,000 Indians served with the Union Army. (See: Parker, Colonel Ely, U.S.)

Indian State

The South was so anxious to enlist help from Indians that
it offered the Cherokee, Chickasaw, Choctaw, Creeks, and
Seminoles their own state in present-day Oklahoma if they
helped the South win the war. Albert Pike, an Arkansas lawyer,
traveled to Indian territory in 1861 to make the offer, which
included representation in the Confederate Congress. (See
Indian Allies of the Confederacy.)

Insurrection

On April 15, three days after guns first fired on Fort Sumter,
President Lincoln proclaimed a state of insurrection. The
president carefully avoided the word *war,* which would have
intimated a clash with a foreign country and helped legiti-
mize the Confederacy's claim to national sovereignty. Coin-
cidental with the proclamation, Lincoln called for 75,000
volunteers to quell the rebellion. At that time, the Union had
only 16,000 professional soldiers under arms, and the war
would ultimately be fought by farmers, shopkeepers, laborers, lawyers, and others who had followed civilian professions.
Except for former West Pointers and others who resigned
commissions in the U.S. Army to fight for the Confederacy
and form the nucleus of a professional officer corps, the
South would field an army and navy of civilian volunteers.
(See: Fort Sumter.)

Intrepid

One of the Union's fleet of hot air observation balloons, the
Intrepid was used during the Seven Days Campaign of 1862.
(See: Antiaircraft Fire; and Balloons, Hot Air.)

Irish

More than 150,000 Irish immigrants served in the Union
Army, many of them refugees from the devastating potato
famine. The Irishmen generally fought hard and well, but
they had a reputation for being difficult to control and for insubordination. The Confederacy also attracted immigran

Celts, and one entire brigade was composed of Irishmen.
See: Irish Brigade.)

Irish Brigade

One of the most storied of all Civil War regiments, this brigade was composed of Irish immigrants, most from enclaves in New York, New England, and Pennsylvania. Formed by Frances Meagher, an influential Irish-American, the brigade consisted of the 63d, 69th, and 88th New York Volunteers, the 166th Pennsylvania, and the 29th Massachusetts. The 29th was later replaced by the 28th Massachusetts, and the 166th was replaced by the 7th New York Artillery. The brigade fought gallantly throughout the war and gained a reputation for its courageous performance. The Irish Brigade's regimental battle flags carried the names of virtually every major engagement in the Eastern Theater, including Gettysburg, Fredericksburg, Chancellorsville, Antietam, Second Bull Run, Malvern Hill, Corinth, Gaines's Mills, Savage's Station, Fair Oaks, Glendale, Yorktown, Alan's Farm, White Oak Bridge, and Bristoe's Station.

Iron Brigade

Considered the North's most elite fighting force, the Iron Brigade (1st Brigade, 1st Division, I Corps of the 1st Army of the Republic) sent advancing Confederate skirmishers at the crest of McPherson's Ridge staggering back with a blistering volley of rifle fire in the opening action at the Battle of Gettysburg. The unit was initially composed of the 19th Indiana and the 2d, 6th, and 7th Wisconsin Regiments and later joined by the 24th Michigan. Distinctive tall black Hardee hats worn by the brigade provided its nickname as the Black Hats. (See: Foreign-Born Soldiers, Union; and Irish Brigade.)

Ironclads

The Union and the Confederacy produced 66 ironclad warships during the conflict, including the famous USS *Monitor*

and the CSS *Merrimac*. Most of the South's revolutionar
warships lost during the conflict were scuttled to preven
capture by the enemy. Only 12 Confederate and Union iron
clads were sunk by enemy action. (See: Hampton Roads
Battle of; *Merrimac,* CSS; and *Monitor,* USS.)

J

Jackson, Lieutenant General Thomas Jonathan "Stonewall," CS

Complex, religious, and fiery-tempered, Jackson fought the Civil War like it was a holy crusade, and when he was accidentally killed at Chancellorsville by his own troops it turned the Confederate victory into a disaster for the South. Jackson and General Robert E. Lee worked together like they were joined at the hip. Lee was calm, determined, and scholarly. Jackson was zealous, spirited, and a talented military tactician and field commander. Both men were master strategists who knew how to get the most out of their men and equipment. When Jackson led his outnumbered forces on an unexpected but perfect march and flanking movement that won the Battle of Chancellorsville, the maneuver went down as one of the most brilliant in military history. But he was never able to follow up with another crippling blow against the enemy the next day, because he was mortally wounded when he was shot by one of his own men while reconnoitering at dusk after the battle. A Virginian, West Point graduate, and former professor at the Virginia Military Institute, Jackson served in the Mexican War, and when his home state seceded he joined the Confederate Army. Named a brigadier general on June 1861, in October, when he was promoted to major general, Jackson was placed in control of the Army of the Shenandoah Valley and maneuvered his outnumbered forces with imagination and guile to keep Union forces in Virginia busy and away from the Confederate capital in Richmond. After a less-than-perfect performance dur-

ing the Seven Days Battles, Jackson bounced back at Second
Bull Run by leading his men on a 51-mile forced march that
brought vital reinforcements to the Confederates in the nick
of time. He was so known for urging his men on to such
rapid marches that the Federals called his troops Jackson's
foot cavalry! Jackson rushed to Lee's rescue a second time at
Antietam and saved the Confederate Army from almost certain destruction. Promoted to lieutenant general in October
1862, Jackson led the II Corps of the Army of Northern
Virginia to victory at Fredericksburg. Then Lee and Jackson devised and carried out the winning strategy that led to
the demoralizing Federal defeat at Chancellorsville—and to
Jackson's death. Jackson was shot in both arms and the chest
by his own men, and when he reported to his old friend and
commander that his left arm had been amputated General
Lee replied, "I have lost my right arm!" At that time, Lee
didn't know that the loss was going to be permanent! Jackson died of pneumonia on May 10, after telling his wife, who
had rushed to help him convalesce at a Guiney Station farm-
house in the Wilderness, "No, no, let us pass over the river
and rest under the shade of the trees." (See: Bee, Brigadier
General Barnard Elliott, CS; and Chancellorsville, Battle
of.)

James, Jesse, and Frank
Sons of a Baptist preacher, the bank- and train-robbing
brothers who were to become the most widely known desperadoes in American criminal history learned their killing
ways riding with border cutthroats William Clarke Quantrill
and "Bloody Bill" Anderson during the Civil War. Jesse was
only 15 when he and Frank rode off from their farm home in
rural Missouri to begin their killing spree aimed at Federal
troops and Union sympathizers. (See: Anderson, William T.
"Bloody Bill"; and Quantrill, Colonel William Clarke, CS.)

James River
Control of the river, extending along the southwest edge of
Virginia's peninsula, was vital to both sides in the war be-

cause it was poised like a dagger pointed at Richmond, the heart of the Confederacy. The river was navigable by shallow-draft gunboats and other craft most of the way north.

"John Brown's Body"

Union volunteers marched off to battle during the early months of the war singing "John Brown's Body," a tune memorializing the abolitionist fanatic's sacrifice. The song depicts Brown as a martyr, and the opening lines read: "John Brown's body lies a' molderin' in the grave. But his soul goes marching on!" (See: "Battle Hymn of the Republic"; Brown, John; and John Brown's Raid on Harpers Ferry.)

John Brown's Raid on Harpers Ferry

During the summer of 1859 abolitionist firebrand John Brown moved his crusade for emancipation from Bloody Kansas to a rented farm in Virginia and, with 21 close followers and financial backing from wealthy northeasterners known as "the Secret Six," began preparations to seize the federal armory at nearby Harpers Ferry, then establish a republic of free blacks in Virginia's Appalachian Mountains. He planned to hole up in the Blue Ridge Mountains and lead a bloody slave revolution with arms and munitions captured during the raid. Under cover of darkness on the evening of October 16, 1859, Brown led his followers to Harpers Ferry, where they seized the arsenal, along with Hall's Rifle Works, captured hostages, and waited for slaves to flock to him from throughout the South and join in the rebellion. The slaves never showed up. Local militia and outraged residents of Harpers Ferry and the surrounding countryside appeared instead and began blazing away with their guns at the abolitionists holed up inside. Some of the attackers swigged heavily from whiskey bottles and others practiced their marksmanship on the dead bodies of two of the raiders while the battle raged. Brown had already moved with his surviving raiders into the armory's fire department engine house when U.S. Army lieutenant colonel Robert E. Lee led a detachment of U.S. Marines to the arsenal. Carrying a white flag,

Lee's aide, Lieutenant J. E. B. "Jeb" Stuart, entered the fire-house for a parley in a last-ditch effort to talk Brown into surrendering and avoiding further bloodshed. Brown stubbornly refused Lee's terms, so Stuart signaled to the marines, then stepped aside as they rushed into the firehouse. Brown's great slave rebellion was over before it started, and after delivering a bitter harangue at his trial in nearby Charles Town he was found guilty of treason and of conspiring with slaves to rebel and murder. Sentenced to death, Brown climbed the gallows steps on December 2 and was hanged. But the fuse had been lighted, and the stage was set for the Civil War. (See Brown, John; Harpers Ferry; Lee, General Robert E., C.S.; Marines, Union; and Stuart, Major General James Ewell Brown "Jeb", C.S.)

Johnny Shiloh
See: Clem, Major General John Lincoln, U.S.

Johnson, Colonel Ole C., U.S.
This Norwegian immigrant was a Wisconsin schoolteacher when he enlisted in the Scandinavian Regiment under Colonel Hans Heg. Johnson was appointed a captain with Company B and after the Battle of Perryville was promoted to major. He fought at Murfreesboro, then at Chickamauga, where the Scandinavian Regiment suffered a nearly 63 percent casualty rate. A lieutenant colonel by that time, Johnson was captured and held at Libby Prison in Virginia until he and two other officers escaped. After 29 days behind enemy lines, the officers finally made their way to safety. Johnson was promoted to colonel and assumed command of the Scandinavian Regiment, leading it through the rest of the war. (See: Heg, Colonel Hans Christian, U.S.; and Wilson, Major Jurgen, U.S.)

Johnson, President Andrew
Although Johnson was a Democrat elected as vice president serving a Republican president, he was unpopular with the Republican Congress. Johnson replaced Lincoln's first-term

vice president, Hannibal Hamlin, in a move by Republicans to balance the ticket during the president's campaign for a second term. Although Johnson and Lincoln worked well together, opposition to Johnson was particularly sharp in the Republican Congress, especially after he moved up to the presidency, because of his policies of reconciliation with the defeated South. A self-educated man from Tennessee who was taught to read by his wife, Eliza, Johnson was a state senator, governor, and congressman before he was elected to the U.S. Senate from his home state. Although Johnson owned several house slaves and wasn't a proponent of emancipation, he strongly opposed secession, and even after Tennessee belatedly joined the Confederacy he was the only senator from the South who refused to resign. In 1862 Lincoln appointed Johnson military governor of Tennessee, and his efforts to restore a civil government in his state that was loyal to the Union paid off when he was selected as Lincoln's running mate in the presidential campaign of 1864. Six weeks after Lincoln's inauguration, Johnson succeeded him as president and began the job under a cloud. He was recovering from typhoid fever when he was sworn in, and his political enemies spread the story that he was drunk. Things went mostly downhill from there, as Johnson followed Lincoln's intent of reconciliation. He pardoned thousands of former Rebels, ex-soldiers and civilians, and pushed for the rapid readmittance of the secessionist states into the Union with restoration of their representation in the U.S. Congress and Senate. Congress was in a mood for revenge, and the differences eventually led the House of Representatives to charge Johnson in February 1868 with 11 counts of impeachment. Johnson considered the two-month trial a farce and refused to attend. He missed being fired from his job by the skin of his teeth when the Senate failed by a single ballot to obtain the necessary two-thirds vote. Johnson's presidency had suffered a death blow, however, and most of his efforts to soften the effects of Reconstruction on the former Rebels were blocked by his political enemies. Johnson managed a final victory on Christmas Day, 1868, when he granted amnesty to all former Confederates who hadn't already been pardoned. Following two unsuccessful bids to win back his old Senate seat after leaving the White House, he was re-elected in 1874. Johnson served only four months of his new term, still fighting an uphill battle against his old enemies, before he died in office in July 1875. (See: Stanton, Edwin.)

Johnson's Island Prison

The 300-acre island on Lake Erie's Sandusky Bay that held Confederate POWs was better than most prison camps in the North and the South. But the fierce winter chill and storms that swept over the island were especially difficult to endure for inmates raised in the Deep South, and it sometimes got so cold that water jugs froze solid. Like many other prisoners, Johnson Island inmates were also so short on food that they resorted to catching and eating dogs and rats. Of the approximate 60,000 POWs who died in the North and South, only about 300 to 400 died on Johnson's Island. (See: Rebellonians.)

Johnson, Willie

This 13-year-old drummer boy with Company D, 3d Vermont, won the Medal of Honor during a series of clashes in the summer of 1862 between General Robert E. Lee's Confederates and General George McClellan's Union forces that became known as the Seven Days Battles. Johnson is the youngest person ever to win his nation's highest award for valor. (See: Seven Days Battles.)

Johnston, General Albert Sidney, CS

A six-foot, one-inch, 200-pound man and a talented, intelligent commander, Johnston was plagued by his role in costly defeats in Kentucky before he was killed at Shiloh in his first major battle in the East. Like General Lee, this Southern aristocrat was wooed by the Union Army and secretly offered a high command, but he chose instead to follow his adopted state of Texas and fight for the Confederacy. Johnston was named to the Confederate Department of the Mississippi, where he made a tactical error by dividing his army while attempting to defend against General Grant's campaign to take control of the Cumberland and Tennessee Rivers. The move cost the Confederacy 15,000 casualties and the double loss of Forts Henry and Donelson, and kept Kentucky firmly in the Union. Grant was also Johnston's opponent in April 1864 at Shiloh, where he courageously took command of scattered Rebel units and was leading an attack on the Union left flank when a bullet severed an artery in his leg. The initial assault was repulsed and Johnston was rallying his troops for a second attack when he dropped unconscious from his saddle and died. (See: Shiloh, Battle of.)

Johnston, General Joseph Eggleston, CS

A West Point graduate, Johnston was injured in the Seminole Wars and in the Mexican War and after duty in the Kansas Territory became quartermaster general of the U.S. Army. Resigning his commission in April 1861 when his home state, Virginia, seceded, he was appointed a brigadier general in the Confederate Army and commanded victorious Southern troops at First Bull Run. After the victory he was appointed to full general and named commander of the Department of the Potomac. Wounded in the Battle of Seven Pines, he was relieved of duty while recuperating, then was named commander of the Department of the West. Due in large part to interference by Jefferson Davis, Johnston's troops suffered mortifying defeats at Chattanooga, Chickamauga, Stones River, and Vicksburg that sullied his reputation. The South was already reeling when he was named commander of the Army of Tennessee and ordered to stop Union general Sherman's march through Georgia to Atlanta. In February 1865, less than a year after turning over the Army of Tennessee to General John B. Hood, Johnston resumed his old command and led his troops against his longtime adversary during General Sherman's march through the Carolinas. By that time the Army of Tennessee, like the rest of the South, was on its last legs and Johnston was unable to do much more than provide annoying harassment to the enemy. On April 26,

Johnston surrendered his troops to Sherman, despite orders from Jefferson Davis to continue the fight. When Sherman died in 1891, Johnston was an honorary pallbearer. When he was urged to put his hat on while waiting in the fiercely cold weather outside the Catholic church in New York City so he wouldn't get sick, Johnston replied, "If I were in there, he'd have his hat off." Johnston died five weeks later of pneumonia. (See: Atlanta, Siege, of; Beauregard, General Pierre Gustave Toutant, CS.; Bull Run, First Battle of; and Seven Pines, Battle of.)

K

Kanawha
The original name selected for West Virginia, after secession from Virginia and formation of a new state covering 24,231 square miles of primarily mountain country. West Virginia's capital, Charleston, is in Kanawha County in the far western area of the Mountain State. (See: West Virginia.)

Kansas-Nebraska Act
This 1854 law permitted the territories to decide by popular vote whether to enter the Union as slave or free states and set off a wave of violence that was especially bloody in Kansas and the neighboring state of Missouri. (See: Bloody Kansas; and Border Ruffians.)

Kautz, Major General August Valentine, U.S.
At the beginning of the Civil War, this Mexican War veteran and Indian fighter was commissioned as a captain of the new 6th U.S. Cavalry Regiment. After fighting in the Peninsular Campaign, he was promoted to the rank of colonel and assigned to the 2d Ohio Cavalry Volunteer Regiment stationed at Fort Scott on the Kansas frontier. By July 1863 he was back in his home state of Ohio and led the successful pursuit and capture of Confederate raider John Hunt Morgan. From April 1864 to March 1865 Kautz was a brigadier general commanding a division of General Benjamin F. Butler's Army of the James. During the latter days of the war, Kautz carried out operations against Confederate supply lines around Richmond and Petersburg and fought at Ream's Station. In

March 1865 he was named to command a division of the black XXV Corps, and he led his troops into the Confederate capital on April 3. After the war he served on the military commission that convicted conspirators in the Lincoln assassination, then returned to the frontier, where he completed his military service. The general was an older brother of Albert Kautz, who served as a young navy officer during the war and later retired as a rear admiral. (See: Morgan's Great Raid.)

Kearny, Major General Philip, U.S.

Widely known as the one-armed general, Kearny was also a millionaire soldier of fortune who served with the 1st U.S. Dragoons and in Algeria with the Chasseurs d'Afrique and became a staff officer for General Winfield Scott during the Mexican War. Kearny was leading a charge in Churubusco when he was severely wounded, leading to amputation of his left arm. But he was quickly back in the saddle, fighting Indians in California and fighting with Napoléon III's Imperial Guard in Italy, where he won the Legion of Honor for leading a daring charge against Austrian forces. At the beginning of the Civil War he was commissioned as a brigadier general in command of a brigade from New Jersey. He fought in the Peninsular Campaign and was promoted to major general in command of a III Corps division after the Seven Days Battles. He then fought at Second Bull Run, before fate caught up with him during the Battle of Chantilly when he mistakenly rode into Rebel lines during a driving rainstorm and was shot to death. (See: Chantilly, Battle of; Flag of Truce; and Kearny Medal.)

Kearny Medal

This military decoration was adopted by the officers of III Corps in November 1862 to honor their fallen commander, Major General Philip Kearny. The medal was designed with a gold Maltese Cross on a circle and awarded to officers who had served "honorably" in battle with General Kearny and whose record was "without stain." (See: Kearny, Major General Philip, U.S.)

Kearsarge, USS
See: *Alabama,* CSS; *Kearsarge,* USS; and Winslow, Rear Admiral John A., USN.

Kennesaw Mountain, Battle of
After throwing back a Rebel attack at Kolb's Farm on June 22, 1864, with heavy enemy losses, Union general William T. Sherman figured their defensive line on Kennesaw Mountain was stretched too thin. Anxious to penetrate the enemy's defensives and blast open a pathway to Atlanta's supply line, the Western & Atlantic Railroad, early on the morning of June 27 Sherman ordered his troops forward in a frontal assault preceded by a massive artillery bombardment. A number of Confederate pickets were overrun, but the strongly dug-in enemy quickly forced the Federals back, inflicting devastating losses. (See: Atlanta, Siege of; and Kolb's Farm, Battle of.)

Kerr Revolver
The British import .44-caliber Kerr revolver was produced by the London Armory Company and was a favorite weapon of Confederate cavalry. It saw more use than all other Southern handguns combined. The revolver had a five-shot cylinder and could be fired either single- or double-action.

Kilpatrick, Major General Hugh, U.S.
Kilpatrick earned a reputation among his peers for reckless courage while fighting in battles including Second Bull Run, Gettysburg, and Big Bethel, where he was wounded. General William Sherman was aware of Kilpatrick's daredevil background when he handpicked him to lead the Army of the Cumberland's cavalry during the Atlanta Campaign and remarked, "I know Kilpatrick as a hell of a damned fool, but I want just that sort of man to lead my cavalry." Despite his gallantry and risk taking, Kilpatrick survived the war. After

leaving the army he continued serving his country as minister to Chile.

King of Spades

When Robert E. Lee took command of the Army of Northern Virginia during the Battle of Seven Pines and withdrew to defensive lines around Richmond, he kept his troops so busy digging trenches that they tagged their new commander with the sarcastic nickname King of Spades. The general had yet to prove himself, and some soldiers revived an earlier nickname stemming from his cautious performance while in command in western Virginia, calling him Granny Lee. (See: Seven Pines, Battle of.)

Kirkland, Sergeant Richard R., CS

See: Angel of Fredericksburg.

Knight, Newton

A former shoemaker drafted into the Confederate Army, Knight refused to fight because of his Union sympathies, so he was allowed to serve with the 7th Mississippi as a hospital orderly. But when he learned his mother's horse had been confiscated by Confederates, he took to the woods and with fellow deserter Jasper Collins formed a band of irregulars to fight the Rebels. Arming himself with a double-barreled 12-gauge shotgun, Knight led the guerrillas, who grew to about 125 men and created havoc while moving about so freely that their neck of the woods in and around Jones County became locally known as the "Free State of Jones." (See: Devil's Den (Mississippi); and Maury, Colonel Henry, CS.)

Kolb's Farm, Battle of

During the Siege of Atlanta, Confederates were dug in along an arc-shaped line on the high sides of Kennesaw Mountain when Union general William T. Sherman ordered a flanking movement aimed at enveloping the enemy force and cutting or capturing their supply line, the Western & Atlantic Railroad. After Confederate general John B. Hood's corps was shifted from the left flank to the right to counter the Union action and moved to its new position near the Mount Zion Church Sherman ordered an attack. It was a bad decision, made without orders from the commander of the Confederate Army of Tennessee, Joseph E. Johnston. Warned ahead of time about the impending assault, Union generals John M. Schofield and Joseph Hooker, each commanding a corps, had their troops firmly dug in and were spoiling for a fight. Hood's forces were hobbled by swampy terrain as they attacked and were raked with artillery and small-arms fire before withdrawing with heavy casualties. Hood's corps suffered about 1,000 casualties. U.S. losses were 350 killed, wounded, or captured. (See: Atlanta, Siege of; and Kennesaw Mountain, Battle of.)

Krzyzanowski, Brigadier General Wladimir, U.S.

The son of a veteran of the Napoleonic Wars, Krzyzanowski immigrated to the United States shortly after the Polish Insurrection of 1846 and organized one of the first militia companies in Washington, D.C., after President Lincoln's call for volunteers. Krzyzanowski hoped to form a Polish Legion from local recruits but only managed to fill four companies. Late in 1861 the War Department joined his companies with six others from New York State, and the new 58th New York Volunteer Infantry Regiment became widely known as the Polish Legion. Krzyzanowski was a fearless leader, and during the Battle of Cross Keys he was armed with only a hand-held bayonet when he led a bayonet charge that saved a vital Yankee artillery position from being overrun. Krzyzanowski also fought gallantly at Second Bull Run, Chancellorsville, Groveton, and Gettysburg, where the Polish Legion suffered more than 50 percent casualties on the first day of battle. Krzyzanowski was reportedly twice passed over for promotion because U.S. senators had difficulty pronouncing his name, but Alaska voters showed more patience. After the war, Krzyzanowski was elected first governor of the new territory.

L

Laird, Son & Company, Shipyard

Despite Great Britain's professed neutrality, several ships were constructed or reoutfitted at the busy Laird shipyard in Birkenhead, England, for the Confederate Navy and privateers serving the South. Among those delivered to Confederate masters were the notorious raider CSS *Alabama*, CSS *Denbeigh*, CSS *Lark*, and CSS *Wren*. Two armored warships that were to be named the CSS *Mississippi* and the CSS *North Carolina* were completed but never delivered because of complaints from the Lincoln government. The juggernauts were equipped with thick side armor and twin turrets and were superior to anything in the Union Navy at that time, but Great Britain settled the international dispute by renaming them the HMS *Wilvern* and HMS *Scorpion* and adding them to the Royal Navy. Two steel-hulled sidewheel blockade runners, the CSS *Albatross* and the CSS *Penguin*, were also under construction at war's end. The Confederacy also acquired ships constructed at other English yards. (See: *Denbeigh*, CSS; *Lark*, CSS; and Maffitt, Captain John Newland, CSN.)

Land Mines

When the Rebels retreated from the Warwick-Yorktown defensive line during the Peninsular Campaign, they left buried land mines behind to slow advancing Union troops. It marked the first time in the history of warfare that land mines were used against an enemy. The hidden killing devices were the brainchild of Brigadier General Gabriel Raines, who instructed his men to bury 8-inch and 10-inch shells just below the surface of the ground after priming them and setting them to explode when stepped on or moved. After the Federals occupied the entrenchments, they used Confederate prisoners to excavate and disarm the devices that soldiers on both sides referred to as "infernal machines."

Lane, James Henry

A veteran of the Mexican War, Lane led the convention of Free Staters in the Kansas Territory that produced the anti-slavery Topeka Constitution, and in 1856 became an abolitionist hero when he organized Free State Volunteers in the defense of the town of Lawrence during the Wakarusa War. Two years later he killed a prominent Free-Soiler in a land dispute, but instead of being sent to prison, he was sent to Washington, D.C., as a U.S. senator when Kansas became a state in 1861. He was reelected in 1865 but fell into disfavor with powerful Republican leaders by supporting President Andrew Johnson's Reconstruction policies. Returning to Kansas, dispirited and exhausted, Lane committed suicide on a farm near Leavenworth. (See: Lawrence Massacre.)

Languages

So many foreign-born soldiers flocked to the colors on both sides that attempting communication, especially in some Union regiments that were packed with immigrants from Ireland, Italy, Germany, Poland, and other European nations, was like building the biblical Tower of Babel. One Yankee regiment had officers and men from 15 different countries, and the colonel's orders had to be passed on in seven different languages. The Union's major general Franz Sigel gave orders in his native German, and at one time they had to be translated to Hungarian, to English, and back to German by his polyglot staff. (See: Sigel, Major General Franz.)

Lark, CSS

This fast little steel-hulled side-wheeler earned the twin distinction of being the last Southern ship to slip in and out of a

Confederate port at the end of the war and the only blockade runner to successfully repel a Federal boarding party. The *Lark* ran aground off Galveston Harbor in early April 1865, and an eight-man guard was posted aboard when two heavily manned launches sent by blockading Union gunboats quietly approached alongside in the postmidnight darkness. The launches were within pistol shot when the guard opened up with a hail of fire that killed the lieutenant in charge and two other sailors. Seven other Yankees were wounded before the survivors made their escape. On May 24, the same morning the CSS *Denbeigh* was burned in the harbor, the *Lark* returned to Galveston, picked up the stranded crew of their sister ship, and successfully slipped back through the blockade into the open sea. (See: *Denbeigh*, CSS.)

Lawrence Massacre

This East Kansas community was a hotbed of abolitionists and Union sympathizers when a bloodthirsty band of Border Ruffians led by William Clarke Quantrill launched a surprise raid, burning the town to the ground and killing about 180 of its male citizens. Quantrill had taught school and stolen the horses of his neighbors there. Some 450 heavily armed raiders struck at 5.00 A.M., on August 21, 1863, riding into town and shooting down every adult male in sight. U.S. senator James Henry Lane, a leading Free-Soiler and one of the prime targets of the raid, escaped by racing through the farm fields in his nightshirt. Women and children were spared, but the bank was cleaned out, taverns were emptied of whiskey, and stores and homes were looted before the killers made their escape. Two months later, while riding back to temporary winter refuge in Texas, the Confederate irregulars surprised a 100-man escort for Union general James G. Blunt and killed 80 Yankees, wounded 18, and rode off with loaded supply wagons. Most of the Bluecoats were shot down after surrendering. (See: Bloody Kansas; Lane, James Henry; and Quantrill, Colonel William Clarke, CS.)

Le Mat Revolver
Many of the best Confederate handguns were imports from
Europe, including the fearsome .40-caliber Le Mat revolver.
The Le Mat featured a nine-shot cylinder for standard pistol
rounds, which revolved around a .63-caliber shotgun barrel.
This arm was said to be a favorite of Confederate general Jeb
Stuart and was considered the gun that packed the most fire-
power of any handgun in the war.

Lea, Colonel Albert Miller, CS
This brilliant military engineer served the South in battles
and in other capacities throughout the war, but he is best remembered for his role in one of the most poignant moments
of the conflict. A West Point graduate and army officer for
the Confederacy, Lea knelt and prayed by his dying son,
an Annapolis graduate and Union naval officer, during the
young man's last moments at the conclusion of the Battle of
Galveston. Lieutenant Commander Edward Lea was second-
in-command of the USS *Harriet Lane* when he was shot in
the navel and mortally wounded during a fierce hand-to-hand
fight with a Confederate boarding party. At Albert Lea's request he was assigned to temporary duty at Galveston after
learning that his son was aboard a ship expected to be involved in the approaching battle. When the Confederate officer
(then a major) found Lieutenant Commander Lea sprawled
on the blood-slicked deck of the ship, it was the first time father and son had seen each other since the beginning of the
war. With his last breath, the navy officer gasped, "Yes, Father, I know you," then died. (See: Galveston, Battle of.)

Lee, Custis
The oldest of General Robert E. Lee's three sons, Custis
began his service with the Confederacy as an army captain
of engineers, constructing fortifications around Richmond.
Most of the remainder of his service was spent as an aide and
courier delivering secret messages to the front for Jefferson
Davis and his staff. On June 25, 1863, Lee was promoted to
brigadier general, and he was named a major general on Oc-

tober 20, 1864. Lee's desire for a frontline assignment was finally realized during the Siege and Battle of Petersburg when he was named to command a regiment in Lieutenant General Richard S. Ewell's division. When Lee was confronted with a large force of Yankees who greatly outnumbered him, he surrendered his men to avoid the useless sacrifice of their lives.

Lee, General Robert E., CS

The scion of an aristocratic Virginia family and son of a Revolutionary War hero, Robert E. Lee turned down an offer from President Lincoln to become general in chief of all the Union armies. Although Lee favored neither slavery nor states' rights, he was intensely loyal to his home state, and after Virginia seceded he resigned his U.S. Army commission to offer his services to the South. Incredibly, despite his 20 years of military experience and service as a teacher at West Point, where he taught many of the professional soldiers who would lead both the Blue and the Gray, Lee was refused a field command and relegated to a job as adviser to Confederate president Jefferson Davis. The man who was to become the icon of a rebellious South was finally given his opportunity on May 31, 1861, when he took command of the Confederate Army after General Joseph E. Johnston was injured at the Battle of Seven Pines during the Peninsular Campaign. Lee renamed his army the Army of Northern Virginia and quickly began whipping his weary, forlorn troops into a formidable fighting force with high morale. Although he was not one of the South's best tacticians and had never before led men in battle, Lee was an excellent strategist. He was also daring and imaginative, and those qualities served him well in five consecutive campaigns during which he repeatedly whipped numerically superior, better-equipped, and better-fed foes. Lee's first task was saving Richmond from advancing Union forces, which held an enormous advantage in manpower and supplies. Union general George McClellan was threatening the Confederate capital with an army of 100,000 men. Major General Nathaniel Banks was raiding

supply depots and tearing up Confederate supply lines in the
lush Shenandoah Valley. And Major General Irvin McDowell was threatening from Northern Virginia, only a short march
from Richmond. Lee couldn't fight them all at once, so he
concentrated all his forces on one of the Union armies, figur-
ing if he could inflict a defeat he would disrupt the activity of
the others. The Army of Northern Virginia attacked McClellan's forces, pushing them back. Then Lee attacked the same
army, which was by then being led by General Joseph "Fighting Joe" Hooker, and inflicted a major, morale-smashing defeat on the Federals at the First Battle of Bull Run. Lee
subsequently fought a bruising battle at Antietam Creek in
Maryland that led to his forced withdrawal to Virginia, won
again at Fredericksburg, and at Chancellorsville, then invaded the North, where he subdued the Cumberland Valley
and small areas of Pennsylvania before locking up in the
most significant battle of the war, at Gettysburg. That was the
beginning of the end, and early in 1884 Lee faced off with
the new general in chief of all the Union armies, Ulysses S.
Grant, in the Wilderness Campaign. Outnumbered two to
one, Lee's army was crushed in a series of battles that led
to a retreat and last-ditch stand at Petersburg, only about
25 miles due south of Richmond. In February 1865 Lee was
at last placed in charge of all Confederate armies, but the war
was already lost. On April 9, 1865, the two generals in chief
met at Appomattox Courthouse and Lee surrendered his
armies to Grant. After the war, Lee was indicted for treason
but never brought to trial. Pardoned, he lived out the rest of
his life as president of Washington College in Lexington,
Virginia. The school was later renamed Washington and Lee
College. General Lee died on October 12, 1870.

Lee, General Robert E., Resignation
Blaming himself for the defeat at Gettysburg, Lee sent a
message to Jefferson Davis on August 8, 1863, offering to
resign. Davis refused the proposal and responded with praise
for the achievements of Lee and his army. (See: Gettysburg,
Battle of; and Lee, General Robert E., CS.)

Lee, Lieutenant General Stephen Dill, CS

A West Pointer and distant relative of Robert E. Lee, Stephen Dill Lee had already served in the U.S. Army for seven years before resigning in February 1861 to join the Confederates. He was on Brigadier General Pierre G. T. Beauregard's staff at Fort Sumter and fought in the artillery at the Second Battle of Bull Run and Antietam. Transferred to Mississippi and promoted to brigadier general, Lee directed artillery at Chickasaw Bayou and Champion's Hill and during the Siege of Vicksburg, where he was taken prisoner. After exchange he was promoted to major general and in May 1864 became commander of the Department of Alabama, Mississippi, and East Louisiana. He was promoted again on June 23, 1864, to lieutenant general and led his troops in the Atlanta Campaign, at the Battle of Ezra Church, and in the Franklin and Nashville Campaign. Lee was wounded during the retreat from Nashville and didn't return to active duty until the final days of the war, when he saw action in the Carolinas Campaign.

Lee, Major General Fitzhugh E., CS

A nephew of Robert E. Lee, Fitzhugh Lee narrowly avoided being expelled from West Point while his uncle was serving as superintendent, but graduated and went west to fight Indians. He was seriously wounded and returned to West Point to teach but resigned to take a commission as a first lieutenant in the Confederate Army. Lee served as a staff officer in the Peninsular Campaign and was promoted to brigadier general in July 1862, then to major general in August. At 27 he was one of the youngest cavalry commanders of the war. Called Fitz by his peers, he led a brigade at Antietam, Chancellorsville, and Gettysburg and was seriously wounded at the Third Battle of Winchester. Following a long recuperation, he served as his uncle's chief of cavalry until the end of the war. After the war he served as governor of Virginia and consul to Havana and was a major general of the U.S. Volunteer Army during the Spanish-American War.

Lee, Major General William Henry Fitzhugh "Rooney," CS

The second son of Robert E. Lee, Rooney began the war in May 1861 as a captain of cavalry and was promoted to major a few days later. He fought in western Virginia, then was named a lieutenant colonel with the 9th Virginia Cavalry. Promoted to full colonel, he joined J. E. B. Stuart's cavalry brigade and participated in the famous ride around Union general McClellan's army. Promoted to brigadier general, Lee led his mixed brigade of Virginia and North Carolina cavalry at Fredericksburg and Chancellorsville. Lee fought in numerous battles throughout the war and was once trampled by horses and left for dead but regained consciousness and made his way back to his command. He was taken prisoner after suffering a severe leg wound at Brand Station, and after exchange he was promoted to major general and named commander of a cavalry division. He led the division throughout the remainder of the war.

Legal Tender Act

A national currency, known as greenbacks, was issued and printed for the first time during the Civil War after passage of the Legal Tender Act. Until that time individual states printed their own money. The new greenbacks were printed with the image of Secretary of the Treasury Salmon P. Chase and were backed by government gold.

Libby Prison

This converted tobacco warehouse in Richmond was the South's best-known prison for captured Yankee officers until the Union launched a raid in 1864 to free the inmates. Libby was then abandoned in favor of other prisons located deeper in the South, including Camp Sumter. Sumter was built in Georgia and became better known as Andersonville. Southern prisons for holding Union soldiers were also located in Danville, Virginia; Salisbury, North Carolina; Mobile, Alabama, and several other locations. (See: Andersonville Prison.)

Liberia

This handsome nineteenth-century tidewater mansion in Manassas, Virginia, was used as headquarters for Confederate general P. G. T. Beauregard, then for Union general Irvin McDowell. The Liberia plantation was also visited by President Lincoln and his secretary of war, Edwin Stanton, before it was converted into a dairy farm after the war. Jefferson Davis is also believed to have walked the halls of the mansion, constructed in 1825.

Limbers

These two-wheeled horse-drawn vehicles had a platform seat for drivers and were used to haul gun carriages or caissons.

Lincoln, Abraham, the Other

The South had its own Abraham Lincoln, but he didn't stick around with his fellow soldiers in Company F, 1st Virginia Cavalry, to see it through to the end of the war. Private Abraham Lincoln, CSA, was listed as a deserter in 1864.

Lincoln Assassination

Despite repeated threats on his life, Abraham Lincoln had only a single bodyguard when he was fatally shot in the head while watching a comedy, *Our American Cousin,* at Ford's Theatre with his wife and friends. He was the first American president to be assassinated. John Wilkes Booth, a handsome actor and member of a prominent theatrical family, had been an invited guest at Lincoln's second inaugural but was a zealous Southern sympathizer and hatched a scheme with fellow conspirators to kill the president and several members of his cabinet. Lincoln's murder was the only assassination that was successfully carried out, although one of his cabinet members was wounded in another attack. Booth died two weeks after the assassination in a shoot-out with Federal troops, who cornered him in a rural Virginia tobacco barn. The other conspirators were also rounded up and imprisoned or hanged. In a statement to the press, Edwin Stanton, Lincoln's outspoken secretary of war, traced the president's assassination to a plot orchestrated by Jefferson Davis and other leading Confederate authorities. The claim was completely false, and although there wasn't a shred of evidence to back up the claim, Stanton's statements fed the Northern animosity against the South. (See: Corbett, Boston, U.S.; Old Capitol Prison; Rathbone, Major Henry, U.S.; and Seward, William Henry.)

Lincoln, First Presidential Election

Lincoln was second choice of many delegates at the Republican national convention of 1860 and after some wheeling and dealing won the nomination for president on the third ballot. A fractious element of the old Whig Party, re-formed as the Constitutional Union Party, selected their own candidate, John Bell, of Kentucky. The Democrats had a more difficult time settling on a candidate, and the first convention in Charleston, South Carolina, broke up when 50 Southern delegates stormed out because the party refused to include a platform providing constitutional protections for slave owners. Then about 100 Southern delegates stomped out of a second convention in Baltimore before the remaining Democrats selected Stephen Douglas as their candidate. The Southerners responded by picking John Breckinridge of Kentucky. By Election Day the race had basically boiled down to a choice between Lincoln or Douglas in the North and Breckinridge and Bell in the South—where Lincoln's name wasn't even on the ballot. Lincoln won 40 percent of the popular vote, along with the electoral votes of the most populous states in the North and West, which, given the divisive conflict within the Democratic Party, was enough to make him the new president.

Lincoln In-Laws

Four of President Abraham Lincoln's brothers-in-law fought for the Confederacy. One was wounded and another was killed in action. Lieutenant David H. Todd, a half brother of the First Lady, was commandant of Libby Prison in Richmond, the Confederate capital city. The relationship of these Rebel soldiers to the president's wife, Mary Todd Lincoln, cast suspicion on her and helped her enemies spread rumors that she was a spy.

Lincoln, Second Presidential Election

Disappointment over failure to register an early victory over the South, and the backbiting political manipulations of secretary of the treasury Salmon P. Chase almost cost Lincoln nomination for a second term. Lincoln won his party's nod after Chase resigned when his disloyalty became publicly known. But the president was facing a more formidable and widely popular Democratic opponent, George B. McClellan, the former general who had disappointed him after being handpicked to lead the Union Army to an early victory. Although McClellan personally favored continuing the war until the Confederacy was solidly defeated, he campaigned on a peace platform, promising negotiations and a quick end to hostilities. Lincoln remained loyal to his original promise to preserve the Union, no matter what the cost. But the president was hobbled by repeated Union defeats on the battlefield and the nation's war weariness, which led to widespread criticism in the press and in Congress. General Sherman's capture of Atlanta and Admiral Farragut's victory at the Battle of Mobile Bay changed the political picture just in time, and the arrogant, posturing "Little Mac" McClellan was soundly thumped in the election. Lincoln captured 55 percent of the popular vote and commanded the electoral college by an even larger margin, 212–21. McClellan won only in his home state of New Jersey, Kentucky, and little Delaware. (See: McClellan, Major General George Brinton, U.S.)

Little Napoléon

One of the nicknames for Union major general George "Little Mac" McClellan.

Little Round Top

This large hill became the scene of some of the fiercest fighting at Gettysburg when Confederates threatened to overwhelm a signal detachment led by Brigadier General Gouverneur K. Warren. Meade had ordered Warren to observe conditions on the flank, and he quickly realized that the hill was a natural gun platform that could be used by Rebel artillery to rake Union troops with devastating fire. Summoned by Warren to help hold the heights, reinforcing Bluecoats, including the 20th Maine Regiment, rushed to the heights where, after hard fighting, they ousted members of an Alabama brigade under Colonel William Oates. While the Rebs who had already gained the summit were being pushed off, the rest of the Alabama Brigade was shattered and repelled by Union troops, including the 140th New York, as they attempted to scale the western face of Little Round Top. (See: Gettysburg, Battle of.)

Longstreet, Lieutenant General James, CS

The Gettysburg corps leader whom Lee called "my old warhorse," Longstreet never planned to become a battlefield commander. Before the war he had set his sights on becoming chief of the U.S. Army Paymaster Department. But when South Carolina seceded, Major Longstreet remained loyal to his home state and traded in his blues for Confederate gray. He was a good tactician, who favored a defensive style, but his calm deliberateness and stubborn reluctance to accept orders he disagreed with brought him into frequent conflict with his superiors. He didn't even hesitate to question General Lee's battle plans. When Lee decided to order a 15,000-man infantry attack on the third day of battle at Gettysburg up Cemetery Ridge against Meade's center, Longstreet didn't hesitate to make his firm objections known. "It is my opinion that no 15,000 men ever arrayed for battle can ever take that position," he declared. Longstreet was right. But Lee was so upset by the open opposition of his subordinate that after Gettysburg, Longstreet and his corps were reassigned to the West, where he fought valiantly at Chickamauga and in other battles. (See: Chickamauga, Battle of; Pickett's Charge; Trenches; and Wilderness, Battle of the.)

Lugenbeal, Private William, U.S.

When the steamboat *Sultana* blew up while transporting former Union prisoners upriver on the Mississippi, Lugenbeal made his own lifeboat from a wooden crate after using his bayonet to kill the previous occupant—a huge alligator. (See: *Sultana*, SS.)

Lundy, William, CS

A discredited veteran of the Civil War, Lundy died on September 1, 1957, and was widely believed at the time to have been survived by only two other veterans. Lundy claimed to have served in the Alabama Home Guard in 1865, even though census records indicate he was born in May 1860, which would have meant he was serving under arms when he was a mere five years old.

Claims of the other two surviving Confederates have also been discredited. (See: Crump, Private Pleasant Riggs, CS; Salling, John, CS; Williams, Walter Washington, CS; and Woolson, Private Albert H., U.S.)

Lutheran Theological Seminary

This imposing building on Seminary Ridge served as an observation post and field hospital for both sides during the Battle of Gettysburg.

Lyon, Brigadier General Nathaniel, U.S.

The first Union general to die in the war, Lyon was killed during the Battle of Wilson's Creek in Missouri on August 10, 1861. The newly appointed commander of about 7,000 Missouri volunteers, Lyon was directing his troops on foot and leading his mount when he was shot in the leg and his horse was killed. He continued to lead his men in an assault on the enemy, was grazed on the head, and staggered toward the rear. Quickly regaining his senses, he was re-forming the men of the 2d Kansas Regiment for a new assault when he was shot in the chest and killed. (See: *General Lyon*, SS; and Wilson's Creek, Battle of.)

M

MacDonald, Angus, CS

A West Point graduate, MacDonald recruited his own company of rangers from the Lower Shenandoah Valley and was known for his unorthodox and non–military academy view that tomahawks were better cavalry weapons than sabers. MacDonald also favored other tactics more commonly employed by Plains Indians, such as striking swiftly in small groups, then retiring from the field.

Machine Gun

The first machine guns barely made their debut in the Civil War when the Confederates used them at Chattanooga and Union major general Benjamin F. Butler fired a few at Petersburg. The Confederates had at least ten Agar guns, better known as the "Devil's Coffee Mill," but they were used sparingly, if at all, and their presence didn't prevent a crippling defeat. Butler was known for an attraction to new forms of weapons and was the first to use the six-barreled revolving cannon known as the Gatling gun. Developed by Dr. Richard Gatling, these weapons fired 250 rounds per minute with a hand crank when they were working properly. The Gatling gun was patented in 1862, but mechanical defects and production problems kept it off the battlefield until the final days of the war. The Agar guns were capable of firing 60 rounds per minute but, like the Gatling guns, didn't always perform as expected. The Confederates also had a one-pound Williams gun that fired multiple rounds, but like the others it was dogged by mechanical problems that hampered its effectiveness.

Maffitt, Captain John Newland, CSN

The first captain of the Confederate commerce raider CSS *Florida,* Maffitt was relieved of his command to recover from yellow fever after a successful seven-month cruise. Maffitt had a nearly 30-year career with the U.S. Navy before resigning his commission to serve the Confederacy. He also captained the ironclad ram CSS *Albemarle* and commanded blockade runners during the final months of the war. (See: *Tennessee,* CSS.)

Magruder, Major General John Bankhead, CS

A cocksure officer who loved the spotlight, Magruder never recovered from a blunder on the last day of battle at Malvern Hill, during the Seven Days Battles in the summer of 1862. He was widely blamed for the crucial Rebel defeat after mistakenly leading his badly needed division down a road away from the fight. By October 1862 the disgraced officer was exiled to the West, where he was put in command of the District of Texas, New Mexico, and Arizona. Called Prince John by peers and subordinates because of his flair and showiness, he was a more talented strategist and leader than some of his peers gave him credit for, and he successfully engineered the Southern victory at the Battle of Galveston. After the war he became a general under the ill-fated Emperor Maximilian in Mexico. (See: Galveston, Battle of; Malvern Hill, Battle of; and Seven Days Battles.)

Mahone, Major General William, CSA

A tavernkeeper's son, Mahone was quickly promoted to colonel after joining the Confederate Army, and participated, in the capture of the Norfolk Navy Yard. He briefly commanded the Norfolk Naval District, before Southern forces were forced to retreat from the area. Mahone fought at Second Bull Run, Fredericksburg, Chancellorsville, the Wilderness, Gettysburg, and Petersburg, where he earned promotion to major general. A Virginian, he was elected to the U.S. Senate after the war.

Mallory, Stephen R.

The Confederate secretary of the navy, Mallory found himself at the beginning of the war facing a rapidly developing Union blockade of Southern ports, more senior officers than it would seem he knew what to do with, and only 12 small ships. The officer problem was the easiest to solve. He assigned older officers to an inactive regular navy that allowed them to save face and hang on to their permanent rank. Younger officers were assigned to a provisional navy, which would allow them to fight and earn promotions. The other problems were closely linked and more difficult to solve. Although the Union also had a shortage of ships to enforce the blockade, they had the shipyards and other industrial resources to solve the problem quickly. The South had neither the needed industry to quickly launch new craft or that to modify existing ships. A former U.S. senator from Florida who was chairman of the Naval Affairs Committee, Mallory believed the South's only chance to penetrate or break a Union blockade would be through the use of swift, heavily armed raiders to harass Yankee shipping and ironclads, and specially outfitted rams with sharp-pointed iron prows to challenge Federal craft manning a blockade. Mallory also sent agents throughout the South to buy privately owned ships that could be used as they were or refitted to use in coastal defense. Other agents headed for England with money in their pockets to buy ships or arrange to have them built. A few Federal ships were also captured in Southern ports at the beginning of the war before they could put to sea and subsequently became part of the Confederate Navy. Southerners and foreigners, especially English, began outfitting privately owned blockade runners, and privateers were equipped with letters of marque, authorizing them to sink or capture Union ships for personal profit. (See: *Merrimac,* CSS; and Privateers.)

Maloney, Private Patrick, U.S.

A husky Irish private in the Union's famous Iron Brigade, Maloney captured the first of Lee's generals ever to be taken prisoner when Rebel infantry were scattered at McPherson's Ridge during the opening volleys at Gettysburg. Maloney proudly turned over his prize, Brigadier General James Archer, to his own commanders. (See: Archer, Brigadier General James Jay, CS.)

Maltese Cross

This emblem was used on the kepi to signify members of the army V Corps.

Malvern Hill, Battle of

General Lee was determined to destroy the retreating Union Army when he launched the last of the Seven Days Battles with a series of fierce attacks on sturdy defenses at Malvern Hill. Union general George B. McClellan was already convinced he had lost the Peninsular Campaign after his defeat at Gaines's Mill and was attempting to conduct an orderly retreat to the James River, where his army could be evacuated by ship. The powerful Union positions on Malvern Hill were buttressed by 100 cannon facing the front and another 150 on the flank that chopped up the Confederates when the attack was launched on July 1, 1862. During daylong assaults led by Brigadier General Lewis Armistead against the enemy lines, the South lost 5,300 men to the enemy artillery's grapeshot and canister before breaking off the fight without gaining an extra foot of ground. Union casualties amounted to about 2,200, far less than the exhausted enemy, but McClellan continued his withdrawal to Harrison's Landing on the James River. Richmond had been saved, and the bloody Peninsular Campaign was ended at last. (See: Armistead, Brigadier General Lewis Addison, CS; Poindexter's Farm, Battle of; and Seven Days Battles.)

Manassas, First Battle of
Alternate name for the First Battle of Bull Run.

Manassas, Second Battle of
Alternate name for the Second Battle of Bull Run.

Manoeuvre Sur Les Derrières, La
Mastered by Robert E. Lee, this was a Napoleonic battle tactic used for enveloping the enemy flank or rear.

Mansfield, Battle of
Major General N. P. Banks was in command of a force of 12,000 men along a road leading to Mansfield and Shreveport, Louisiana, when they were attacked and so badly mauled that it brought a quick end to the Union's ill-fated Red River Campaign and Camden Expedition of 1864. Banks's troops had disembarked from a flotilla of transports on the Red River and were expecting to hook up with another Union army when they engaged a force of Confederates about three miles south of Mansfield on April 8. The Federal column was led by cavalry and followed by a supply train, and several thousand infantrymen marched behind the 350 wagons. The Federals were dangerously strung out in a thin column extending more than 20 miles, and when 8,800 Confederates, led by Major General Richard Taylor, attacked, it was a slaughter. Although reinforcements even farther to the rear arrived before the fighting stopped, the Federals were routed and suffered one of the most humiliating defeats of the war. Banks's army took 2,200 casualties, including 1,500 captured. Nearly 1,000 valuable horses and mules were also captured or killed. Taylor's fighting Confederates from Texas and Louisiana also captured 200 supply wagons and 20 artillery pieces. The Rebels had approximately 1,000 casualties. (See: Bailey, Major General Joseph, U.S.; Banks, Major General Nathaniel Prentiss, U.S.; Red River Campaign; and Taylor, Major General Richard, CS.)

Marines, Confederate

On March 16, 1861, less than four weeks before the first shots were fired at Fort Sumter, volunteers for the Confederate marines began signing up at Montgomery, Alabama, the first capital of the Confederacy. Some 1,600 officers and men eventually served, although the new corps never had more than 600 men, about the size of one Confederate infantry regiment, under arms at any one time. Like their brothers in the army and the navy, many of the recruits resigned or simply left the U.S. Marine Corps to fight for the South. Confederate marines were stationed aboard both Confederate raiders and ironclads as sharpshooters and to repel boarders at sea and were used to quell disturbances and to provide security for navy yards. Marines were stationed with the James River Squadron at Camp Beall, named for the Corps' commandant, Colonel Lloyd Beall, and Drewry's Bluff, protecting the river approach to the Confederate capital. During the First Battle of Drewry's Bluff in 1862, marine sharpshooters deployed along the banks of the James River, helping to suppress fire from Federal gunboats. Two years later marine skirmishers fought alongside the Army of Northern Virginia in the Second Battle of Drewry's Bluff and were instrumental in helping block Union General Ulysses S. Grant's assault on Richmond. The last major engagement the CS marines participated in was the Battle of Sayler's Creek on April 6, 1865. Some CS marines guarded the treasury of the Confederate States, and when Richmond was evacuated at the end of the war some CS marines served with other bodyguards for Confederate president Jefferson Davis. (See: Beall, Colonel Lloyd J., CS; and Sayler's Creek, Battle of.)

Marines, Union

The fledgling U.S. Marine Corps was authorized during the first year of the war to expand its strength to 3,000 men but had trouble attracting enough volunteers because until 1864 there were no signing bonuses for marines as there were for men joining the army or the navy. The term of service was also longer. The marines nevertheless eventually fielded a force of 4,167 officers and men. Of those, 148 were killed in action. With such a small force at his disposal, Marine commandant Colonel John Harris shied away from using his men for waterborne invasions and utilized the marines primarily to man shore batteries and to guard ships, forts, and naval installations. But a battalion of marines fought at First Bull Run (Manassas) and participated in landings at New Orleans and the attack on Fort Fisher at Charleston, South Carolina. Seventeen Civil War marines were awarded the Medal of Honor for conspicuous bravery. Just two years before the war broke out, marines captured abolitionist John Brown while putting down the insurrection at Harpers Ferry, and nearly 30 years before that marines tracked down Nat Turner to end a grisly slave rebellion. (See: Brown, John; and Harpers Ferry.)

Mason, James
Mason was the Confederate emissary to England, and his capture by the Union along with fellow emissary John Slidell, while aboard the British ship HMS *Trent*, sparked the Trent Affair. (See: Trent Affair.)

Mason-Dixon Line
The name for the line that is generally considered the demarcation point between North and South during the Civil War was taken from a pair of British astronomers who conducted a survey aimed at settling a boundary dispute. Charles Mason and Jeremiah Dixon conducted the survey between 1763 and 1767 to establish the boundary between Maryland and Pennsylvania. The line extends along the northern borders of the two states and Delaware, and long after the dispute was officially settled many Maryland residents claimed their state was shortchanged and unfairly lost territory to Pennsylvania. (See: "Dixie.")

Maury, Colonel Henry, CS
After a guerrilla band of Union sympathizers in Mississippi refused an offer of amnesty from General Leonidas Polk,

in early 1864 he ordered Colonel Maury to clean out the troublemakers and make the area safe once more for Confederates. Maury was given command of a battalion of sharpshooters, along with cavalry and horse artillery, and after several months reported that he had rid the area of about 100 guerrillas but still hadn't run down their leader, Newton Knight, and about 20 of his hard-core followers. Knight was wounded when 100 cavalrymen surprised him at a Christmas Day wedding but escaped with his men into the swamps and survived the war. (See: Devil's Den; and Knight, Newton.)

Maynard Carbine
This was a .35- and .50-caliber Confederate breech-loader. A trigger guard released the breech, which then accepted a custom metallic cartridge.

McCausland, Brigadier General John, CS
McCausland was 91 when he died in 1928 and was the last surviving general to have served in the Confederate Army.

McClellan, Major General
George Brinton, U.S.
Diminutive in size but with a huge ego, McClellan had a talent for training and organization and was loved by his men. They affectionately tagged him with the nickname Little Mac. President Lincoln, who appointed McClellan as general in chief of all the Union armies after the retirement of General Winfield Scott, believed that McClellan was the man who would lead Union troops to a victory that would bring a quick end to the War of Secession. McClellan had the background and credentials to do the job. The son of a wealthy Philadelphia family, he entered West Point at 16 and graduated second in his class. He fought in the Mexican War, was sent to Europe to observe the Crimean War, and as the Civil War was shaping up was appointed a major general of the Ohio Volunteers, in command of the Department of the Ohio. When he chased the Confederate Army from western Virginia, he was promoted to major general of the regular army.

He was appointed commander of the Army of the Potomac after the Union defeat at First Bull Run. But McClellan was a better administrator than fighting general, and the Mexican War veteran was hobbled by an overdose of caution, indecision, and a reluctance to commit his troops to battle. His overabundance of caution led him to lose one opportunity after another to destroy the Southern armies and bring an early end to the war. Even after the president gave McClellan a direct order in January 1862 to engage the enemy, he waited another two months before beginning the Peninsular Campaign against Robert E. Lee. By July 1862, Lincoln was fed up with his reluctant commander's shilly-shallying and replaced him with General Henry Wagner Halleck as general in chief of all the Union armies. General John A. Pope was named to lead all Union troops north and west of Virginia, and McClellan was left with only the Army of the Potomac. He vaulted back to overall command after Pope's demoralizing defeat at Second Bull Run on September 1, 1862. Continually pushed by the president to fight, McClellan frittered away his opportunities to destroy Lee's army at Antietam. At last, after McClellan refused a direct order from the president to move forward, Lincoln removed him from command and McClellan returned to private life. At one point, President Lincoln had become so exasperated with the commander's reluctance to fight that he sent him a cable, advising: "If you're not using the Army, I'd like to borrow it!" (See: Antietam, Battle of; Sharpsburg, Battle of; Halleck, Major General Henry Wagner, U.S.; Lincoln, Second Presidential Election; Pope, Major General John A., U.S.; and Scott, Lieutenant General Winfield, U.S.)

McClellan Saddle
George B. McClellan was a promising young U.S. Army officer in 1859 when he designed a cavalry saddle that was simpler and less costly than those previously used. The saddle featured an open rawhide-covered seat, wooden stirrups, a girth strap of wool yarn, and a thick harness leather skirt along with saddlebags and a thimble to hold the rider's car-

bine muzzle. The saddle was used by both the Union and the
Confederacy.

McClellan's Silent Army

Although the fighting was so fierce during the one-day Battle of Antietam that entire regiments ceased existing, one-third
of Union general George B. McClellan's mighty 75,000-man
Army of the Potomac never fired a shot.

McDowell, General Irvin, U.S.

After reluctantly accepting command of the Union Army,
McDowell led his green, mostly volunteer troops, to defeat
at the First Battle of Bull Run, where he proved his ability as
a military strategist and his glaring failure as a field commander. The battlefield defeat was a shock to the North and
to Lincoln, who promptly replaced McDowell with General
George B. McClellan. McDowell had an opportunity to re-
deem himself at Second Bull Run, where he led a corps, but
was relieved of command shortly afterward and did not play
a significant role in Union plans for the remainder of the war.
(See: Bull Run, First Battle of.)

McLean, Willmer

All McLean wanted out of life was to be left alone with his
farm and his family, but he was fated to play a different role
in history. The First Battle of Bull Run, the first major clash
of the Civil War between North and South, was fought on
property that included his Virginia farm. McLean and his
family escaped injury, although a Union artillery shell ripped
through his summer kitchen. That was too close for McLean,
so he left the Manassas area and bought another farm several
miles west of Richmond, where he figured he could till his
fields in peace and be safely isolated from the war. Barely
three years later General Lee surrendered the Confederate
forces to General Grant in the front parlor of the McLean
home in the little crossroads town of Appomattox Court
House. (See: Appomattox Court House.)

McPherson, Major General
James Birdseye, U.S.

Appointed in 1863 as commander of the Army of the Tennessee, McPherson was the highest-ranking Union officer to be killed during the Civil War. Accompanied only by an orderly, the general was rushing to the front on July 22, 1864, in response to a fierce Confederate attack when he ran into a line of enemy skirmishers. Ignoring a demand to halt, McPherson tipped his hat to the Rebels and was wheeling his horse around to escape when he was fatally wounded by a volley of enemy fire. Ironically, John Bell Hood, who was his roommate at West Point where McPherson graduated number one in the Class of 1853, was in command of the Southern troops who fired the fatal volley during the clash on the outskirts of Atlanta. (See: Atlanta, Battle of.)

Meade, Major General George G., U.S.

A West Pointer trained as an engineer, Meade distinguished himself at the Battle of Fredericksburg, where his Pennsylvania reservists smashed through the Rebel line held by Stonewall Jackson. The assault marked the only clear-cut victory of the day for the Union. The performance earned Meade his promotion from brigadier general of volunteers to major general, and he rapidly moved up to a position as a corps commander. A fighting general who was best when leading a defensive battle, he was greeted warmly by the troops when Lincoln named him commander of the Army of the Potomac after dumping Hooker. Meade's qualities as a stern disciplinarian and cautious perfectionist served him well on most occasions but drew criticism from contemporaries and from some historians for causing him to miss a chance to bring an early end to the war by not pursuing the shattered Rebels following Pickett's disastrous charge at Gettysburg. (See: Gettysburg, Battle of; and Pickett's Charge.)

Meagher's Zouaves

Company K of the 69th New York State Militia marched off to war wearing elaborately embroidered shirts and baggy

pants and was one of the few militia units to fight throughout
the entire war. But before the war ended, the men of Company K had exchanged their bright uniforms for more practical Union blue.

Mechanicsville, Battle of

General Robert E. Lee got off to a poor start in the first of the
Seven Days Battles after taking over the Army of Northern
Virginia following the critical wounding of the former commander, Joseph E. Johnston. General George "Little Mac"
McClellan's Army of the Potomac was only six miles outside
Richmond, almost near enough to begin bombarding the
Confederate capital with siege guns, when Lee devised a
three-part plan to force the enemy to climb out of the trenches
and fight. Part 1 called for 47,000 men in three divisions
to launch a frontal attack against a lone corps of Union
troops under General Fitz John Porter on the north side of
the Chickahominy River. Meanwhile, in part 2, Confederate
general Thomas "Stonewall" Jackson would be turning the
enemy's right flank and sweeping around on the Federal rear.
Finally, in part 3, a division led by General Ambrose P. Hill
would cross the Chickahominy at Meadow Bridge and clear
the Federal troops out of Mechanicsville. Once all the troops
had crossed, the four divisions led by Hill and by General
James Longstreet would move down the north side of the
riverbank, destroying what was left of Porter's corps, and
capture the Federal supply depot at White House Landing.
On June 26, 1862, the Confederates, including Jackson's reinforcements, who numbered nearly 90,000 men, opened the
fight that is best known as the Battle of Mechanicsville. (It is
also known as the Battle of Beaver Dam, Beaver Dam Creek,
or Ellerson's Mill.) Regardless of whichever name the battle
is known by, the unexpected tardiness of Stonewall Jackson
and a rash decision by General Hill to begin the attack led to
a disaster for Lee. The battle plan called for Hill to wait until
he heard the sounds of Jackson's guns at dawn signaling the
beginning of the attack before ordering his troops across the
river. When Jackson still hadn't started the battle by midafter-

noon, Hill at last ran out of patience and ordered his five brigades to cross the river. After an easy crossing of the Chickahominy, Hill's troops swept through Mechanicsville before confronting Porter's forces. The Yankees had dug in on strongly fortified high ground on the far side of Beaver Dam Creek. In late afternoon, Hill ordered his five brigades to charge across open fields into the Union lines, which were commanded by 36 cannon. Hundreds of Rebels dropped under the hail of cannon, rifle, and musket fire. Lee dispatched two divisions as reinforcements, and Hill sent them to their deaths in another doomed charge. When nightfall ended the fighting and the dead and wounded were counted up, it was revealed that General Lee's first battle as commander of the Army of Northern Virginia had cost the Confederates 1,485 men. The Union had 361 casualties. (See: Seven Days Battles.)

Medal of Honor
Not the Congressional Medal of Honor, which is the highest decoration a soldier can be awarded today, the Medal of Honor, the Union's top military award, was the only medal available during the Civil War.

Meigs, General Montgomery C., U.S.
This West Point graduate didn't have a glamour job like Generals Grant or McClellan, but he played a key role in the eventual Union victory by keeping troops supplied with everything from tents and blanket rolls to uniforms and shoes that didn't fall apart when they got wet. Although Meigs wasn't responsible for supplying food and weapons, as quartermaster general of the army he kept Union troops far better equipped than their Confederate counterparts, who were chronically short of supplies and equipment throughout the war.

Memminger, Christopher
This South Carolinian was the Confederacy's first secretary of the treasury, and early in the conflict he attempted to keep the war machine going by issuing war bonds. After a brief

flurry of activity immediately following the capture of Fort Sumter, sales plummeted and the Confederate government was forced to approve a Federal income tax and other unpopular assessments on the Southern populace.

Memorial Day

Commander in Chief John A. Logan of the Grand Army of the Republic established this national day of observance in 1868 to honor members of the armed forces who died while on active duty. (See: Grand Army of the Republic.)

Merrimac, CSS

Anxious to develop a secret weapon to break the Union blockade of Southern ports, Confederates built the formidable ironclad ram from the bare bones of the first iron-plated warship ever constructed on American soil, the USS *Merrimac.* The original *Merrimac* was a three-masted wooden steam frigate outfitted by the Union with four-inch-thick steel plates, but it was burned and scuttled at the Gosport Navy Yard near Norfolk in April 1861 to keep it out of enemy hands. The Confederates raised the wreck from the shallows of the Elizabeth River 40 days later and rebuilt it into a new iron-plated juggernaut that was even more awesomely intimidating than the old. The 1,275-ton ironclad was launched and christened on February 17, 1862, as the CSS *Virginia,* but the Union and most later Civil War historians continued to describe it by its earlier name. Despite the *Merrimac*'s 723 tons of armor plating, it was smaller, faster, and more maneuverable than it had been in its previous incarnation. The ship was also constructed with 10 cannon, including two guns fired from a revolving turret. The revolving turret was an innovation that permitted fire from any direction without waiting for the ship to be pulled into position so that a salvo could be launched from fixed-place cannon and gave the captain tremendous advantages in maneuvering during battle. The armament was capped off with a prow outfitted as a 1,500-pound cast-iron ram. Flag Officer Franklin Buchanan was named to command. (See: Hampton Roads, Battle of; Ironclads; and *Monitor,* USS.)

Merrimac, CSS, Sinking of
The CSS *Merrimac* survived its historical battle with the USS *Monitor* by only two months before it was set afire and blown up on May 10, 1862, to prevent its capture when Union forces took Norfolk and the Gosport Navy Yard. (See: Hampton Roads, Battle of; Ironclads; and *Monitor,* USS, Sinking of.)

Mexican War
Many of the officers who led the North and the South earned their military spurs during the war with Mexico from 1846 to 1848. Jefferson Davis, who was to become president of the Confederacy, forged a close friendship with Braxton Bragg, later one of the South's leading generals, while they were both young officers in Mexico. General Winfield Scott, commander in chief of Union armies at the beginning of the war; General McClellan, the man who succeeded him; and General Ulysses S. Grant, who eventually led the Union to victory, were also veterans of the Mexican War. The political struggle over exactly what to do and how to govern the new territories wrested from Mexico at the conclusion of the conflict was also at the center of much of the conflict between North and South. Southerners cited the U.S. Constitution's Fifth Amendment property rights to justify bringing slaves into the new territories. The North, led by vocal abolitionists in New England and the Midwest, vociferously opposed any expansion of slavery.

Mexican-Americans, Confederacy
See: Benavides, Colonel Santos, CS.

Mexican-Americans, Union
Several hundred Mexican-Americans fought for the Union, but poor treatment caused some to defect to the Confederacy.

Military Organization, Confederate

With so many of the South's generals being former West Pointers, the Confederate Army was organized similarly to, but not exactly the same as, that of the Union. Confederate divisions and corps were typically larger than those of their enemy. Four infantry regiments formed a brigade, like those of the Union foe. But divisions were formed from four brigades, one more than the Union. And Southern corps were composed of four divisions, which usually exceeded the number of those on Union organizational charts. (See: Military Organization, Union.)

Military Organization, Union

The Union Army was organized with four infantry regiments forming a brigade, three brigades making up a division, and two or more divisions comprising a corps. Small armies could consist of a single corps, and larger armies were made up of two or more. (See: Military Organization, Confederate.)

Minesweepers

Most Union ships sunk during the war were lost to the floating water mines called torpedoes, so the first minesweeper was constructed as a countermeasure. The new naval defensive weapon ferreted out the floating bombs, then blew them up or otherwise neutralized them. (See: Torpedoes.)

Minié Ball

These standard bullet-shaped projectiles were fired from the rifled muskets used on both sides from the beginning of the war. Designed by two French army officers, Henri-Gustave Delvigne and Clude-Etienne Minié, the bullet's hollow base expanded, forcing its sides into the grooves or rifling of the gun barrel. That action caused the bullet to spiral in flight, giving it greater range and accuracy.

Missionary Ridge

Confederate forces were firmly dug in along the natural fortification during the Battle of Chattanooga when Union

troops and artillery commanded by Major General William
T. Sherman opened a major attack along the north end of the
Rebel lines. When the Yankees were unable to accomplish
a breakthrough, General Ulysses S. Grant directed Major
General George H. Thomas to order a separate assault on the
Confederates at the base of the ridge to draw the enemy away
from Sherman's front. Many of the more-experienced Confederates withdrew, but others stayed and fought until they
were overrun. After taking control of the ridge, acting without orders, the spirited Federal troops continued up the slopes
of Lookout Mountain, routing the Rebels and placing Chattanooga firmly in the hands of the North. (See: Battle Above
the Clouds; Chattanooga, Battle of.)

Mitchell, Corporal Barton W., U.S.

This foot soldier with the 27th Indiana played a crucial role
in blocking Southern plans for a smashing victory at Antietam when he discovered General Lee's battle plans wrapped
around three cigars left lying at a campsite near Frederick,
Maryland. Mitchell gave Lee's handwritten Special Order
191 to a superior, and it was passed up the chain of command
to Union general George B. McClellan. (See: Antietam, Battle of; and Special Order 191, Mystery of.)

Mobile Bay, Battle of

After more than two years of urging the secretary of the navy
to approve a combined land-sea assault to capture Mobile
Bay and close it to blockade runners, the Union's rear admiral David Farragut at last got the go-ahead in the summer of
1864. The long delay had given Admiral Franklin Buchanan,
the Confederate commander at Mobile, plenty of time to
strengthen his defenses, and he took full advantage of the opportunity. Fort Morgan at the western tip of Mobile Point and
Fort Gaines on Dauphin Island were on opposite sides of the
only dependable deepwater channel in the bay. But the forts
had been neglected and had only a few old-fashioned guns
and hardly enough gunners to man them. And Grant's Pass, a
narrow shallow-water channel northwest of Dauphin Island,

was virtually unprotected. Buchanan ordered the construction of Fort Powell to guard Grant's Pass, beefed up the garrisons, and added additional modern guns to the existing forts. While all that was going on, Brigadier General Gabriel J. Rains was using his expertise with torpedoes (floating mines) and other defensive devices to close off the main channel into the bay to enemy forces. Rains spread 180 torpedoes across the deepwater channel, leaving only a narrow 500-yard safe area that would require ships entering the bay to pass directly under the powerful guns at Fort Morgan. A complex field of pilings was added to the mines to make passage by an enemy ship or fleet even more difficult. Finally, Buchanan assembled a small polyglot fleet of wooden gunboats, armored rams, and the pride of his makeshift navy, the newly launched casemated ironclad the CSS *Tennessee.* Farragut had gathered a fleet of 18 ships led by four monitor-class ironclads, the USS *Manhattan,* USS *Chickasaw,* USS *Winnebago,* and, the most recently arrived, USS *Tecumseh.* At daybreak on August 5, 1864, Farragut's ironclads led his invading fleet into Mobile Bay. A force of 5,000 Union soldiers under the command of Major General Gordon Granger had been landed on Dauphin Island two days earlier and surrounded Fort Gaines. At 6:45 A.M. the *Tecumseh* fired the first salvos at Fort Morgan. In minutes the Fort Morgan batteries and Farragut's ships were raking each other with blistering fire. The Confederate fleet, with the *Tennessee* at the front, moved in just behind the minefield and began adding their firepower to that of the forts. The powerful *Tecumseh* turned from its course and headed straight for the *Tennessee,* blundering into a mine and sinking bow-first two minutes after the explosion. The *Tecumseh*'s sudden cross-channel move had fouled up the line of the other Union ships, and they stacked up behind the ironclads like sitting ducks for the Confederate artillery. Farragut's flagship, the *Hartford,* was turned into a slaughterhouse, the deck covered with such a grisly slick of blood and body parts that it was almost impossible to stand or move about on it. At that time, Farragut uttered his famous command, "Damn the torpedoes—full speed ahead!" and the *Hartford* and the USS *Metacomet* passed safely through the minefield into the lower bay, where they came face-to-face with the Confederate defenders. The slow-moving *Tennessee* headed for the *Hartford* to ram the flagship but was easily evaded, so the Confederate ironclad headed for other Union ships that were also negotiating the minefield. The lumbering, awkward ironclad failed to inflict serious damage but a short time later, after sailing out of sight, reversed course and came steaming back toward Farragut's reassembled fleet in the Navy Cove. At the conclusion of a bruising battle, Farragut's ships crippled the Confederate juggernaut, and at 10:00 A.M., three hours after the Battle of Mobile Bay began, the *Tennessee* hoisted the white flag. The surrender of the pride of the Confederate fleet and the capture or flight of the other ships was the beginning of the end for the forts protecting the channel. After nearly three weeks of steady bombardment by the Union fleet and ground forces, the last holdouts at Fort Morgan capitulated and the Battle of Mobile Bay was over. The city of Mobile remained in Confederate hands until April 12, 1865, when its surrender was no longer significant. (See: Buchanan, Admiral Franklin, CSN; Farragut, Admiral David Glasgow, USN; *Tecumseh,* USS; and *Tennessee,* CSS.)

Monitor, USS

Despite knowledge of the CSS *Virginia* (*Merrimac*) under construction in a Southern shipyard, Union officials who were running naval affairs in Washington were in no rush to produce their own ironclad. The navy's Ironclad Board refused to budge until Swedish-born inventor John Ericsson lit a fire under them with a spirited pitch to build a super metal-plated warship for the bargain price of $275,000 in a mere 90 days. The board was so impressed that they gave him the go-ahead and, generously, 10 extra days to the deadline. The Continental Iron Works in Brooklyn was contracted to handle the construction of a flat-bottomed warship with a shallow 10-foot, 6-inch draft, a wooden deck covered with two layers of half-inch iron plates, and armor hanging over the sides to protect against rams and strikes at the waterline by enemy shell fire. A cylindrical revolving 9-foot-high gun turret protected by eight layers of 1-inch-thick iron plating, was the strangest feature of all. Two 11-inch Dahlgrens were mounted in the turret. The 172-foot-long warship was much smaller than the *Merrimac* and looked nothing like any ship that had ever before plied the rivers or seas. Ericsson's unique ironclad was launched and christened as the USS *Monitor* and made its maiden voyage in New York's East River on January 30, 1862—18 days after the construction deadline. Lieutenant John Worden was placed in command and quickly recruited an all-volunteer 57-man crew. On March 6, 1862, the *Monitor* left New York Harbor with a two-gunboat escort, headed off to meet with the squadron blockading Hampton Roads before sailing up the Potomac River to protect Washington. (See: Hampton Roads, Battle of; *Merrimac, CSS,* Sinking of; and Revolving Turrets.)

Monitor, USS, Sinking of
Like its Confederate nemesis during the historic battle at Hampton Roads, the *Monitor* didn't survive into the new year. The strange-looking Union ironclad foundered and sank on the chilly night of December 30, 1862, during a fierce storm off Cape Hatteras, taking 16 men down with her. The rest of the crew were rescued by the steamer *Rhode Island.*

Montgomery, Alabama
See: Cradle of the Confederacy; and Republic of Alabama.

Mooney, Father Thomas H.
A New York City priest, Father Mooney said mass for Union troops but got into trouble with his bishop after christening a cannon in Arlington, Virginia, for the Irish 69th New York Regiment.

Morgan, Brigadier General John Hunt, CS
A veteran of the Mexican War who was a first lieutenant with the 1st Kentucky Regiment, Morgan was daring, gallant, and

fearless. But the cavalry officer who became one of the Confederacy's most famous raiders was predictably impetuous and got into trouble with his superiors and the enemy because of his headstrong tendency not to follow orders. From his early youth, Morgan displayed a violent streak and a love for the military. He left Transylvania University after engaging in a duel, and while trying his hand at being a merchant after returning from Mexico he organized a pro-Southern militia called the Lexington Rifles. Kentucky was officially neutral when the Civil War began, but when Morgan was linked to the smuggling of rifles to Southern sympathizers a warrant was issued for his arrest and he fled from Lexington to join the Confederate Army. This experienced warrior was commissioned and led a cavalry charge at Shiloh before returning to the Western Theater, where he quickly attained prominence as leader of a brigade of mounted raiders. After leading several raids through Kentucky and an excursion into Indiana and Ohio that led to his capture, imprisonment, and escape, he returned to his home state to accept a new assignment. The escaped raider quickly discovered that he was more popular with the Southern press and the public than he was with the Confederate command, which was still smarting because he had disobeyed orders by crossing the Ohio River on his raid. Things went from bad to worse when Morgan was accused of involvement in a bank robbery in Sterling, Kentucky, which had been pulled off by some of his men, apparently without his knowledge. He was at the home of a friend in Greeneville, Tennessee, on September 4, 1864, awaiting a court-martial when Federal troops suddenly launched a surprise attack. Morgan was trying to escape when he was shot down in the street by a former Confederate who had deserted the South to join the Union Army as a private. (See: Morgan's Great Raid.)

Morgan's Great Raid

Cavalry officer John Hunt Morgan led several destructive strikes through Kentucky, but it is for his daring thrust into the Northern states of Indiana and Ohio that he is best remembered. Morgan led two regiments through Kentucky from July 4 to August 1, 1862, that played a significant role in slowing the advance on Chattanooga by Union general Don Carlos Buell's Army of the Ohio. Morgan and his brigade were on the march again in October. And on Christmas Day, 1862, he led another lightning strike that disrupted the Union supply line for five weeks when he ripped up the L & N Railroad and caused Major General William Starke Rosecrans to divert 7,300 advancing troops. But it was Morgan's final strike against the enemy that inspired the Southern home front when news spread about "Morgan's Great Raid." In the summer of 1863 the dashing brigadier general hatched a plan to ride through Kentucky and enlist recruits while tearing up Union supply and communication lines and deflecting enemy forces from Tennessee. General Braxton Bragg, commander of the Confederate Army of Tennessee, approved the proposal, which included an assault on Louisville. But Morgan never mentioned that he also planned to cross the Ohio River and carry the war into the North. Although it was understood by Morgan and his superiors that he would remain south of the Ohio, on July 8 he commandeered civilian boats just west of Louisville and crossed the rain-swollen river into Indiana. The next day, lead elements of Morgan's 2,450-man brigade clashed with a hastily gathered force of about 400 Indiana Home Guards just outside the little settlement of Corydon. Composed primarily of old men and poorly trained farmers and shopkeepers, most of the defenders were taken prisoner and later released. Morgan's troopers suffered 41 casualties. The state militias in Indiana and Ohio had already been mobilized when Morgan began leading his troopers east, burning and destroying bridges, railroads, and supplies. The militia and Union cavalry led by Brigadier General Edward H. Hobson were in pursuit, and crossings and boats along the river were blocked off when Morgan led his force into Ohio at Harrison on July 13. Six days later two brigades attacked and almost completely encircled the raiders at Buffington Island, near the West Virginia border. About 900 Confederates were captured or killed, but Morgan and about 400 of his men escaped through a wood during the night. The survivors continued northeast before they were cornered just outside Salineville in Columbiana County near the Pennsylvania state line by Union forces led by Brigadier General James Shackelford. On July 26, exhausted, outnumbered, and with no way to escape, the raiders surrendered. The unauthorized raid had netted almost 6,000 Union soldiers and state militia who were taken prisoner and released. Railroads were also ripped up at more than 60 locations, 34 bridges were destroyed, thousands of Federal troops had been diverted from other campaigns, and for the first and only time in the war Northern states other than Pennsylvania were invaded by Confederate troops. Morgan was locked in the maximum-security Ohio State Prison at Columbus. On November 26 he dug a tunnel and escaped through air shafts with six of his men. Morgan and four of the escapees made their way safely back to Kentucky. (See: Morgan, Brigadier General John Hunt, CS.)

Morgan, J. P.
Famous Wall Street genius J. P. Morgan made a killing when he financed the purchase of 5,000 rifles from an arsenal in New York for $3.50 each, then sold them to the Union Army for $22 each. While Morgan was pocketing a 25 percent commission, plus interest, Union soldiers were shooting their thumbs off with the defective rifles. (See: Robber Barons.)

Mosby, Colonel John Singleton, CS
A former Virginia lawyer, Mosby was a Confederate Army private when J. E. B. "Jeb" Stuart took him under his wing after recognizing him as a soldier with unique talents who didn't shy away from violence. Under Stuart's tutelage, Mosby became a superb scout, then blossomed into one of the South's most feared raiders. The deceptively frail-appearing warrior jumped from private to lieutenant with the 1st Virginia Cavalry, eventually moving up the line to colonel of Mosby's Virginia Cavalry Regiment. Mosby repaid Stuart's faith in him when he helped set the stage for his patron's

famous three-day ride around McClellan's army to scout out Union positions during the Peninsular Campaign. Mosby rode ahead and scouted out the region in advance. After being captured and exchanged in the summer of 1862, Mosby was authorized by Stuart to raise a band of partisans to fight in northern Virginia's Loudon Valley. Mosby quickly raised a battalion, but by the end of the war the raiders had grown to a regiment. Even though he had moved up to command, Mosby thrived on scouting and continued to personally gather intelligence before his raids, often doing so in disguise. Mosby's partisan rangers ripped up Union supply and communications lines, captured food and munitions, and even penetrated Union defenses surrounding Washington, D.C. His best-remembered exploit occurred early in 1863 when he boldly rode through Union lines into Fairfax Court House with a handful of men and took a Union general prisoner without firing a shot. The Union Army was so embarrassed and frustrated by Mosby's raids and feats of derring-do that it began executing captured rangers. After the Union's young general George Custer executed six of Mosby's raiders, the Confederate responded in kind. Mosby executed seven of Custer's men and left a note on one of the bodies pointing out that all future captives would be treated normally, as prisoners of war, unless Custer committed some new atrocity. That was the end of the executions. Mosby disbanded his command after General Lee's surrender at Appomattox. After the war, Mosby became a strong political supporter of President Grant and was appointed as the U.S. consul in Hong Kong. (See: Ford, Antonia; Stuart, Major General James Ewell Brown "Jeb," CS; and Stoughton, Brigadier General Edwin H., U.S.)

Murfreesboro, Battle of

Confederate general Braxton Bragg was hoping to sit out the winter in the East Tennessee rail junction along the bank of Stones River when Union general William S. Rosecrans showed up with his 41,000-man Army of the Cumberland at the end of December 1862 looking for a fight. Bragg, who had 35,000 men in his Army of Tennessee, struck first. Just before dawn on December 29, his troops smashed into the Union's right flank, driving it back three miles. A total Union disaster was averted by a gallant stand made by General Philip Sherman's division, which held the line at the cost of huge casualties. But Bragg was so certain that he had defeated the enemy that he telegraphed Richmond at the end of the day that the Confederate Army of Tennessee had won a decisive victory. But the Yankees still had plenty of fight in them, and Rosecrans moved a division across the river to extend his defensive line. Bragg ordered General John C. Breckinridge to attack. After failing to convince his superior officer that an assault across open ground was sheer folly, Breckinridge reluctantly ordered his men forward. The Yankees met the assault with a blistering barrage from 58 cannon and withering rifle fire that cost Breckinridge's brave Confederates 1,500 casualties in one hour. The Battle of Murfreesboro ended with a smashing Union victory that left Tennessee firmly in Union hands. On January 4, 1863, Bragg led his shattered army in a humiliating retreat. (See: Stones River, Battle of.)

N

Namozine Church

The Army of Northern Virginia was retreating toward Amelia Courthouse on April 3, 1865, when a Union cavalry brigade caught up with the Confederate rear guard near Namozine Church in Amelia County and the two forces met in a brief but fierce skirmish. Confederate general Rufus Barringer was captured, and casualties amounted to 75 men on both sides.

Napoléon

These smoothbore, muzzle-loading field artillery pieces were named Napoléons because they were developed under the direction of Napoléon III. Napoléons fired a 12-pound projectile and were the basic light artillery weapon of both the North and the South. The guns were originally cast in bronze, but because that metal was so scarce in the South, iron was substituted for the Confederate cannon.

Nashville, Battle of

A furious general in Chief Ulysses S. Grant was en route to Nashville when Union general George Henry Thomas stole the march on the man who was coming to relieve him of command by leading an immediate attack on a ragged Confederate Army dug in just outside the heavily fortified city. Thomas was a cautious commander who was playing it safe and conserving his manpower when he allowed Rebel general John B. Hood's exhausted, poorly clothed, and hungry troops to sit and freeze for a while after they showed up in

the hills south of Nashville on December 2, 1864. But Grant
was in a hurry to get the Civil War over with and was aware
that Thomas's troops, reinforced by soldiers commanded by
General John McAllister Schofield, who had marched from
Franklin, outnumbered the Rebels by almost two-to-one.
Grant wired Thomas a direct order to attack, but the Nashville
commander refused to move forward until a sleet storm blew
itself out. Early on December 15, Thomas finally ordered his
troops forward. Three Union corps shattered the Confederate
left while infantry and cavalry backed up the main assault all
along the line. Shortly before nightfall, outnumbered and
outfought, Hood's Rebels fell back to new positions a couple
of miles away. The next afternoon the Bluecoats once more
surged forward. They were temporarily pushed back when
the weary Confederates made a gallant stand at Overton Hill,
but by nightfall Hood's left flank was entirely surrounded by
artillery and Union blue. A cold rain was falling again when
the Federals crashed through the Confederate line, routing
the enemy. Almost an entire Southern division was taken
prisoner, along with valuable artillery and other supplies.
Survivors of the rout were pursued through the hills for
two weeks, all the way to Tupelo, Mississippi. The battle cost
Hood's forces approximately 1,500 casualties, while about 400
Union soldiers were killed. And it was only through the
valiant efforts of General Nathan Bedford Forrest's cavalry,
which fought a magnificent rear-guard action, that roughly
5,000 members of Hood's once-mighty Army of Tennessee
managed to escape with their freedom and their lives. Less
than one month after the disaster at Nashville, Hood resigned
his command and the remaining troops were assigned to oppose General William Sherman's destructive march through
the Carolinas. (See: Forrest, Lieutenant General Nathan Bedford, CS; and Hood, Lieutenant General John Bell, CS.)

Nelson, Major General William, U.S.
A husky six-foot, two-inch 300-pound bear of a man with a
ferocious temper that seemed to justify his nickname, Bull,

Nelson was a seasoned military veteran who was a naval lieutenant at the Washington Navy Yard when the war started. He
switched military services a few weeks later when the adjutant general of the U.S. Army picked him for special duty
mustering volunteers in Kentucky. Nelson established Camp
Dick Robinson and was made brigadier general, U.S. Volunteers, before moving up to major general following the Battle of Shiloh. But Nelson was also a native Kentuckian who
made it plain he didn't think much of soldiers from the
neighboring state of Indiana. He called them poor trash. In
the summer of 1862, when Confederates invaded Kentucky
and headed for the state capital at Frankfort, Nelson was ordered to hold up the Rebel advance until reinforcements
arrived—and most of his troops were Hoosiers. The day before the Confederates attacked on August 30, Nelson went to
Lexington, leaving Brigadier General Mahlon D. Manson in
charge of the main Union forces in Richmond. By the time
Nelson returned on the afternoon of the battle, his troops
were in full retreat. According to some witnesses, Nelson
cursed the fleeing men and shot or chopped some of them
down with his saber. Nelson himself was wounded in the
thigh, but a veteran of the battle later wrote that the injury
was inflicted by one of the general's own men. Bad blood between the Kentuckian and the Indianans Nelson so detested
may have been a contributing factor when he was shot to
death by a fellow Union officer from Indiana, Brigadier General Jefferson C. Davis. (See: Davis, Brigadier General Jefferson Columbus; and Richmond, Virginia.)

New Market Heights, Battle of

Fourteen black Union soldiers won Medals of Honor for
their valor during this battle on September 29, 1864. The
3,000 black troops engaged in the battle suffered 1,773 casualties, more than one-third of the total Union losses of 3,291.

New Orleans
The largest city in the South, with 150,000 residents at the beginning of the war, New Orleans didn't even put up a fight before Union troops occupied the city.

Nicknames, Confederate
Johnny Reb was the most common nickname for Confederate soldiers. At other times they were simply referred to as Rebs or Gray.

Nicknames, Union
During the Civil War, the nickname Billy Yank was as common for the ordinary Union fighting man as was GI Joe nearly a century later during World War II. Union soldiers were also known by other nicknames, including Bluecoats, Bluejackets, Yanks, and Yankees.

Niter Corps
The name for Confederate ordnance officers who searched the South before locating large deposits of the crucial crystalline compound used in the production of gunpowder in limestone caves in eastern Tennessee, northern Alabama, Georgia, and Arkansas. The Confederacy also created potassium nitrate (niter) by digging shallow pits and filling them with dead animals, manure, and vegetable matter, then dousing the whole disgusting mess with stagnant water and the noxious contents of chamber pots collected from patriotic Southerners.

Nuns
Roman Catholic nuns volunteered and served as nurses during the war, and more than half were from other countries, including 289 from Ireland. Others were from Germany and France.

O

Old Capitol Prison

Four convicted conspirators in the Lincoln assassination, George Atzerodt, David Herold, Lewis Paine, and Mary Surratt, were hanged in the Old Capitol courtyard on July 7, 1865. Four months later, on November 10, 1865, Heinrich "Henry" Wirz, the former commandant of the Andersonville Prison, starred at a hanging there. Found guilty at a military tribunal of "murder in violation of the laws and customs of war" and of other charges, Wirz was the only Confederate tried, convicted, and executed for war crimes. The condemned man stoically mounted the gallows while soldiers lined the walls cheering and chanting, "Andersonville, Andersonville," until he dropped through the trapdoor. The prison building was constructed about 1800 and was used as a tavern and lodging house until it was leased by Congress in 1814 to temporarily replace the U.S. Capitol Building that was burned by the British. When a new Capitol building was built in 1825, the old structure saw various uses until the Civil War, when the then-vacant building was converted into the Old Capitol Prison. It was used for Union and Confederate prisoners as well as for prisoners of state. In addition to the Lincoln conspirators and Wirz, Confederate spies Belle Boyd and Rose O'Neal Greenhow were two of the more notorious inmates. (See: Andersonville Prison; Lincoln Assassination; Paine, Lewis; and Wirz, Captain Heinrich "Henry," CS.)

Oldest Soldier

Although some Confederates were known to have been in their early seventies when they marched off to war, the record for being the oldest recruit apparently belongs to a Yankee. In November 1862 when Curtis King enlisted in the 37th Iowa, he was 80 years old. North Carolina's E. Pollard listed his age as 62 when he joined the 5th Infantry, but historians believe he was in his seventies. Pollard served only briefly before he was discharged because of old age and rheumatism.

Olustee, Battle of

Also known as Ocean Pond, the Battle of Olustee pitted nearly equal forces of about 5,000 men against each other and was one of the bloodiest clashes of the war in terms of percentages of casualties. The battle, on February 20, 1864, was fought out in North Florida's pine forests just west of Jacksonville on February 20, 1864, and cost the Union 1,861 casualties and the Confederates 946. Although it was Union troops who broke off the fight, Jacksonville remained in Union hands for the rest of the war.

Ord, Major General Edward Otho Cresap, U.S.

After graduation from West Point in the class of 1839, and fighting in Florida's Seminole Wars, Ord spent most of his early military career in California and chasing Indians in the Pacific Northwest. He was back east attending artillery school at Fort Monroe, Virginia, when he joined in putting down John Brown and his raiders at Harpers Ferry, then returned to the West Coast. Ord was stationed at the Presidio in San Francisco when the Civil War began. Returning east, he was commissioned as a brigadier general of volunteers and assigned to the Army of the Potomac to help defend Washington, D.C. He fought against J. E. B. Stuart's cavalry at Dranesville, then was promoted to major general and transferred to the Western Theater. Ord was wounded at Hatchie, Mississippi, and it was several months before he was able to return to duty just in time to participate in the Siege of Vicks-

burg. Ord then held commands in Louisiana and fought in
the Shenandoah Valley before he was again wounded at Fort
Harrison. After a three-month convalescence, he was named
to command the Army of the James and fought during the
Siege of Petersburg. The U.S. Army base Fort Ord in California is named after him.

Outhouse Johnstone
This humiliating nickname dogged Lieutenant Colonel Robert
Johnstone throughout the rest of his military career after he
fled in his undershirt and hid under an outhouse to avoid capture by Confederate ranger John Singleton Mosby in Fairfax
Court House, Virginia. The 5th New York Cavalry officer left
his wife to keep the partisans busy at the front door while
he scrambled outside into the backyard. (See: Stoughton,
Brigadier General Edwin H., U.S.)

P

Paine, Lewis

The hulking half-witted son of a Baptist minister and Confederate Army veteran, Paine attacked and seriously injured U.S. secretary of state William Henry Seward as part of the Lincoln assassination plot. On April 14, 1865, the night the president was killed, Paine talked his way into the victim's home, smashed Seward's grown son over the head with a pistol, then dashed upstairs, where the secretary was in bed recovering from a bad fall, and repeatedly stabbed him with a knife. Paine was dragged off his victim by Seward's son and a male nurse but broke away and escaped. He was quickly tracked down and was hanged with three other conspirators at the Old Capitol Prison. Seward recovered from his injuries and continued his cabinet job under the new president. (See: Booth, John Wilkes; Old Capitol Prison; and Seward, William Henry.)

Palmetto Ranch, Battle of

Ironically, the last major battle of the Civil War was fought more than a month after Lee's surrender and was won by the Confederates at Palmetto Ranch, near Brownsville, Texas. Also known as the Battle of Palmetto Hill, the clash was a series of skirmishes that began after Union colonel Theodore Barrett broke a cease-fire agreement that had halted fighting along the Rio Grande in March. On May 11, 1865, he sent 300 horse soldiers to attack Confederate outposts. When Union lieutenant colonel David Branson learned that Mexicans south of the river had tipped off the enemy about his movements, he ordered an immediate attack on a Confederate supply dump at Palmetto Ranch. The Rebels were scattered in the initial clash but returned in greater force and chased the Yankees out. When Barrett learned of the rout, he left his headquarters with 200 men of the 34th Indiana Volunteer Infantry and joined up with Branson, and the reunited Yankee force fought their way back to Palmetto Ranch. They destroyed the remaining supplies before the back-and-forth battle was concluded by a Confederate cavalry attack that cleared Palmetto Ranch and sent the retreating Yankees back to Boca Chica, where they were evacuated by ship before daylight on May 14.

Parker, Colonel Ely, U.S.

The highest-ranking American Indian officer in the Union Army, Parker transcribed the terms of Robert E. Lee's surrender at Appomattox Court House. A full-blooded Seneca born on a tribal reservation in New York State, Parker was denied a commission when he first attempted to enlist in the Union Army. But the need for quality fighting men led to a change of attitude by the army. General Grant was pursuing the 1864 Petersburg Campaign when he named Parker his military secretary, with a rank of lieutenant colonel. (See: Appomattox Court House; and Indian Allies of the Union.)

Parker, Richard

Judge Parker sentenced abolitionist John Brown to be hanged when the injured terrorist was lifted from his cot and held up by deputies to face the court following his conviction in Charles Town, Virginia (now West Virginia), for conspiracy, treason, and murder. Brown responded to the death sentence by remarking, "I feel no consciousness of guilt."

Parrott Guns

Named after Robert Parker Parrott, the inventor of the uniquely reinforced cast-iron cannon, these formidable muzzle-loading rifled artillery pieces were widely used by the North and less often utilized by Southern artillerists, who were generally restricted to guns captured with Union forts or gunboats. The rifled guns were more accurate at longer range than their smoothbore predecessors. Parrott was a West Point graduate and U.S. Army captain of ordnance when he resigned his commission in 1836 to become superintendent of the Iron and Cannon Foundry at Cold Springs. The facility later became known as the West Point Foundry. (See: West Point Foundry.)

Patients and Penitents, Battle of
The vital rail and supply link of Petersburg, a few miles south of Richmond, was lightly defended when Confederate general Pierre G. T. Beauregard cobbled together a collection of local militia, old men, drummer boys, and the sick and injured to repulse an assault by a strong Union force under the command of Major General Quincy Gillmore. The clash on June 9, 1864, marked the beginning of the 10-month Battle and Siege of Petersburg. Known by some as the Battle of Patients and Penitents and by others as Old Men and Young Boys, the encounter pitted 4,500 Union foot soldiers and cavalry against 2,500 defenders and led to about 120 total casualties. The Union forces withdrew after they were unable to break through the Rebel lines. (See: Petersburg, Siege and Battle of.)

Pelham, Major John, CS
While commanding the horse artillery for J. E. B. "Jeb" Stuart's cavalry, Pelham, movie star handsome before there were movies, proved to be as gallant and brave as he was good-looking. Known as "the boy major," he was only 24 when he was killed in March 1863 in the Battle of Kelly's Ford. At least three young Southern belles reportedly dressed in mourning clothes after learning of his death.

Pemberton, Lieutenant General John Clifford, CS
A Pennsylvanian, Pemberton graduated from West Point, where most of his close friends were from the South. A firm

believer in states' rights, he even married a Virginia woman, and when the Civil War began this Mexican War veteran and cavalry officer volunteered his services to the Confederacy. Two of Pemberton's brothers fought for the Union. Given the rank of brigadier general, John Pemberton was named to command the Department of South Carolina and Florida. In January 1862 he was promoted to major general, and in October he moved up to the rank of lieutenant general in command of the Department of Mississippi and East Louisiana. Pemberton was in command of the garrison at Vicksburg in 1863, which he was forced to surrender after a long siege and receipt of conflicting orders from his immediate superior, General Joseph E. Johnston, and from Confederate president Jefferson Davis. No command commensurate with Pemberton's rank was available after Vicksburg, so he stepped down and accepted a commission as a colonel of artillery. He served with the artillery until the end of the war. (See: Vicksburg, Battle of.)

Pendleton, General William, CS
The Confederate chief of artillery for the Army of Northern Virginia, Pendleton was also an ordained Episcopal priest who preached when he wasn't directing his guns at the enemy in combat. The handsome bearded Virginian looked so much like Robert E. Lee that troops sometimes confused the two officers for each other.

Peninsular Campaign
If the ill-fated Peninsular Campaign of 1862 had been led by a more aggressive Union general, the Civil War might have ended years before the Confederate surrender at Appomattox and thousands of lives could have been saved. But General George Brinton McClellan was in command of the powerful 130,000-man Army of the Potomac that was landed by ship at the tip of the Virginia Peninsula between the James and York Rivers. McClellan, "Little Napoléon" to many of his troops and the Northern press, had talked President Lincoln out of attacking strong Rebel forces gathered at Manassas, a

short 10 miles from the Union capital and nerve center at Washington, D.C. Instead, Little Napoléon planned to take the pressure off Washington by marching his army up the lightly defended peninsula and capturing the Confederate capital. The strategy was sound and provided the Union with an opportunity to cut the head and heart from the Confederacy with a single bold stroke. But McClellan was the wrong man for the job. Although he was in command of the largest army ever assembled on the North American continent and was supported by more than 300 cannon, with a strong navy presence, McClellan's personal leadership flaws caused him to botch the job. Poor timing and bad luck also had a lot to do with the failure. McClellan's army was preparing to secure the old tobacco port city of Yorktown near the peninsula's tip when the navy support evaporated, because the Rebel's ironclad juggernaut, the CSS *Merrimac,* had steamed into the Chesapeake Bay off Hampton Roads and was keeping the sailors busy. Then the general learned his maps were no good, because surveyors had marked roads incorrectly. Confederate general "Prince John" Magruder contributed to the confusion and misery when he wisely dammed up the shallow Warwick River, transforming most of the crossings into swamps or rushing torrents. Then it started to rain! Lincoln added the coup de grâce when he demanded 40,000 of McClellan's troops to shore up the shaky Washington defenses. McClellan was demoralized, and he hesitated almost a month before finally giving in to Lincoln's insistent prodding and ordering the attack on Yorktown. On May 4 the Yankees walked into the city and took over its forts unmolested, because the Confederates had abandoned it the day before. By that time, political and military decisions had trimmed McClellan's army to 100,000, still twice the 50,000 that General Joseph E. Johnston had available to defend the Confederate capital. Another powerful Union force of 40,000 soldiers commanded by Major General Irvin McDowell was on the march only a short distance away. Despite the bad weather and confusion, McClellan's army drove close enough to Richmond so that soldiers could see church steeples before Johnston finally turned to fight. He fought and lost the Battle of Seven Pines, where he was critically wounded, leading to his replacement by General Lee. Lee led the Confederates through the Seven Days Battles. At the conclusion of the fighting, the Confederacy had lost 20,000 men and the Union 15,000, but the Southern crisis was over. The Siege of Richmond was lifted, and McClellan, loudly complaining to Washington that he could have won if he had only had a larger army, was retreating down the peninsula to where the navy was waiting to evacuate his troops. (See: Seven Days Battles.)

Pennypacker, Major General Galusha, U.S.

When 17-year-old Union officer Galusha Pennypacker was brevetted as a major general, he became the youngest person on either side to attain that rank during the Civil War. Born June 1, 1844, he wasn't even old enough to vote until a few weeks after the war ended. Pennypacker, who grew up in the home in Valley Forge, Pennsylvania, used by George Washington as a headquarters during the Revolutionary War, enlisted at 16 and despite his youth was quickly elected captain, then rose through the ranks while fighting at Drewry's Bluff, Cold Harbor, Fort Fisher, and Petersburg. Shortly before his twenty-first birthday, near the end of the war, he was named as the Hero of Fort Fisher for his courageous leadership. Pennypacker remained in the U.S. Army after the war, serving in the South during Reconstruction and on frontier duty in the West. He died in Philadelphia in 1916. (See: Cold Harbor, Battle of; Drewry's Bluff, Battle of; Fort Fisher; Hero of Fort Fisher; and Petersburg, Siege and Battle of.)

Perryville, Battle of

After leading his Army of Tennessee through the Cumberland Mountains, General Braxton Bragg captured Frankfort, the state capital of Kentucky, and reached the outskirts of Louisville and Cincinnati. But Confederate hopes of claiming the Bluegrass State for the South were dashed a few weeks later on October 7 and 8, 1862, when Bragg's forces clashed with the 55,000-man-strong Army of the Ohio under the command of Major General Don Carlos Buell at the small crossroads town of Perryville. After initial Confederate advances the Rebel attack faltered, and short of men and supplies, Bragg was forced to withdraw back through the Cumberland Gap into eastern Tennessee. The withdrawal ended the Rebel threat to Kentucky. (See: Bragg, General Braxton, CS; and Buell, Major General Don Carlos, U.S.)

Petersburg, Siege and Battle of

General Lee was jealously shepherding his ragged and rapidly dwindling Army of Northern Virginia in the final days of the war when General Grant figured out a scheme to force him out of the trenches by attacking Petersburg, the lifeline to Richmond. Five major railroads connected in the city, and it was only 25 miles due south of Richmond. If the vital supply base fell, Union armies would be knocking at the back door of the Confederate capital. Grant's Army of the Potomac was also exhausted. The army had been decimated by the terrible bloodlettings at Antietam, Fredericksburg, Spotsylvania, the Wilderness, and most recently Cold Harbor. Grant was ready to replace the bludgeon of frontal attacks with the more imaginative maneuver of launching a flank attack by sweeping around under Richmond and marching through Petersburg to pounce on the capital from below. The defenses of the city of 18,000 were spotty. The primary defense was the Dimmock Line, 10 miles of trenches fortified with 55 artillery batteries. But some areas of the line were almost undefended. General Pierre G. T. Beauregard, who became one of the South's first heroes of the war for his performance at Charleston before political infighting led to his temporary banishment to the West, was in command of the seriously undermanned garrison with a brigade of only 2,200 men. At almost exactly 7:00 P.M. on June 15, 1864, the Siege and Battle of Petersburg began. Major General William F. "Baldy" Smith, commanding the XVIII Corps, the leading element of Major General Benjamin Butler's Army of the James, ordered an artillery barrage, followed by a charge.

The Bluecoats, including cavalry led by Smith and Brigadier General August Kautz, quickly swept through the Dimmock Line and captured forts, guns, and prisoners. The defenders fell back to a new defense at Harrison Creek, but instead of continuing on and capturing the city as it could have done, the XVIII Corps was ordered to halt the advance and dig in for the night. Beauregard and Lee took the opportunity to rush reinforcements to the city until they had gathered a defensive army of about 10,000 men to face the 60,000 already massed against them by Butler and Grant. General Ambrose P. Hill provided more Confederate reinforcements, Union forces were beefed up to 100,000 men, and North and South settled in for what would become a nearly 10-month siege. Soldiers died in dozens of skirmishes before Major General Ambrose E. Burnside tried to break through the defenses by tunneling under enemy positions and lost 4,400 men in the debacle known as the Battle of the Crater. As the siege continued, Union forces grew again to 100,000, but although General Lee personally joined the defenders, their supply line had been cut off and they were left virtually without food. The city was continuously bombarded by Union artillery, which included a huge rail gun, a mortar called the Dictator that fired 218-pound shells up to two and a half miles. Soldiers and civilians were forced into dugouts and suffered terribly. At last after months of back-and-forth skirmishes and battles ranging from Petersburg to Richmond, and a humiliating defeat by General Philip Sheridan's cavalry at Five Forks that cost the Confederates its last rail line into the city, General Lee was forced to throw in the towel. On April 2, one week before Lee's surrender at Appomattox, he withdrew from Petersburg and wired Jefferson Davis that Richmond was doomed. Union troops marched and rode into both cities the next day, and on April 5 President Lincoln toured Richmond. (See: Beauregard, General Pierre Gustave Toutant, CS; Crater, Battle of the; Hill, Lieutenant General Ambrose Powell, CS; and Rail Gun.)

Photography, Battlefield
Mathew Brady is the most famous of the Civil War photographers who for the first time in history brought the horrors of war to the home front. But several other notable photographers filmed the dead and the dying, as well as generals and sergeants and privates as they prepared for battle or tended to chores in encampments. In those early days of photography, pictures were routinely posed and many industrious shutterbugs weren't above moving an arm or a leg or the entire body of a dead soldier to make a picture more dramatic or improve the composition. Some other famous photographers in addition to Brady include George Barnard, George Cook, Alexander and James Gardner, and Timothy O'Sullivan.

Physicians
At the beginning of the war, both sides in the conflict were woefully unprepared for the crush of sick and injured whom medical officers would be required to care for. The Union had fewer than 100 military doctors and the Confederacy, only 24. Even those who were available were poorly trained, and most had never attended medical school but learned their trade by serving as apprentices. By the end of the war, the Union had 13,000 doctors treating sick and injured soldiers and sailors and the Confederacy had 4,000.

Picacho Pass, Skirmish at
Although almost all the Confederates whom the California Column was ordered to clear out of the New Mexico and Arizona Territories had withdrawn before the Union soldiers arrived, Union scouts fought a small skirmish with Rebel pickets they encountered at Picacho Pass. Three Union scouts were killed, and two were wounded. The Confederates lost one killed, four wounded, and three taken prisoner. The action at Picacho Pass is considered to be the farthest west that any engagement between Billy Yanks and Johnny Rebs occurred. (See: Carlton, Major General James Henry, U.S.)

Picket

One or more soldiers on guard duty to protect their unit from surprise attack.

Pickets, Small

Fashioned from tree branches between one and a half and three feet long and sharpened at one end, small pickets were driven into the ground along defensive positions to slow down or impale a careless or unlucky attacker. The pickets were commonly placed in varying order at the edges or bottoms of ditches to injure or slow down attackers so they would be exposed to defensive fire for longer periods of time.

Pickett, Major General George, CS

As a general, Pickett appeared to be snakebit and had the bad luck to be immortalized for leading his men to slaughter in a doomed charge at Gettysburg. After graduating last in his class at West Point in 1846, Pickett fought Indians on the frontier and in the Mexican War before resigning his commission as a U.S. Army captain to fight for the Confederacy. Pickett fought during the Peninsular Campaign at Williamsburg and Seven Pines and was wounded at Gaines's Mill. After a long recovery he was named to divisional command and foraged in southeastern Virginia with General Longstreet before leading the ill-fated charge at Gettysburg. Pickett later fought at New Bern, Drewry's Bluff, and Cold Harbor. His bad luck caught up with him again when he and cavalry general Fitzhugh Lee were away from their commands at a picnic on April Fools' Day, 1865, when Union general Philip Sheridan launched a surprise assault on the Confederates at Five Forks. By the time Pickett learned of the attack, his confused, disorganized troops were fleeing the field. Grant took advantage of Pickett's blunder to order attacks all along the Confederate line, forcing a Southern collapse and the evacuation of Petersburg and Richmond. On April 8 a furious General Lee relieved Pickett of command and sent him home to await orders. But Pickett remained on duty and surrendered his army to the Union the next day. (See: Pickett's Charge.)

Pickett's Charge

The disastrous Confederate charge that was forever branded with Major General George Pickett's name on the third day of the Battle of Gettysburg was devised by General Robert E. Lee and was under the overall command of Lieutenant General James Longstreet. Longstreet was a reluctant collaborator and strongly objected that the Union positions were too strong to overcome with a frontal attack but was overruled by Lee. But it was Pickett, a handsome, flashy Virginian, who braced himself in the saddle, shook his shoulder-length hair, and urged 15,000 men forward to cross a mile and a half of open fields facing the center of the Union lines on Cemetery Ridge. The so-called charge, which began with the Southerners walking at about a hundred yards a minute, was preceded by one of the heaviest artillery barrages of the war. Lee's artillery pounded the Union lines for two hours before the attackers walked, then broke into a running charge against the enemy breastworks. The attackers were outnumbered and outgunned, and when the charge collapsed and the survivors finally staggered back to their own lines only about 5,000 men were still on their feet and alive. General Lee rode out to meet the survivors, removed his hat, and apologized, then ordered Pickett to re-form his division in preparation for a possible counterattack. "General Lee, I have no division," Pickett replied. "Come, General Pickett," Lee said. "This has been my fight, and upon my shoulders rests the blame." (See: Gettysburg, Battle of; and Pickett, Major General George, CS.)

Pinkerton, Allan

The founder of the famous detective agency was named by Major General George B. McClellan as chief of Union intelligence. Pinkerton quickly proved that he was better at civilian detective work than at snooping for military information. He was blamed for repeatedly overestimating the strength of enemy forces and passing on other misinformation. (See: Greenhow, Rose O'Neal.)

Pioneers
Military construction engineers.

Pittsburg Landing, Battle of
Another name for the Battle of Shiloh.

Plymouth, Battle of
The ironclad CSS *Albemarle* engaged two Federal ships and played a crucial role in the Confederate recapture of the North Carolina coastal port of Plymouth on April 19, 1864. The powerful ram sank the USS *Southfield* and drove off the USS *Miami.* Although the land and sea assault led by Confederate brigadier general Robert Hoke was successful, the port fell again to the Federals on October 31. (See: *Albemarle,* CSS.)

Poindexter's Farm, Battle of
An alternate name for Malvern Hill, the sixth and last of the Seven Days Battles. (See: Malvern Hill, Battle of.)

Polecat
Many of flamboyant Confederate general Count Camille Armand Jules Marie de Polignac's backwoods fighting men wanted nothing to do with trying to properly pronounce their commander's tongue-twisting name. So they took the easy way out. They called him Polecat—but not to his face! (See: Prince de Polignac, Major General Count Camille Armand Jules Marie, CS.)

Polish Legion
See: Krzyzanowski, Brigadier General Wladimir, U.S.

**Polk, Lieutenant General
Leonidas "Bishop," CS**
After giving up a career as an Episcopal bishop to become a major general for the Confederacy, Polk quickly set about proving that he was more courageous than capable as a field commander. There was no question about Polk's bravery, especially after he led four assaults against strong Union forces

at the Battle of Shiloh. But his failings as a corps commander were also obvious and were reflected by his performances at Perryville, Murfreesboro, and Chickamauga. A big part of his problem was a reluctance to obey orders to the letter, without giving the commands his own unique twists. Polk had been promoted to lieutenant general when he was struck and killed by an artillery shell on June 14, 1864, during the Atlanta Campaign. He had just ridden up to share copies of a religious pamphlet with two other generals gathered on a hill to observe Confederate defenses when a Union battery spotted the group and began firing.

Poltroonery

That was just one of the caustic nouns used by veteran Indian fighter George Crook to describe the behavior and military performance of fellow officers he served with and observed after he was brought east to serve with the Union during the Civil War. (See: Crook, Major General George, U.S.)

Pope, Major General John A., U.S.

A vain show-off who was unpopular with his men, Pope developed a reputation for blaming others for his own failings after he led the Army of Virginia to defeat at the Second Battle of Bull Run. The army was formed in June 1862 with Pope in command after failure of the Peninsular Campaign. In the new army's first major action, Pope was defeated by Stonewall Jackson at Cedar Mountain near Culpeper, Virginia. When Pope faced off with Jackson it was at Manassas (Bull Run) and after intense fighting the Union commander was so certain he had won, he cabled Washington with news of his perceived victory. Shortly after Pope sent the wire, his command was devastated by a fierce artillery barrage and infantry attack, and he fled back to Washington with the remnants of his army. Pope's place in the limelight ended at Second Bull Run, and the force was merged with the Army of the Potomac under the command of General George B. McClellan. (See: Bull Run, Second Battle of; and Frémont, Major General John C., U.S.)

Port Hudson, Siege of

As part of the campaign against Vicksburg aimed at taking control of the Mississippi River, Major General Nathaniel P. Banks launched an attack on Port Hudson, at the southern end of the Confederate defenses. On May 23, 1863, 30,000 Union troops of XIX Corps, Army of the Gulf, launched a frontal assault on the 6,800-man Rebel garrison commanded by Major General Franklin Gardner, opening what some historians consider to be the longest battle of the Civil War. The outnumbered defenders from the 3d District, Department of Mississippi and East Louisiana, beat back the first Union attack, and Banks's forces settled into a siege. The Confederates occupied a strong position atop high bluffs overlooking a bend in the river a few miles north of Baton Rouge, Louisiana, and their position was fortified with artillery that were as seriously threatening to an attacking army as they were to shipping on the vital waterway. When Banks ordered another major assault on June 14, the Bluecoats were again repulsed. But on July 9, after learning of the fall of Vicksburg, General Gardner realized that the battle for the Mississippi was lost and that continued resistance was futile, and negotiated a surrender. The Union suffered an estimated 5,000 casualties and the Confederates, 7,208. (See: Banks, Major General Nathaniel Prentiss, U.S.; Farragut, Admiral David Glasgow, USN; and Vicksburg, Battle of.)

Port Republic, Battle of

The June 9, 1862, battle in Rockingham County, Virginia, pounded the final nail in the coffin of Federal efforts to oust Major General Thomas J. "Stonewall" Jackson's forces from the Shenandoah Valley. Only one day earlier, Confederate brigadier general (later major general) Isaac R. Trimble had routed Union forces at the Battle of Cross Keys. At Port Republic about 3,500 Bluecoats under Brigadier General Erastus Tyler faced off with a numerically superior force of 6,000 under Jackson's overall command east of the south fork of the Shenandoah River. Rebel assaults across the bottomland were repulsed with heavy casualties, before the

Union left was finally turned. After Federal counterattacks failed to budge the Southerners, Tyler was forced to order a retreat. The Federal withdrawal after the twin defeats at Cross Keys and Port Republic left Jackson in solid control of the upper and middle valley. Jackson's Army of the Valley was also free to go to the assistance of Confederates defending Richmond against Major General George B. McClellan's Union army. Union casualties at Port Richmond numbered 1,002, and Confederate losses amounted to 816. (See: Cross Keys, Battle of.)

Porter, Major General Fitz John, U.S.

Unfairly blamed by Major General John A. Pope for the Union defeat at Second Bull Run, Porter was convicted at court-martial of disobeying orders and misconduct in the face of the enemy, then sacked from the Union Army. Porter's sentence was later remitted by President Chester A. Arthur and his army commission was restored by a special act of Congress. (See: Pope, Major General John A., U.S.; and Porter's Balloon Ride.)

Porter's Balloon Ride

Major General Fitz John Porter got a closer look at enemy defenses than he planned when he climbed aboard an observation balloon as the sole rider, the lone cable snapped, and the balloon floated directly over the Confederate lines during the Siege of Yorktown. While the startled Rebels aimed rifle and musket fire at the balloon, Porter coolly leaned over the observation basket with a telescope pressed to his eyes, studying enemy fortifications and troops strength, until a fortunate change of wind returned him to his own lines. When the balloon crashed into a tent in the Union encampment and Porter clambered out of the canvas unscathed a brass band struck up a welcome-home tune. (See: Balloons, Hot Air; and Porter, Major General Fitz John, U.S.)

Porter, Rear Admiral David Dixon, USN

The son of a naval hero of the War of 1812, Porter served in the Mexican Navy in the 1820s. After accepting an appointment as a U.S. Navy midshipman, he fought against his old shipmates during the Mexican War. During the Civil War, Porter served on blockade duty, joined the New Orleans expedition, commanded the Mississippi Squadron, and participated in a joint operation with the army to capture Vicksburg. Early in 1865, he played a leading role in the capture of Fort Fisher and Wilmington, N. C. Porter was promoted to vice admiral in 1866, and to admiral in 1870. (See: Fort Fisher, Battle of; and Vicksburg, Battle of.)

Price, Pap

A prewar state governor and U.S. congressman, Price was the Confederate leader in Missouri. He gained his military experience during the Mexican War.

Prince De Polignac, Major General Count Camille Armand Jules Marie, CS

The scion of a distinguished French family, Prince de Polignac served with the French army in the Crimean War before resigning his commission and traveling to Central America to pursue his interests in botany. Offering his services to the Confederacy, he was commissioned as a lieutenant colonel and assigned as chief of staff to General Pierre G. T. Beauregard. Prince de Polignac fought at Shiloh and Corinth before he was promoted to brigadier general and led victorious Confederates during the Red River Campaign. He was promoted to major general in June 1864 and in March of the following year was sent to France to seek assistance for the Confederacy from Emperor Napoléon III. Prince de Polignac was in Paris when he learned of the Confederacy's surrender, and retired to his estate in France. He died on November 15, 1913, after outliving all the Confederacy's other major generals. (See: Foreign-Born Soldiers, Confederacy; and Polecat.)

Prisoners of War, Confederate

About 214,000 Confederate POWs were sent north to Union prisons. Approximately 26,000 of the Rebs died there, roughly 12 percent of those imprisoned.

Prisoners of War, Union

Some 211,000 Union soldiers were captured during the war, and 194,000 were sent to Southern prisons. Approximately 30,000, or 12 percent, died. (See: Andersonville Prison; Old Capitol Prison; and Wirz, Captain Heinrich "Henry," CS.)

Privateers

Caught short without a navy to speak of, in his first naval policy statement of the war Confederate president Jefferson Davis invited shipowners to apply for letters of marque and reprisal. Similar to those issued by warring nations in the past, the documents were essentially licenses to turn ships into privateers and sink or capture Union merchant ships for personal profit. Ships and cargo could be sold as captured contraband of war, and the Confederate States promised payment of 20 percent of the value of Federal warships that were destroyed. Lincoln responded by branding Confederate privateering as piracy, declaring that the Union was indivisible and consequently the Confederacy was not a sovereign nation with the authority to license privateers. Furthermore, England, France, and other nations had signed the 1856 Declaration of Paris, outlawing privateering as a form of warfare. Davis responded by pointing out that the United States did not sign the declaration and argued that therefore his decision to use privateers against the Union was justified. Two of the most famous privateers were the *Jefferson Davis* and the *Georgia*.

Prolonge

A stout rope with a hook and toggle on a gun carriage that is used to maneuver an artillery piece over a short distance when it is not practical to attach it to a limber.

Prostitution

Thousands of prostitutes serviced soldiers on both sides of the conflict, and in 1863 Washington, D.C., had 450 bawdy houses and more than 7,000 working girls. The Confederate capital and other Southern cities offered similar pleasures to homesick soldiers. Prostitutes also frequently dressed as soldiers and worked out of encampments or simply followed behind the troops.

Q

Quaker Cannon
The nickname for logs placed in artillery positions to deceive the enemy by making them appear to be heavy guns. Some of the wooden cannon were painted black.

Quaker Warrior
Samuel C. Means abandoned the Quaker tenet of pacifism and took up arms after Rebels confiscated his horse and equipment to run his mill in Loudon County, Virginia. The lapsed Quaker raised a cavalry company in Maryland from among disaffected Virginians who fled there because they supported the Union, and named it the Loudon Rangers. But Means was determined to do his fighting on the Maryland-Virginia border and resigned his commission after refusing to join his command with the 3d West Virginia Cavalry fighting in West Virginia.

Quantrill, Colonel William Clarke, CS
One of the most bloodthirsty killers of the war, Quantrill led a wild band of rascals and renegades through Kansas and Missouri, burning, looting, and slaughtering civilians and Yankee soldiers. Some of the Wild West's most notorious bandits and desperadoes, including Jesse and Frank James, Cole and Jim Younger, and "Wild Bill" Anderson, rode with Quantrill's Raiders. Quantrill was an Ohio schoolteacher when he trekked west to Kansas, then accompanied an army provision train to Fort Bridger, Utah. After working for a while as a professional gambler, becoming linked to several murders

and robberies, and being named on an arrest warrant, he fled back to Bloody Kansas and joined a group of abolitionists planning to free some slaves. Three of the men were killed after Quantrill betrayed them. Quantrill then recruited about a dozen fellow renegades, and they fought alongside Confederates at the Battle of Wilson's Creek in Oakhills, Missouri. By late 1861 Quantrill and his rapidly expanding force of irregulars struck out on their own to harass small Union patrols and camps. In November 1862 Quantrill's raiders slaughtered 12 unarmed teamsters and were declared by Union authorities to be an outlaw band. After helping capture Independence, Missouri, Quantrill was rewarded with a commission as captain in the Confederate Army and later promoted to colonel. After carrying out a bloody raid on Lawrence, Kansas, which was strongly abolitionist and pro-Union, and carrying out the Barter Springs Massacre, the raiders spent the winter in Texas. After the raiders committed a series of atrocities, the Confederates themselves chased Quantrill out. By late spring of 1864 his authority over the band of roughly four hundred raiders was eroding, and one of his former lieutenants was elected as the new leader. After concocting, then abandoning a wild scheme to assassinate President Lincoln, the guerrilla chieftain led 33 remaining loyal followers to Kentucky early in 1865. They were near Taylorsville on May 10 when a force of Union irregulars surprised them and Quantrill was shot through the spine. He was 27 when he died on June 6 at the military prison in Louisville. (See: Anderson, William T. "Bloody Bill"; James, Jesse and Frank; and Lawrence Massacre.)

R

Rail Gun

A 13-inch seacoast mortar named the Dictator was the first artillery piece ever mounted on a railroad car and fired at the enemy. The railcar was strengthened by Union engineers with extra beams and iron rods to withstand the shock and vibration from firing the 17,000-pound mortar, which hurled a 218-pound shell almost two and one half miles. Transported on the City Point Railroad, the Dictator was used by Federal artillerymen during the Siege and Battle of Petersburg and was considered a critical factor in the victory. The massive gun was cast in 1862 at the Fort Pitt Foundry. (See: Petersburg, Siege and Battle of.)

Railroads

At the beginning of the war, the Union had nearly 20,000 miles of railroads, more than all the rest of the world combined. Railroad lines in the new Confederacy were dwarfed by comparison, with a mere 9,000 miles of track. The Union also had 96 percent of the railroad equipment. Ironically, it was the South that for the first time in the history of warfare used rails to move troops to battle. In preparation for the First Battle of Bull Run in July 1861, Confederate general Joseph E. Johnston transported 18,000 troops to Manassas Junction by rail, delivering his soldiers to the battlefield not only quickly but also rested and prepared to turn the tide of battle against the Union and mark up the first Confederate victory of the war. Thereafter, the outcomes of several battles were decided for both sides in large part through the efficient or timely use of railroads to move troops and supplies. The tides of battle changed at Bull Run, Chickamauga, and Chattanooga after the timely arrival by rail of fresh troops to reinforce the ultimate winners.

Railroads, Movable Repair Center
Union major generals George Henry Thomas and Daniel McCallum spearheaded development of the world's first workable railroad repair and transportation center that could be moved to support the advance of troops. (See: Thomas, Major General George Henry, U.S.)

Raines Brothers
General Gabriel J. Raines and his younger brother, George Washington Raines, were West Point graduates who put their fertile minds to work for the Confederacy with devastating results for the Union. They were explosives experts who created the coal bomb to blow up ships, water mines, and land mines, and although they denied having anything to do with the insidious devices they were also credited with devising the first booby traps. While Gabriel kept busy in the South's newly formed Torpedo Bureau, his little brother, George, made most of the gunpowder used in the torpedoes, mines, and other Confederate munitions. Although he was a newcomer to the gunpowder-manufacturing trade, he had taught chemistry, geology, and mineralogy at West Point. (See: Coal Bombs.)

Ransom Bond
When Confederate commerce raiders captured a Union ship, they sometimes negotiated its release on ransom bonds based on the value of the cargo. The agreements, which permitted Yankee captains to sail away with their ships and crews, called for the bond to be paid to the Confederacy six months after a peace treaty was signed between the warring parties. The bonds were never paid, because after April 1865 the Confederacy ceased to exist.

Rapidan River

Both sides in the conflict were exhausted after the Battle of Gettysburg in July 1863, and after Lee retreated into Virginia the two huge armies faced each other from opposite sides of the Rapidan for the rest of the year. Both North and South appeared to be satisfied with occasional raids and light skirmishing, while catching their breath and resting up for the terrible bloodletting ahead on such battlefields as Chickamauga, Chattanooga, Chancellorsville, and Atlanta.

Rathbone, Major Henry, U.S.

This Union officer was stabbed in the arm with a seven-inch dagger when he grappled with John Wilkes Booth after the actor and Southern sympathizer fatally shot President Lincoln. Rathbone and his fiancée, Clara Harris, were the only people among nearly a dozen invited by the Lincolns who actually showed up and joined them in the theater box. (See: Booth, John Wilkes; and Lincoln Assassination.)

Ream's Station, First Battle of

A division of Federal troops led by Brigadier General August V. Kautz was tearing up track along the Weldon Railroad during the Richmond-Petersburg Campaign when they unexpectedly ran into a strong force of Confederates on June 29, 1864. They were barring the way to Ream's Station, which the Union raiders had believed was held by Federals. Major General James Wilson, already fighting off Confederate general William H. F. "Rooney" Lee's cavalry, quickly brought up his division to support Kautz. But the Union forces were almost totally surrounded by the Rebels. At noon Major General William Mahone's infantry attacked the Union front while Brigadier General Fitzhugh Lee's cavalry moved against the left flank. Separated by the fierce Confederate assault, the Federals were forced to abandon their artillery and burn their wagons. Wilson and his troops fought their way through the attacking Rebels, then fled to Blackwater River, turned north and finally reached Union lines on July 2. Kautz led his troops across country to Union lines at Petersburg, which they reached safely shortly after sunset. Total casualties for both sides in the clash amounted to about 600 men.

Ream's Station, Second Battle of

Two months after the first encounter, a second battle was fought at Ream's Station and, like the first, resulted in a Confederate victory. This time the Federals' crack II Corps was shattered and Major General John Gibbon was so humiliated when three fresh, untried regiments refused to join the fight that he resigned his command. Major General Winfield Scott Hancock was in overall command of Union forces and the Confederates were led by Major General Henry Heth in the encounter. The II Corps had marched south along the railroad, protected by cavalry while tearing up track on August 24, 1864, and the Confederates attacked the next day. Heth's Rebels quickly overran the poorly defended Union position at the station, capturing nine artillery pieces and hundreds of prisoners. Hancock broke off the fighting and withdrew to the Union's main defense line near the Jerusalem Plank Road. Total casualties in the battle amounted to 3,492 men, most of them Federals.

Rebel Yell

This high-pitched, piercing shriek worked for the Confederates as well as similar battle cries had worked for American Indians and other warriors around the world—it put spirit into their own troops and terrified the enemy. The yell was believed to have been used for the first time at the First Battle of Bull Run when, after hours of bloody fighting, troops commanded by General Pierre G. T. Beauregard launched a fierce counterattack that panicked and scattered Union defenders. After that, the shrill, keening rebel yell quickly spread throughout the Confederate Army.

Rebellonians

The name adopted by a group of Confederates at the Johnson's Island prison on Lake Erie, who staged minstrel shows for their fellow inmates. (See: Johnson's Island Prison.)

Reconstruction

Reconstruction was supposed to be much like an early Marshall Plan, the farsighted program that helped rebuild Europe after the devastation of World War II. But the effort to restore the economy of the South, initiate black suffrage, and bring the rebellious states back into the fold didn't work out all that smoothly. Lincoln's assassination, his well-meaning successor's inability to control Congress, other political infighting, and a desire for revenge simply deepened many of the old enmities and drew the painful process out for 12 years. (See: Carpetbaggers.)

Recruiting Abroad

The Union was so hungry for recruits to feed its war machine that recruiters were stationed abroad to sign up young foreigners for the army and navy. Joseph Pulitzer, who later became one of the wealthiest and most powerful newspaper barons in the world, was only 17 when he was recruited by an agent in Hamburg, Germany. Pulitzer was previously turned down by the French Foreign Legion and the British army in India because he was so puny and had poor eyesight. He was assigned to the 1st New York Lincoln Cavalry and served as an orderly.

Recruitment Brokers

Eager for commissions earned for enlisting substitutes to serve in place of wealthy draft-age men, some unscrupulous recruitment brokers signed up male inmates of a New York insane asylum for the Union Army. Other recruits reported for duty missing arms or legs or with bad eyesight or feeble minds.

Redlegs

A common nickname for artillery men derived from the red stripe worn on their trousers. (See: Zouaves.)

Red River Campaign

In the early spring of 1864, at the strong urging of General in Chief Henry Halleck, the Union launched the Red River Campaign in the Western Theater with three major objectives: (1) drive the Rebels from the rich plantations of Louisiana and Arkansas and occupy Texas to obtain cotton for hungry Northern mills; (2) discourage a Southern alliance with the French in Mexico; and (3) choke off supplies to the Confederate military. The South had already lost Vicksburg and Port Hudson on the Mississippi, and the Federals commanded by Major General Nathaniel P. Banks, commander of the Gulf, planned to take control of the Red River north to Shreveport and invade Texas. The operation kicked off with a march north to Alexandria, where Banks's army of 17,000 was to be joined by 10,000 troops from General William Tecumseh Sherman's Mississippi command under General Andrew J. Smith and another 15,000 under Major General Frederick Steele. Eventually, troops led by Banks and another column under Steele were expected to launch a two-pronged invasion to subdue and occupy much or all of Texas. Smith's troops were carried upriver by a flotilla of 12 gunboats and 30 transports commanded by Admiral David D. Porter, and the combined army-navy force occupied Alexandria a week before General Banks showed up with his troops. Steele, who was marching across country from Little Rock, Arkansas, was delayed by bad spring weather, and stiff Confederate resistance also arrived too late to participate in the action at Alexandria. Bad weather and an unseasonably low water level on the Red River continued to make things difficult for the Federals, and one of the few bright spots was the capture of 250 Confederates during a brief, fierce skirmish near Henderson Hill on March 21. After a series of clashes, the retreating Rebels under the overall command of General Richard Taylor had fallen back to Mansfield, where Banks led his army to an overwhelming and embarrassing defeat. The Confederates pursued Banks's demoralized Yanks to Pleasant Grove, where they launched an attack that was repulsed. But the Union Army had endured enough. Banks ordered his troops to fall back to Grand Ecore, signaling an end to the Union's largest military campaign west of the Mississippi River. (See: Banks, Major General Nathaniel Prentiss, U.S.; Mansfield, Battle of; Porter, Rear Admiral David Dixon, USN; Smith, Major General Andrew Jackson, U.S.; Steele, Major General Frederick; and Taylor, Major General Richard, CS.)

Regiments, Cavalry

Most cavalry regiments on both sides of the conflict were composed of twelve companies, two more than the infantry. Only about 14 percent of the Union's fighting men were cavalry, and the percentage of Confederate horse soldiers was slightly higher.

Regiments, Infantry

At full strength, infantry regiments from both the North and the South were comprised of 1,000 men. Regiments were formed from 10 companies of 100 men each. About 80 percent of the Union's Army troops were foot soldiers, and the rest were cavalry or artillery.

Repeating Rifles

Today's modern armies are equipped with rifles and handguns capable of rapid fire of metal cartridges and designed with reload mechanisms that trace their genesis back to the Civil War. While most Billy Yanks and Johnny Rebs were equipped with old-fashioned, slow-loading rifled muskets, the Union produced about 400,000 repeating rifles that were distributed primarily to cavalry units. The new rapid-loading, rapid-firing rifles were formidable weapons. At Chickamauga a single brigade laid down such a withering hail of fire with repeating rifles that a Confederate advance was seriously slowed, allowing retreating Federals to avoid annihilation.

Republic of Alabama

A banner proclaiming the new republic flew over the state capital at Montgomery for 12 days between the time Alabama seceded and the Confederacy was established. (See: Cradle of the Confederacy.)

Resplendent Surrender

Robert E. Lee was facing the most agonizing experiences of his life when he prepared to meet Ulysses S. Grant to discuss surrender terms but dressed his best for the occasion. The Southern general wore his finest dress uniform, a crimson sash, red-stitched boots with spurs attached, and a pair of long Confederate gray gauntlets and buckled to his side a jeweled sword that had been presented to him by a group of female admirers in England. Then he rode off to the historic Palm Sunday meeting at Appomattox Courthouse.

Revolving Turrets

The USS *Monitor* was the first warship ever equipped with a revolving turret for its guns. The innovation helped revolutionize naval warfare. (See: *Monitor,* USS.)

Reynolds, Major General John F., U.S.

Commander of the crack 10,000-man I Corps at Gettysburg, Reynolds was directing the defense of a ridge northwest of town when he was killed by a Rebel sharpshooter. Reynolds was the highest-ranking officer on the field at the time, and a short time after he fell the XI Corps, which had come up as reinforcement, broke and ran, followed by the shattered I Corps. Reynolds's I Corps suffered almost 60 percent casualties in the short, bloody clash. Reynolds was captured in June of 1862, and exchanged after two months. According to some reports he was offered command of the Army of the Potomac following "Fighting Joe" Hooker's drubbing at Chancellorsville but declined. (See: Gettysburg, Battle of.)

Rich Mountain, Battle of

Major General George B. McClellan was in overall command of Union Army operations in western Virginia when Confederates under the command of Brigadier General Robert Selden Garnett and Lieutenant Colonel John Pegram were defeated at the Battle of Rich Mountain on July 11, 1861. The Confederates suffered 300 casualties, to 46 for the North. Although Brigadier General William Starke Rosecrans was the field commander, the victory played a major role in vaulting McClellan to leadership of the Army of the Potomac. (See: Garnett, Brigadier General Robert Selden, CS.)

Richmond Rifle Musket

This Confederate firearm was produced in the South with machinery taken from the Harpers Ferry Armory. The rifle was a near-exact replica of the U.S. Model 1855/61. The .58-caliber shoulder arm employed a percussion cap and featured a butt plate and brass nose cap.

Richmond, Virginia

The Confederate capital in northern Virginia was the object of repeated Union efforts to capture it, including the ill-fated Peninsular Campaign of General George B. McClellan early in the war. Richmond not only was the Confederacy's political nerve center, but it also contained the biggest chunk of the lightly industrialized South's manufacturing facilities, including its only heavy weapons factories. Despite its proximity to Washington, D.C., and its outnumbered defenders, the battered and bloodied city remained in Southern hands until it was ordered evacuated during the dying Confederacy's final hours.

Rienzi

Union general Philip H. Sheridan's horse, which shared fame with its owner for a breakneck 20-mile dash while rallying hundreds of panicked troops. Surrounded by wagons and walking wounded, they were fleeing a surprise dawn attack by Rebels at Cedar Creek in Virginia's Shenandoah Valley. Alarmed by what appeared to be a Union rout while he was attending a strategy meeting in Washington, Sheridan waved his hat and yelled at the terrified soldiers to follow him back to their encampment at Cedar Creek. When Sheridan arrived at the camp, he learned that the Rebel attack was already petering out and that Lieutenant General Jubal Early had failed to follow up on the initial Confederate success. (See: Early, Lieutenant General Jubal Anderson, CS.)

Rifled Muskets

The Minié ball–firing rifled muskets that most soldiers fighting for the North and South were provided with after the first few months of the conflict were a solid improvement over the old-fashioned smoothbore, long-barreled shoulder arms previously used in warfare. The old smoothbores were notoriously inaccurate and weren't of much use even at 100 yards. A skilled sniper using the new rifled muskets could take out a target from as far as a half-mile away. But loading the muskets was still a frustrating, time-consuming affair that could easily lead to confusion during the heat of battle. The muskets fired Minié balls that were devastating to human flesh and bone—when they struck their target. (See: Repeating Rifles.)

Rob Roy

Commanded by William Watson, this Confederate blockade runner carried cargo from Bermuda, the Bahamas, and Cuba. The islands were favorite stopovers for ships sailing between Great Britain and the blockaded Southern ports. A skillful captain could earn as much as $5,000 per month, and some blockade runners made 30 to 40 trips before they were captured or their vessels sunk.

Robber Barons

Big-time Wall Street speculators and fast-money artists dodged the draft and made millions of dollars on the war while their fellow Americans were fighting and dying on the battlefield. J. P. Morgan, John D. Rockefeller, Andrew Carnegie, and Jay Gould were among the kings of capitalism who paid $300 each to hire substitutes to take their places in the draft, then applied their talents to gold speculation and other money-making schemes. Every time the Union Army suffered a defeat, the price of gold rose against the dollar and Morgan and his friends cleaned up. Lincoln was so outraged at their greed that he declared it was his hope that every gold speculator would have his head shot off. (See: Morgan, J. P.)

Robinson Crusoe of the Civil War

If the story of Henson G. Raines is true, he was a modern-day Robinson Crusoe who was marooned on an island for 10 years after the burning and sinking of the SS *General Lyon* only a few days before General Lee's surrender at Appomattox. After mysteriously turning up at Guy Hospital in London, Raines said he had survived with a Lieutenant Butler by clinging to a door until they were picked up by a schooner, then dumped on a small island. According to the account, Butler died shortly afterward and Raines remained alone on the island like the fictional castaway until he was rescued by the British man-of-war HMS *Vengeance*. Although the story is widely discounted today, records in Illinois disclosed that a Henson G. Raines enlisted as a private in Company K of the 56th Illinois Infantry on November 7, 1861, and drowned during the *General Lyon* disaster. (See: *General Lyon,* SS.)

Rock of Chickamauga

Commander of the XIV Corps, Major General George H. Thomas earned his nickname as the Rock of Chickamauga for his valiant stand at Snodgrass Hill that repulsed repeated attacks by overwhelming Confederate forces. The stubborn defense of Thomas's lone corps, supported by the reserve, covered the disorganized retreat of the routed Federals and saved Rosecrans's army from being completely shattered. (See: Chickamauga, Battle of; and Thomas, Major General George Henry, U.S.)

Rosecrans, Major General William Starke, U.S.

Rosecrans helped train the Ohio State Militia, then joined with Major General George B. McClellan to lead the Ohioans in a campaign that cut the new state of West Virginia off from Virginia. Rosecrans succeeded his fellow Ohioan after the First Battle of Bull Run as commander of the Department of Western Virginia. In June 1862 Rosecrans took over from General John Pope as commander of the Army of the Mississippi, and that October he became commander of the Army of the Ohio after General Don Carlos Buell was relieved for lack of aggressiveness. A West Point graduate who had left the military to become a successful Cincinnati businessman, Rosecrans was a smart, aggressive leader who looked after his men and was better at defense than attack. While commanding the Army of the Mississippi, he won two important battles in that state. After he took over from Buell, Rosecrans quickly led his renamed Army of the Cumberland on the offensive, and his forces fought to a tactical draw at the Battle of Stones River. In June 1863 he opened the weeklong Tullahoma Campaign, and lured the Confederate Army of the Tennessee to Chickamauga, where he suddenly lost his nerve. After losing the bruising fight to Confederate general Braxton Bragg and barely avoiding total destruction of his army, Rosecrans was relieved of command. He was sent west and finished out the war in Missouri. (See: Stones River, Battle of.)

Rosser, Major General Thomas Lafayette, CS

Rosser was a lieutenant of artillery when he shot down one of Union general George B. McClellan's observation balloons and was rewarded for the feat with promotion to captain. (See: Balloons, Hot Air.)

S

Sabers

By the time the Civil War began, sabers were the dinosaurs of the cavalry. Firearms had made it increasingly difficult for cavalry to get close enough to the enemy to cut or slash, and the curved swords were also awkward to carry. But the old glamour and dash of the swords were still inspiring, and it was rarely, if ever, that horse soldiers clashed without at least one or a few waving their sabers and urging their companions forward.

Sabine Pass, First Battle of

An attempt to strengthen the Union blockade of the Texas coast and open the state to invasion from the sea led to the First Battle of Sabine Pass. Acting Master Frederick Crocker commanded Union naval forces consisting of two schooners and a steamer. The Confederates had about 25 horse soldiers, a 30-man garrison at Fort Griffith, and other artillerists manning a battery at Sabine Pass leading inland to Port Arthur. Early on the morning of September 25, Crocker ordered his ships into the pass to begin bombarding the Confederates. The defenders were unable to retaliate because their ancient batteries couldn't reach the attacking ships, and the Confederate commander, Major J. S. Irvine, ordered their guns spiked and the garrisons evacuated during the night. The town of Sabine Pass was surrendered the next day.

Sabine Pass, Second Battle of

Confederates had reoccupied the garrisons at the pass when the Union launched a new attack by land and sea that led to a humiliating defeat and provided a new hero for the South, Lieutenant Richard "Dick" Dowling. The land forces were commanded by Major General William Franklin and the ships once again by Crocker, who had been promoted to captain. The invading force was much larger than before, and Crocker was in charge of a small fleet of four gunboats and 11 transports loaded with thousands of troops gathered to lead a thrust inland and begin the occupation of Texas. Dowling had slipped back into the abandoned Fort Griffith with 44 men, most of them tough, difficult-to-control Irish immigrants who had gotten into various scrapes and were considered expendable by the Confederates. But Dowling had known for months that an attack was coming and had scraped up a handful of more modern artillery pieces, improved others, and trained his men daily by ordering practice fire on range markers set afloat in the Sabine River. They were ready and raring to go when the first of the Union gunboats began steaming up the pass and into the river at 6:00 A.M. September 8, 1863. Dowling's brawling Irishmen had been turned into disciplined soldiers who were crack shots, and they fired barrage after barrage into the Union fleet. Crocker was quickly forced to order a withdrawal from the pass, after suffering 230 casualties, the loss of one captured gunboat, and several others damaged.

Salient

The portion of fortifications, line of defense, or systems of trenches that jut out toward enemy positions.

Salling, John, CS

When Salling died in Virginia on March 16, 1959, newspapers around the country announced that only one Civil War veteran was left alive. According to historian William Marvel in *Blue & Gray* magazine, that wasn't the case. Salling and the other reputed survivor, as well as several other claimants who already died, were imposters who misrepresented themselves as Civil War veterans, according to the author. Marvel wrote that Salling was born in Virginia in March, 1858, and was only seven years old when General Lee surrendered at Appomattox Court House. (See: Crump, Private Pleasant Riggs, CS; Lundy William, CS; Williams, Walter Washington, CS; and Woolson, Private Albert H., U.S.)

Saxton, Major General Rufus, U.S.

After serving as a quartermaster and in field command, Saxton spent the last years of the war enlisting and organizing blacks to serve in the Union Army. A preacher who fought in the Seminole Wars, Saxton was in command of Georgia's Sea Islands. At the conclusion of the war he became assistant commissioner of the Freedman's Bureau in charge of Georgia, Florida, and South Carolina and promoted the Port Royal Project to show that ex-slaves would work to become self-sufficient if provided with land and other opportunities. Saxton was awarded a Medal of Honor for his performance commanding the defenses of Harpers Ferry in 1862. (See: Special Field Order #15.)

Sayler's Creek, Battle of

Robert E. Lee's troops were starving and foragers were unable to find more than a few scraps of food when Union troops caught up with the tattered corps of Generals George Thomas Anderson and Richard Ewell at the little town of Sayler's Creek. Anderson and Ewell lost the supply trains they had been assigned to protect, along with more than 7,000 men, in the uneven battle on April 6, 1865. Lee's once-proud Army of Northern Virginia had been reduced to 15,000 soldiers who had virtually no food or other supplies and were armed with little more than muskets and sabers to face a well-fed, well-supplied Union army of 80,000. The Confederacy had less than a week to live.

Scandinavian Regiment

See: Heg, Colonel Hans Christian, U.S.; Johnson, Colonel Ole C., U.S.; and Wilson, Major Jurgen, U.S.

Schimmelfennig, Brigadier General Alex, U.S.

A former Prussian officer, Schimmelfennig led General Oliver O. Howard's 3d Division at Gettysburg. At the beginning of the battle, when General Jubal Early's division charged against the Union's right flank, the Prussian led his men in a headlong dash for the rear, and he spent most of the rest of the battle hiding in a storm cellar. (See: Early, Lieutenant General Jubal Anderson, CS; Gettysburg, Battle of; and Howard, Major General Oliver Otis, U.S.)

Schofield, Lieutenant General John McAllister, U.S.

Schofield Barracks, the army base in Hawaii that was bombed and strafed by the Japanese during the World War II attack on Pearl Harbor, is named after this Civil War general. Schofield fought at Wilson's Creek in Missouri, in General Sherman's Atlanta Campaign, and at Franklin and Nashville, Tennessee, and ended the war as a major general. After the conflict he served as President Andrew Johnson's secretary of war and later succeeded General Sheridan as commanding general of the U.S. Army. Schofield retired in 1895 as a lieutenant general.

Schurz, Major General Carl, U.S.

One of several German students and young military officers forced to flee their homeland after a failed revolution, Schurz immigrated to the United States and served as an officer with the Union Army. A committed abolitionist, he campaigned for Lincoln, was U.S. envoy to Spain, negotiated with foreign governments for the president, and as a soldier recruited German immigrants for the army and served under General John Frémont in the Department of the West. Promoted to brigadier general, Schurz commanded the 3d Division of the Army of Virginia from June to September 1862 and fought at the Second Battle of Bull Run, then commanded the 3d Division of the Army of the Potomac until April 1863. Schurz also fought at Fredericksburg, Chancellorsville, and Gettysburg. He was promoted to major general after Fredericksburg. After the war he was elected to the U.S. Senate in 1869 and in 1877 became secretary of the interior under President Rutherford B. Hayes.

Scott, Lieutenant General Winfield, U.S.
Lincoln's general in chief at the beginning of the conflict between the states, the old soldier had commanded all American army forces during the Mexican War. Although Scott was an excellent strategist, when the Civil War began he was 75 and in ill health. After a string of early Union defeats he was retired and replaced with General George B. McClellan.

Scurvy
Starving or underfed prisoners of war on both sides suffered terribly from disease, and a lack of fresh vegetables or citrus led to thousands of cases of scurvy because of a lack of vitamin C. First the skin of victims became discolored and hair and teeth fell out, then weakness and lethargy occurred—and finally death.

Secession
Despite all the talk about secession, few people in the North and in foreign countries actually expected the Southern states to follow through on their threats. Then, with the election of Republican Abraham Lincoln, who was antislavery and supported by powerful abolitionist forces, the South concluded that secession was its only choice. The Southerners reasoned that since sovereign states formed the Union, sovereign states could withdraw if they believed the Federal government was about to make them submit to laws harmful to them. The North was more populous and industrially developed and wealthier and would use those advantages to impose its will on them, the Southerners believed. South Carolina became the first state to secede when it passed the Ordinance

of Secession on December 20, 1860. By February 1, 1861, Mississippi, Florida, Alabama, Georgia, Louisiana, and Texas had followed suit. Virginia, Arkansas, and North Carolina joined the Confederacy soon after the fall of Fort Sumter, and by June 8, when the Ordinance of Secession was signed in Tennessee, 11 states had opted to form the Confederate States of America. (See: Confederate States of America; Fort Sumter; and Lincoln, First Presidential Election.)

Secession Winter

The raucous four-month interval between President Lincoln's election on November 6, 1860, and his inauguration on March 4, 1861. The South was horrified by the election of the political leader from Illinois they called a baboon and "the worst type of black Republican." Fire-eating extremists throughout the South used fear of the new president and his Republican policies to stoke a rising tide of violence. On April 12, 1861, less than six weeks after Lincoln was inaugurated, Rebel shore batteries in Charleston began firing on Fort Sumter.

Sedgwick, Major General John, U.S.

Sedgwick fought bravely at the Battle of Seven Pines, in the Seven Days Battles, and in other clashes, but he is probably best remembered for his poorly timed remark about the perceived inability of Rebel snipers to hit their targets from long distances. He was overseeing the placement of artillery at Spotsylvania when a frightened soldier sprawled onto the ground as snipers began firing from about eight hundred yards. "Why, what are you dodging for?" Sedgwick upbraided the cowering Bluecoat. "They could not hit an elephant at that distance." Before the soldier had a chance to reply, a sniper's bullet struck Sedgwick in the cheek. He died instantly.

Seminary Ridge

Named for the Lutheran Theological Seminary overlooking Gettysburg, this ridge that stretched along the front of the town was the main Confederate stronghold during the final two days of the pivotal Civil War battle. (See: Heth, Major General Henry, CS.)

Semmes, Captain Raphael, CSN

A Maryland orphan who was 16 when he became a navy midshipman, Semmes later excelled in the Norfolk officers' training school and marched into Mexico City with U.S. Army comrades during the Mexican War. As secretary of the U.S. Lighthouse Commission in Washington, Semmes became friendly with Mississippi senator Jefferson Davis. Semmes resigned his U.S. commission in February 1861 and offered his services to the Confederacy. After a trip north to recruit mechanics and buy naval supplies, Semmes talked his way into command of the packet ship *Habana,* which was to be turned into the first Confederate Navy commerce raider. Semmes refitted the steamer, installed an eight-inch pivot gun and four 32-pound howitzers, renamed his new raider the *Sumter,* and recruited a crew. Then he sailed off to pillage Union merchant shipping and sink Federal gunboats. Semmes's first victim was the *Golden Rocket,* a 700-ton bark he captured and burned off the coast of Cuba. Semmes and the *Sumter* had captured 18 ships in six months before putting in at Gibraltar for repairs and to load on coal. But the U.S. consul intervened to block the sale of coal to the Confederate raider, and Semmes found himself stranded there while the USS *Tuscarora,* the USS *Ino,* and the USS *Kearsarge* sailed to Gibraltar and blockaded his ship. The captain was forced to discharge his crew before the *Sumter* was sold to a Liverpool merchant. Semmes was ordered to England to take command of the *Enrica,* a new ship under construction at a shipyard there. He recruited a crew, including Executive Officer John Kell, and took command of the 220-foot-long raider in the Azores. He renamed her the CSS *Alabama.* (See: *Alabama,* CSS; and *Alabama,* CSS, and *Kearsarge,* USS, Battle of.)

Seven Days Battles

Newly in command of the Army of Northern Virginia after Joseph E. Johnston was critically wounded at the Battle of

Seven Pines, Robert E. Lee began the Seven Days Battles with an assault on heavily entrenched Federals at Mechanicsville on June 26, 1862. Lee's 40,000-man army had been reinforced by Stonewall Jackson's army from the Shenandoah Valley, and the new commander hoped to demolish the Union right flank and capture its supply base at White House Landing. The Confederates were beaten back at Mechanicsville with heavy losses. The next day, June 27, Lee attacked again at Gaines's Mill, capturing the supply depot and pushing Union general George B. McClellan back across the Chickahominy River. Pursuing the fleeing Federals, Lee fought two indecisive battles: at White Oak Swamp, also known as Savage's Station, on June 29, and at Glendale, also known as Frayser's Farm, on June 30. McClellan finally managed to pull away from Lee's pursuing Confederates and assemble a strong force at Malvern Hill to cover his retreating army while it was falling back to the James River. Sensing victory, Lee ordered a series of frontal assaults that were beaten back by artillery, and McClellan's main forces completed the retreat to the sanctuary of Harrison's Landing and the protection of a Union Navy fleet. With McClellan retreating to Washington, D.C., to lick his wounds without posing a further threat to Richmond, Lee broke off the Seven Days Battles. (See: Gaines's Mill, Battle of; Glendale, Battle of; Malvern Hill, Battle of; Mechanicsville, Battle of; and White Oak Swamp, Battle of.)

Seven Pines, Battle of

Richmond was under siege on May 31, 1862, when General Joseph E. Johnston moved against the huge Union Army of the Potomac led by Major General George B. McClellan at the intersection of three roads called Seven Pines just six miles outside the Confederate capital. Johnston's Army of Northern Virginia had just 50,000 men to face McClellan's 100,000, and another 40,000 Federals under Major General Irvin McDowell were nearby at Fredericksburg. Johnston devised a plan to split his army into three columns and send them along separate roads to converge on the Union Army and destroy it at Seven Pines. The plan called for adherence to a strict timetable and close coordination of movement. Almost immediately, everything began going wrong for the South and the battle quickly turned into a Confederate disaster. A downpour the night before the assault turned already rain-soaked roads into muddy bogs, and commanders and troops couldn't keep to the demanding timetable. Johnston's maps were incomplete, most of his immediate subordinates were unaware of his overall battle plan, brigades were lost in the heavy woods, regiments attacked their own men, and the muddy roads were so packed with troops that artillery couldn't get through the mess. Johnston's army arrived at Seven Pines a bit at a time and managed to force the Federals back. But despite repeated assaults, the Rebels couldn't break through the lines and achieve a victory. When Johnston hurried to the front to get a closer look at the action and try to sort things out, he was struck in the shoulder by musket fire and hit in the chest by a shell fragment. He was rushed to the rear with what was believed at the time to be a mortal wound but eventually recovered and returned to duty. The next day, Confederate president Jefferson Davis's military adviser, Robert E. Lee, took over the Army of Northern Virginia. He ordered the army to retreat to the defenses around Richmond, and the Battle of Seven Pines, also known as the Battle of Fair Oaks, ended with no clear-cut winner. Losses were heaviest among the Confederates, who had about 6,000 casualties. The Union lost 5,000 men.

Seward, William Henry

A New York senator who lost the Republican presidential nomination to Lincoln, Seward was tapped by the new commander in chief to serve as secretary of state in a move aimed at healing political wounds. An experienced and cunning politician, Seward was barely in office before he urged Lincoln to head off a war with the South and unite the nation by picking a fight with England, France, or some other national power. The president turned a firm thumbs-down on the plan. (See: Lincoln Assassination; and Paine, Lewis.)

Sewell's Point, Battle of

Two Union gunboats traded shots with Confederate batteries on Sewell's Point at Norfolk, Virginia, on May 18–19, 1861, in efforts to enforce the blockade of Hampton Roads. Except for a total on both sides of 10 casualties, little serious damage was done, and the results were inconclusive.

Sharpsburg, Battle of

An alternate name favored in the South for the Battle of Antietam. (See: Antietam, Battle of.)

Shenandoah, CSS

The former British merchant steamer *Sea King* was refitted, armed with eight guns, renamed the CSS *Shenandoah,* and sent off to ravage the Yankees' 58-ship whaling fleet in the North Pacific. After capturing several merchantmen in the Atlantic, the *Shenandoah* continued on to the Pacific where it pounced on the whalers, sinking or boarding about a dozen before discovering newspapers on one of the ships reporting General Lee's surrender. But the news stories also quoted some Confederates as vowing to continue the war, and the *Shenandoah*'s captain, James Iredell Waddell, continued capturing and sinking more whalers until he learned from the crew of a British bark that the war was indeed over. (See: Waddell, Captain James Iredell, CSN.)

Sheridan, General Philip Henry, U.S.

Leaving the Western Theater with Grant, Sheridan became a Northern hero when he led the Army of the Potomac's cavalry on a destructive sweep that chased the Confederates from the lush Shenandoah Valley. While Sheridan relentlessly pursued and clashed with the South's brilliant raider and cavalry leader Lieutenant General Jubal Early, the Confederacy's former breadbasket was turned into a charred wasteland. Sheridan defeated Early's exhausted troops at Winchester, Fisher's Hill, and Cedar Creek before finishing them off at Waynesboro. Earlier, Sheridan commanded his troopers during the Overland Campaign and was at Yellow Tavern when the Confederacy's great cavalry leader General J. E. B. "Jeb" Stuart was killed. After the Shenandoah Valley lay in ruins and cleared of Confederates, Sheridan rejoined Grant during the Siege of Petersburg and crashed through Confederate defenses at Five Forks. Sheridan's cavalry, with infantry support, then blocked General Lee's escape at Appomattox, leading to the Southern surrender. A West Point graduate and the son of Irish immigrants, the scrappy warrior began his military service on the frontier and in the Far West. After beginning the Civil War as a quartermaster, he quickly talked his way into field command. He was placed in command of the 2d Michigan Cavalry and vaulted from captain to colonel overnight. Sheridan fought in many other battles in the West, including Chickamauga, Murfreesboro, and Chattanooga. After the war he was stationed in Texas, where he sent a firm message to the French to stay out of Mexico, again fought Indians on the frontier, and in 1869 was promoted to lieutenant general by his old friend President Grant and named General of the Army. Shortly before Sheridan's death in 1888, Congress revived the rank of full general, and he received his fourth star from President Grover Cleveland.

Sheridan's Women

General Philip Sheridan wasn't a recognized rake like his peer "Fighting Joe" Hooker and was probably surprised to learn that females had infiltrated his command. One, a teamster, and the other, a private in a cavalry regiment, were just two of hundreds of women who posed as men to do their patriotic duty as soldiers for both the Union and the Confederacy. Sheridan's belles were exposed when they got drunk and tumbled into a river. Their true sex was discovered after they were hauled out of the drink and their rescuers ripped open their shirts to resuscitate them. Sheridan interviewed the women before they were relieved of duty and later described the tough-talking, hard-cursing teamster as a "she-dragoon." The gentlemanly general declined to reveal the names of the women, the aliases they used, or the units they served in. (See: Women Soldiers.)

Sherman, Major General Thomas W., U.S.

A career soldier and artillery officer from Rhode Island, Sherman lost his right leg on May 27, 1863, while leading a column at the Siege of Port Hudson. After an eight-month convalescence, he returned to duty with the Department of the Gulf. Sherman retired from service on December 31, 1870.

Sherman, Major General William Tecumseh, U.S.

After his destructive march through Georgia and the Carolinas, Sherman became the most hated man in the old Confederacy. Ironically, the native Ohioan whose middle name was once his first name and was taken from the brilliant Shawnee Indian chief Tecumseh, had a warm affection for the South. But that didn't stop him from turning thumbs-down on a commission in the Confederate Army at the beginning of the war. A West Point graduate who fought in the Mexican War before returning to civilian life, Sherman accepted an appointment as colonel with a Union infantry regiment. After fighting at First Bull Run, he was promoted to brigadier general and sent to Kentucky. Then he was made commander of the Department of the Cumberland but almost immediately began quarreling with his superiors and the press. Sherman was accused of being unstable, and the accusations were true. He suffered a nervous breakdown and even considered suicide, before snapping out of his depression. Years later he cited his former mental problems while defending the Union's general in chief, Ulysses S. Grant, against critics who accused him of being an alcoholic. "Grant stood by me when I was crazy, and I stood by him when he was drunk," Sherman declared. The two great generals were a lot alike and believed firmly that if wars were fought, they should be fought as total war. Stern and as demanding of his men as he was of himself, Sherman preferred attack to sophisticated maneuvering and defense. In March 1862, after recovery from his breakdown, Sherman was named commander of the 5th Division, Union Army of the Tennessee. He was wounded at the Battle of Shiloh. In July 1862 he was named commander of the District of Memphis, and he participated with Grant in several battles leading to the capture of Vicksburg. After Grant became the Union's general in chief, Sherman was named to command of the Military Division of the Mississippi and told to capture Atlanta. After carrying out his assignment, he evacuated civilians, then burned the southern industrial center to the ground. Sherman spent the final weeks of the war leading his troops through Georgia and the Carolinas on his famous March to the Sea. Lee had already surrendered to Grant when Sherman accepted the surrender of General Joseph E. Johnston's shattered Confederate Army of Tennessee on April 26, 1865. Sherman continued his military service after the war and in 1869 succeeded Grant as commander in chief of the U. S. Army. (See: Johnston, General Joseph Eggleston, CS.)

Shiloh, Battle of

Poor command decisions mixed with a large number of untried troops in both armies played key roles in the outcome after Confederate general Albert Sidney Johnston opened a surprise dawn attack on Union troops encamped along the Tennessee River on April 6, 1862. Five divisions of Major General Ulysses S. Grant's 42,000-man Union army were spread out around Pittsburg Landing and the Shiloh church, with another division only six miles away. Johnston had amassed an army of 40,000 men. Grant was waiting at the landing for another Union army of 51,000 men to launch a campaign aimed at capturing Memphis. General William T. Sherman was the Union's on-the-scene commander when Johnston's army suddenly plunged through the thick timber and across the rough fields into the Yankee camps. Grant was across the river waiting for General Don Carlos Buell and the second army. Sherman and other officers bravely rallied panicked troops, who held on until Grant arrived. Grant committed his final six divisions and sent word to advance units of Buell's army to hurry and join the battle. On the second day of battle, the reinforced Union forces launched a fierce counterattack that forced the Confederates to withdraw. Although Union losses amounted to 13,050 casualties, compared to 10,700 for the Confederates, General Johnston was killed, and although both sides claimed victory, Shiloh went into most history books as a draw. (See: Johnston, General Albert Sidney, CS.)

Shiloh, Johnny
See: Clem, Major General John Lincoln, U.S.

Shoddys
This derogatory term was coined for cheap, poor-quality dark blue woolen jackets rushed to production for Union troops responding to President Lincoln's call for 500,000 volunteers after the debacle at First Bull Run. Many of the 30,000 jackets were made of coarse, itchy, bargain-basement material and poorly put together and began to fall apart or disintegrate after minimal use. (See: Bull Run, First Battle of.)

Sibley Tents
Named for their inventor, Henry H. Sibley, who later became a brigadier general for the Confederacy, these tents were huge canvas cones with a pole in the center and an opening at the top for ventilation. The tents were designed to accommodate 12 men but often sheltered as many as 20 and were heated by small stoves in cold weather. The Confederacy replaced the Sibleys later in the war with smaller tents that were easier to pack up and carry.

Sickles, Major General Daniel, U.S.
Prior to the war, Sickles's main claim to fame, or infamy, was shooting to death the son of the composer of "The Star-Spangled Banner," then being the first man ever to win acquittal of murder charges on grounds of insanity. Philip Barton Key was shot for carrying on an affair with Sickles's wife, but the gunman had a reputation of his own for skirt chasing that followed him to the battlefield. As a general, Sickles became notorious with fellow generals Daniel Butterfield and

then general in chief "Fighting Joe" Hooker for wild drinking and womanizing parties that other officers charged had turned the headquarters into a combination barroom and brothel. Although Sickles loved to kick up his heels, he was courageous on the battlefield and after advancement to brigadier general commanded a brigade, then a division, and finally a corps, at battles including Seven Pines, the Seven Days Battles, Gettysburg, and Chancellorsville. He lost a leg after it was struck by a shell at Gettysburg and years later donated it to an army medical museum, where he sometimes visited the amputated limb to pay his respects. Although Sickles had powerful friends in Washington, he made the mistake while recuperating of quarreling with Meade over the Gettysburg commander's performance as a general. Consequently, he spent the rest of the war carrying out special missions for the War Department and was never given another field command. After retiring from the army as a major general, Sickles was named U.S. minister to Spain by President Grant and created more scandal with his skirt chasing before being elected to Congress. He also served as chairman of the New York State Monuments Commission until he was forced out of the job by a financial scandal. (See: Butterfield, Major General Daniel, U.S.; and Hooker, Major General Joseph "Fighting Joe," U.S.)

Sigel, Major General Franz, U.S.
The wartime leader of the German-American community, Sigel was barely adequate as a general, but his support was politically important to the Union. (See: Languages.)

Signal Corps, U.S.
The U.S. Signal Corps was established in June 1860 and was the army's new kid on the block when the war began. For a while the Corps worked with civilian operators of the Federal Military Telegraph System, but after less than three years it was shoved aside in favor of civilians and confined its operations to visual signaling. (See: Federal Military Telegraph System; and Wig-Wag Signaling.)

Silk Dress Balloon
See: Balloons, Hot Air.

Sioux
Hostilities erupted with the Sioux Indians during the early stages of the Civil War. The trouble began when the Wahpeton Sioux in Minnesota began warring against settlers and spread into North Dakota. Although badly needed by the Union for the war against the South, Federal troops were sent west to quell the Indian uprising. Battles were fought at Birch Coulee and Killdeer, and a major engagement occurred during the Battle of Whitestone Hill. The worst defeat in the history of the Sioux nation was suffered at the Battle of Whitestone Hill when 3,000 warriors were either killed, wounded, or taken prisoner by U.S. cavalry. Other Indians, including Apache and Comanche, also took advantage of the war between North and South to flee reservations, launch raids, and attempt to recover lost tribal lands.

Skirmishers
Soldiers who are sent out in advance of the main body of troops to scout or probe the enemy position. The word also applies to soldiers who engage in a skirmish, or small fight.

Skylark
The name of one of Confederate cavalry general J. E. B. Stuart's favorite mounts.

Slaves, Freed
An estimated 4 million slaves were freed as a result of the war.

Slocum, Major General Henry Warner, U.S.
A veteran of the Seminole Wars who roomed with Philip Sheridan at West Point, Slocum was the Onandaga County treasurer in New York when the war began and he was elected colonel of the 27th New York Volunteer Infantry from Elmira. Slocum fought at First Bull Run, where he was wounded

in the thigh, and after recovery was promoted to brigadier general and assigned to Washington defense duty. Then he fought in the Peninsular Campaign at the Siege of Yorktown, West Point, Gaines's Mill, Glendale, and Malvern Hill. Promoted to major general in July 1862, he fought at Crampton's Gap on South Mountain, Maryland, and at Antietam, Fredericksburg, and Gettysburg. He led the Army of the Potomac's XII Corps at Culp's Hill. His field savvy drew praise from senior officers after he helped prevent a disaster when General Meade told him to move his entire corps to shore up the Union left and Slocum talked him into leaving the 3d Brigade in place to avoid a collapse on the depleted right. After the XI and XII Corps were transferred to the Union Army of the Tennessee, Slocum fought at Wauhatchie and Lookout Mountain before he was assigned to command of the District of Vicksburg. He was then named to command the XX Corps for General Sherman's Atlanta Campaign and ultimately led his men in to occupy the city after it was abandoned by the fleeing Confederates. Slocum remained with Sherman as commander of the Army of Georgia on the March to the Sea, then ended the war in the Carolinas, fighting in his final battle at Bentonville. Slocum returned to New York State and served in Congress after the war. (See: Atlanta, Siege of.)

Smallpox
This dreaded disease struck the high and mighty as well as exhausted foot soldiers as it raged through the North and South. Even President Lincoln contracted the ailment and was suffering from smallpox when he delivered his historic Gettysburg Address.

Smith, General Edmund Kirby, CS
An Indian fighter and veteran of the Mexican War, Smith was a major with the U.S. Army's 2d Cavalry in Texas when he joined the Confederacy after refusing to surrender his command to local state military forces. Smith rose quickly through the Confederate command structure and after ser-

vice in the Shenandoah Valley was promoted to brigadier general. He was severely injured while leading a brigade at First Bull Run. After recovery he was promoted to major general and served briefly as a division commander in northern Virginia. In March 1862 the West Pointer and native Floridian was reassigned to command of the Department of Tennessee, and he spent the remainder of the war fighting in the Western Theater. He joined with General Braxton Bragg in the Kentucky Campaign, earning promotion to lieutenant general, and fought at Perryville and Stones River before he was sent even farther west to the Trans-Mississippi. After the fall of Vicksburg, Smith and his troops were isolated from Richmond, and although they generally maintained formal military structure and discipline, Smith was forced to use many of the tactics of irregulars. He acquired food and supplies by seizing them for the Confederacy, made his own promotions of senior officers to general, and made many other decisions that would normally have been funneled through Richmond if the lines of communication were more open. His own promotion to full general was formally approved by the Confederacy. Smith's forces trounced Union general Nathaniel P. Banks during the abortive Red River Campaign and launched an aborted invasion of Missouri before he was forced to confine operations to hit-and-run guerrilla tactics as the Confederacy was in its death throes. The Confederate capitulation at Appomattox had occurred more than six weeks earlier and a subordinate had surrendered Smith's army in New Orleans, but the general was still in a fighting mood and unsuccessfully attempted to recruit more troops in Houston on May 25. He was in Galveston on June 2 when he finally threw in the towel. Smith's army was the last significant Confederate fighting force left. He was the old Confederacy's last living full general when he died in Tennessee in 1893. (See: Palmetto Ranch, Battle of; Red River Campaign; Taylor, Major General Richard, CS; and Watie, Brigadier General Stand, CS.)

Smith, Major General Andrew Jackson, U.S.

Smith fought in the Red River Campaign, and led Federal troops to victory at the Battle of Tupelo in Mississippi. The Pennsylvanian was at the head of a force of 14,000 men and had orders to prevent Major General Nathan Bedford Forrest's Confederate cavalry from raiding Union supply lines during the Atlanta Campaign when the forces clashed on July 14, 1864. Forrest headed a force of 6,000 men, reinforced by 2,000 men led by Lieutenant General Stephen Dill Lee. Lee was in overall command at 7:30 A.M. when the Confederates attacked at Tupelo, and the Yankees beat back a series of badly coordinated assaults while inflicting heavy losses. After several hours, Lee broke off the fighting, with General William T. Sherman's supply lines still intact. (See: Red River Campaign.)

Smith Percussion Carbine

The .50-caliber Smith was one of the most commonly issued firearms to Union cavalry. It fired a rubber-encased or foil-wrapped brass cartridge, which was inserted into a down-hinged barrel that dropped when a catch at the front of the trigger was pressed. It wasn't a perfect weapon, and problems sometimes occurred when the rubber cartridges stuck in the breech after the gun became hot.

Sneak Thief

Major General George Custer helped himself to a small table as a souvenir after witnessing Lee's surrender to Grant at the home of a farmer in Appomattox Court House, Virginia. (See: Custer, Major General George Armstrong, U.S.; and McLean, Wilmer.)

Sniper

The term for a sharpshooter who targets individual enemy to bring them down at extreme ranges. Snipers were used by both sides in the war, and the most famous were the 1st and 2d U.S. Sharpshooters, commanded by Hiram Berdan. Berdan's sharpshooters used weapons including the Sharps rifle model 1899, James target rifle, Morgan rifle .46-caliber, and Leonard target rifle. (See: Berdan, Major General Hiram, U.S.)

Soapsuds Brigade

Washerwomen who traveled with the armies to clean uniforms were commonly referred to as members of the Soapsuds Brigade and were allowed to live with their husbands in special areas of encampments known as "suds row." They were the only women in the camps with official status, and all other females who traveled with the armies, including the wives of officers, were known simply as camp followers. The Union Army allowed four laundresses to travel with each company.

Solid Shot

A solid artillery projectile that is oblong or spherical, depending on whether the cannon it is fired from is rifled or smoothbore. Solid shot is primarily used against fortifications.

Spar Torpedoes

Bombs attached to the ends of long poles, the explosive devices were transported by submarine or torpedo boat and rammed home against the sides of enemy ships. Both sides used spar torpedoes and aimed the devices at the waterline. (See: *Albemarle,* CSS; and Torpedoes.)

Special Field Order #15

On January 16, 1865, following a meeting in Savannah four days earlier with leading blacks and Secretary of War Edwin M. Stanton, General William T. Sherman issued Special Field Order #15. The order set aside land for exclusive settlement by blacks and provided for each family to receive "40 acres and a mule." The order designated the Sea Islands and a 30-mile inland tract for the exclusive settlement. (See: Freedmen's Bureau; Howard, Major General Oliver Otis, U.S.; and Saxton, General Rufus.)

Special Order 191, Mystery of

The Confederate officer who so negligently lost General Lee's Special Order 191 outlining battle plans on the eve of the Battle of Antietam, allowing it to fall into Union hands, was never publicly identified. Apparently, he was never punished. (See: Antietam, Battle of; and Mitchell, Corporal Barton W., U.S.)

Spencer Repeating Rifle

The most sought-after breech-loader of the war, the Spencer was capable of a rate of fire of up to 14 rounds per minute. It was a .52-caliber 47 inches long and held seven cartridges in a tubular magazine fed through the buttstock.

Spoils of Mexico

The United States won a resounding victory in the conflict of 1846–48 with Mexico, but the new territories seized from the defeated nation to the south made the Civil War inevitable. As the captured territories prepared to enter the Union, battle lines were drawn over whether they would be accepted as slave or free states.

Spotsylvania, Battle of

After the terrible blooding at the Battle of the Wilderness, Ulysses S. Grant did a strange thing for a Union general. Instead of ordering his army to fall back and lick its wounds while he explained to official Washington why he hadn't performed better, the new general in chief ordered the Army of the Potomac to continue marching south. Grant was intent on cutting General Lee off from the Confederate capital at Richmond. When Grant's war-weary troops learned that their commander was still spoiling for a fight, they cheered and broke into song. Lee quickly figured out what Grant was up to and raced south to the little crossroads town of Spotsylvania, where the Army of Northern Virginia began building defensive breastworks in preparation for another fight. The low walls were constructed in a rough V shape, with the point on high ground holding 22 cannon aimed directly ahead where the attack was expected to come from. The Confederates called the defensive strongpoint the Mule Shoe. The nearly two-week-long Battle of Spotsylvania, or Spotsylvania Court House, began on May 8, the day after the Battle of the Wilderness ended. Grant opened with an unsuccessful attack on Lee's left flank, then turned his attention to the Mule Shoe near the center of the Confederate line. Late on May 10, following a devastating Union artillery barrage, Colonel Emory Upton led a division in a frontal assault, breaking through the lines and capturing a big haul of prisoners before being forced back. Two days later, Grant ordered another even bigger assault on the Mule Shoe. This time the 15,000 men were led by Major General Winfield Scott Hancock in a predawn assault that split the Army of Northern Virginia down the middle, pushing back the defenders and taking most of a division prisoner. With the Bluecoats now in the trenches built by the Confederates, Lee planned a counterattack. Like he had at the Wilderness, Lee planned to lead the charge himself, before he was dissuaded by concerned subordinates. The two armies fought at close quarters, in hand-to-hand combat, for almost 20 hours straight, and gunfire was so withering that trees were cut in half by flying metal. It was after midnight when Lee finally called off the attack. Exhausted, the two sides sparred and parried with each other for the next few days. On May 18 Grant tried another frontal assault that accomplished nothing. On May 19 Lee launched a major assault on Grant's right, but the Union line held. At last Grant ordered his army to move farther south to Hanover Junction, and Lee responded by racing the Army of Northern Virginia ahead of the Yankees to build a new line of defense. The Battle of Spotsylvania was over, but at a cost to the Union of 17,500 casualties. The Confederates had 10,000 men killed, wounded, or captured.

Springfield Rifle Musket, Model 1861

The rifle musket became the favorite shoulder arm of Union soldiers after the Federal armory in Springfield, Massachusetts, began producing them a few months into the war. Within two years the armory produced more than 250,000 of the rifles and 20 private manufacturers were contracted to turn out another 450,000 at a cost between $15 and $20 each. The Model 1861 was considered a much better arm than the smoothbores that troops used prior to its introduction.

Stanton, Edwin

After Lincoln's assassination, Stanton was fired from his cabinet post as secretary of war by the new president, Andrew Johnson. The dismissal was considered a violation of the Tenure of Office Act, which required congressional approval before the president could fire a cabinet member, and political opponents of Johnson's lenient Reconstruction policies used the incident to bring impeachment charges against him. (See: Johnson, President Andrew.)

Staples, Private John Summerfield, U.S.

Hoping to encourage the hiring of substitutes to serve in the place of draftees who preferred not to take up arms, the president paid $500 to this 20-year-old Pennsylvanian who was discharged from the Union Army after contracting typhoid. The substitute agreement was a symbolic gesture on Lincoln's part, but two other future presidents, Chester A. Arthur and Grover Cleveland, were both of draft age and paid substitutes to take their place in the army.

Stars and Bars

Historians aren't certain if the famous Rebel flag was designed by an army major from Louisburg, North Carolina, or a Prussian woman who was a gifted musician and painter at the Marion Female Seminary in Alabama. According to the accounts of some witnesses, Major Orren Randolph Smith is the real father of the flag. But other sources indicate that Nicola Marschall produced three flag sketches, including the Stars and Bars, which featured two horizontal red stripes separated by one white stripe, with a circle of white stars on a dark blue field in the upper left corner. The first flag had 7 stars, the number of states that had seceded at that time, but the design was later altered to show 13 stars, the final number that joined the rebellion. (See: Battle Flag, Confederate.)

Starvation Parties

During the Seven Days Battles, when Union forces were so close to Richmond that cannon fire could be clearly heard, and two years later during the siege of nearby Petersburg, food and other comforts were in short supply in the South's capital city. So Richmond hostesses threw starvation parties, where no food was served and the only drink was water, but there was plenty of patriotic talk about supporting the hard-fighting sons of the South and defeating the hated Yankees.

Steele, Major General Frederick, U.S.

When the North launched the ill-fated Red River Campaign and Camden Expedition, plans called for an eventual two-column invasion of Texas. One of the columns was to be led by Major General Frederick Steele, marching south across the country from Little Rock, Arkansas, to meet in Shreveport, Louisiana, with the second army, led by Major General Nathaniel P. Banks. But Steele was delayed by a combination of unusually wet spring weather and stiff Confederate resistance and never reached the rendezvous point. Before the Red River Campaign was launched, Steele had marched northwest from Helena on the Arkansas border with Mississippi and captured Little Rock. Linking up with Banks in Shreveport was a different story. Steele was at the head of 17,000 troops when his leading division clashed with a strong force of 3,000 Confederate dismounted cavalry while crossing the Little Missouri River. A few miles south at Prairie De Ann, the Yankees clashed with an even larger Confederate force. By that time, heavy rains were turning roads to glue, Confederate resistance was strengthening, and Steele turned his army away from Shreveport and toward Camden, Arkansas. He expected to link up there with Brigadier General John M. Thayer, who was bringing a strong contingent of reinforcements from Arkadelphia, then move the combined force on to Shreveport. After a light skirmish at White

Oak Creek on April 12, 1864, Steele's troops marched the final 18 miles into Camden the next day. But hard fighting was still ahead, and in a clash at Poison Spring on April 18 the Confederates captured a supply train and scattered Union forces. At Mark's Mill a week later, the Rebels inflicted 1,500 casualties on the Federals and captured another supply train. The Rebels had 300 casualties. That was enough for Steele, and he turned his bedraggled, rain-soaked troops back toward Little Rock. After fighting off a strong Rebel attack on April 29 and 30 at Jenkins Ferry and crossing the Saline River, Steele's weary Federals completed their retreat to Little Rock. A West Pointer from New York, earlier in the Civil War Steele commanded a brigade in Missouri, led the 15th Army Corps in the Yazoo Expedition, and fought in the Vicksburg Campaign and at Chickasaw Bayou. Following the war he remained in volunteer service until March 1867 and died the following January. (See: Red River Campaign.)

Stephens, Alexander Hamilton

Like many political and military leaders of the South, the Georgia politician who became the vice president of the Confederate States of America strongly opposed secession. Although he was a fierce advocate of slavery and states' rights, Stephens was convinced that secession would lead to a devastating war that would destroy the country. But in January 1861 when his arguments against joining the rebellion fell on deaf ears at the Georgia state convention on secession he remained true to his Southern roots. Hamilton reluctantly added his signature to the Ordinance of Secession, then traveled to the first capital of the Confederacy in Montgomery, Alabama, where he helped draft the new constitution. Instead, he was selected by the provisional congress to be the new vice president of the CSA. A lawyer, Stephens was also a seasoned politician and public servant, who had served in the Georgia State Legislature, then in the U.S. House of Representatives and in the U.S. Senate, where he defended slavery and championed states' rights. Like many others in the new administration, Stephens didn't get along well with Jefferson Davis and opposed the CSA president's efforts to create a strong centralized government, impose taxes, institute the draft, and suspend the writ of habeas corpus. For his part, Stephens pushed for the rapid sale of cotton in Europe before the Union blockade of Southern ports was strengthened. After the Confederate capitulation, Stephens was imprisoned at Fort Warren in Boston until October 1865, when he was freed and returned to Georgia. He was re-elected to the U.S. Senate in 1866, but vengeful Republicans intent on punishing former Rebels refused to allow him to take his seat. Stephens was given a friendlier welcome two years later when he was elected to the Georgia State House of Representatives, where he served until 1882, when he was elected governor. He had barely begun his term before his death in 1883. (See Davis, Jefferson Finis.)

Stone, Brigadier General Charles Pomeroy, U.S.

This Mexican War veteran was a division commander in charge of Union troops attempting to cross the Potomac and capture Leesburg when he became the scapegoat for the debacle at Ball's Bluff. Stone was carrying out vague orders from McClellan in October 1861 to try to scare the Confederates out of Leesburg, Virginia, with a show of force when he sent four companies to reinforce Harrison's Island, which splits the Potomac River just off Ball's Bluff. When a scouting party mistakenly reported a Confederate encampment just over the top of the bluff, Stone sent several companies ashore, leading to the fateful clash with the Confederates who had been watching the activity from a few miles away. The Yankees were slaughtered, and McClellan and Washington bigwigs quickly settled on a fall guy. Ignoring McClellan's own faulty decisions, communications mix-ups, and blunders by the president's close friend Colonel Edward D. Baker, the finger of guilt was pointed at Stone. He was accused of failing to reinforce the men at Ball's Bluff with troops from nearby Harrison's Island and the Maryland shore of the Potomac—and for other reputedly faulty command decisions. The general was arrested and confined without charges, and although he was eventually released without a court-martial, his career was shattered. The political fallout also affected others, and an offer to retire from Union general in chief Winfield Scott was accepted by President Lincoln and the reality of the war was so dramatically and horribly brought home to government officials that Congress established the Congressional Joint Committee of Conduct of the War. (See: Baker, Colonel Edward D., U.S.; Ball's Bluff, Battle of; Evans, Brigadier General Nathan G. "Shanks," CS; and Scott, Lieutenant General Winfield, U.S.)

Stone Fleet
Only a few days after Charleston was leveled by a devastating fire in December 1861, Union sailors added to the city's misery by scuttling 16 ships and boats across the harbor entrance as part of the new Northern blockade of Southern ports. Early in 1862 the last remaining channel into the harbor was blocked by 14 more scuttled watercraft. The British and French complained that the action was unnecessarily cruel, and Union authorities responded that there were no plans to create permanent injury to the harbor. Within a few months, the sunken hulks referred to as "the stone fleet" settled permanently into the mud and were no longer a threat to shipping lanes. (See: Divine Retribution.)

Stones River, Battle of
Alternate name for the Battle of Murfreesboro. (See: Murfreesboro, Battle of.)

Stoughton, Brigadier General Charles B., U.S.
Stoughton was a colonel with the 4th Vermont Volunteers when he lost an eye during battle at Funkstown, Maryland, and was discharged in 1863. He was the brother of another brigadier general, Edwin H. Stoughton. (See: Stoughton, Brigadier General Edwin H., U.S.)

Stoughton, Brigadier General Edwin H., U.S.

Stoughton is best remembered not for his accomplishments as a military leader but for the embarrassing circumstances of his capture by Confederate partisan ranger John Singleton Mosby. A man of reckless courage, Captain Mosby led a raiding party of 29 partisan rangers 10 miles behind Union lines into Fairfax Court House, Virginia, on the rainy night of March 9, 1863, and captured Stoughton, two captains, 30 soldiers, and 58 horses without firing a shot. After a night of partying, the general was roused from sleep with a resounding slap on his bottom and awakened with a roar of anger. "Do you know who I am, sir?" he demanded of the stranger standing over him. "I reckon I do, General. Did you ever hear of Mosby?" the raider responded. "Yes, have you caught him?" Stoughton replied. "No," Mosby said, "but he has caught you." When President Lincoln learned of the humiliating incident so near Washington, D.C., he disgustedly remarked that he wasn't so upset over losing a general but hated to lose so many good horses. (See: Ford, Antonia; Mosby, Colonel John Singleton, CS; and Outhouse Johnstone.)

Stowe, Harriet Beecher

When her violently antislavery novel *Uncle Tom's Cabin* was published in 1852, it inflamed passions on both sides of the issue and made Mrs. Stowe the most hated woman in the South. Simon Legree, the chief villain in the book, was depicted as such a brute that his name became a synonym in the dictionary for a cruel taskmaster or slave driver. By the end of the year *Uncle Tom's Cabin* sold 300,000 copies, and within five years sales topped a half-million. In 1862 when Abraham Lincoln met Mrs. Stowe, he remarked, "So you're the little woman who wrote the book that made this great war." The author was the sister of Henry Ward Beecher, a nationally prominent clergyman and a leader of the abolitionist movement. (See: Abolition; and Beecher's Bibles.)

Stuart, Major General
James Ewell Brown "Jeb," CS

The handsome, bold-spirited leader of the Army of Northern Virginia's cavalry, Stuart was hailed as a Southern warrior-king after his inspiring ride around Union general George McClellan's army during the Peninsular Campaign. While making the three-day circuit to gather intelligence on enemy positions, troop strength, and movements for Robert E. Lee, Stuart and his 1,200 troopers captured prisoners, arms, and equipment and disrupted enemy operations. The legendary Confederate hero was already a seasoned warrior when the Civil War began. After graduating thirteenth in his class at West Point, the native Virginian was assigned to the Texas frontier as a second lieutenant. A year later he was sent to Bloody Kansas to help keep the peace between Free-Soilers and Copperheads, and a year after that he was seriously wounded while fighting Cheyenne Indians. After helping Robert E. Lee arrest abolitionist zealot John Brown at Harpers Ferry, Stuart returned to Kansas and was there when the Civil War began, and he resigned his commission to fight for the Confederacy. He was commissioned a lieutenant colonel in the 1st Virginia Cavalry. Stuart was promoted to brigadier general after commanding his 1,200 troopers at First Bull Run, then led them on the famous ride around the Army of the Potomac on the Virginia Peninsula. His reputation was at its zenith in July 1862 when he was promoted to major general and named to command the cavalry forces of Lee's Army of Northern Virginia. Stuart fought at the Second Battle of Bull Run, Antietam, and Fredericksburg and briefly assumed command of the army's II Corps after General Stonewall Jackson was killed at Chancellorsville. Stuart was on a reconnaissance mission for a planned new invasion of the North when his troops encountered Union cavalry, leading to the Battle of Brandy Station. After a rare disappointing performance at Gettysburg when he rashly attempted to repeat his famous ride on the peninsula, leaving Lee hobbled early in the battle by a lack of intelligence, Stuart quickly redeemed himself during the Wilderness Campaign. On May 11,

1864, Stuart was shot below the ribs on the right side when his outnumbered troopers clashed with a strong Union cavalry force led by General Philip H. Sheridan at Yellow Tavern. The mortally wounded general was loaded into an ambulance and rushed to Richmond, where he died the next day. (See: Brandy Station; Gettysburg, Battle of; and Yellow Tavern, Battle of.)

Submarine
See *Hunley,* CSS.

Sultana, SS
This side-wheel steamboat was packed with more than 2,000 Union soldiers paroled from Southern prisons and at least another 250 civilians, army guards, and crew members on April 27, 1865, when the boilers exploded and the grossly overloaded vessel burned and sank. The exact number aboard when the boat blew up on the Mississippi River a few miles north of Memphis is unknown, but most estimates range from 2,021 to 2,500. Only 783 of those aboard were pulled from the river alive, and 200 of those later died of burns and other injuries. Destruction of the *Sultana* marked the second major catastrophe in five weeks involving civilian ships contracted as transports by the Union. It was also the worst maritime disaster in American history. (See: *General Lyon,* SS; and Lugenbeal, Private William, U.S.)

Sumner, Major General "Bull" Vase, U.S.
A visiting French military officer accompanying McClellan's staff as a military observer wasn't favorably impressed by "Bull" Sumner, despite the Union general's advanced years, experience, handsome white beard, erect posture, booming voice, and fighting nickname. The Comte de Paris wrote of Sumner in his journal: ". . . the grand old man, wizened, white bearded, had an air of stupidity that perfectly expresses his mental state." Sumner's peers and Civil War historians generally agree that Sumner, at 61 one of the old-

est Union officers on active duty when the conflict began, performed poorly in command while serving in the Peninsular Campaign, at Fredericksburg, and in other battles.

Sumter, CSS
See: Semmes, Captain Raphael, CSN.

Surrender at Harpers Ferry
The violence at Harpers Ferry didn't end with John Brown's aborted insurrection. During the South's first invasion of the North, Confederates recaptured the strategically and industrially valuable town, along with the 12,500 Bluecoats stationed there. Led by Major General Thomas J. "Stonewall" Jackson on September 15, 1862, the Confederates swept out of Maryland and, after taking the bluffs and ridges overlooking the town, pinned down the Yankees with withering cannon and small-arms fire. Union forces were forced to raise the white flag. The surrender marked the largest single capture of Federal troops during the entire war. But Jackson barely had time to get his prisoners, along with 13,000 small arms and 47 pieces of artillery captured in the action, out of town before Federal forces were back in control. The strategically located community with the vital armory and rail and canal center at the northern end of the lush Shenandoah Valley changed hands eight times between 1861 and 1865 and was repeatedly left blackened and in ruins. Virginia had seceded from the Union only a few hours before Federal troops set fire to the armory and arsenal in an attempt to keep the prize out of the hands of the Confederates. Although the arsenal and 15,000 guns and other armaments were destroyed, the armory fire was extinguished by the advancing Virginians and the vital weapons-manufacturing equipment saved to be shipped south. Two months later, when the Confederates left Harpers Ferry they burned the factory buildings and blew up the railroad bridge. (See: John Brown's Raid on Harpers Ferry.)

Sutlers

Many people profited from the war, but to soldiers the most visibly present profiteers were the sutlers who trailed along with the armies on both sides, selling everything from newspapers, socks, and shoelaces to candy and tobacco. The merchandise was frequently shoddy, but the prices were first-class expensive. Soldiers, often frightened and lonely, quickly forked over their hard-earned dollars for the merest taste of normalcy and home. But when soldiers were in a mood for mischief, they sometimes abused the merchants whom they considered to be parasites and looted their stores.

T

Taps

This mournful bugle call is said to have been used for the first time at a military funeral by Calef's Battery A, 2d Artillery, over the grave of Lieutenant John Haskell, killed in action against the Confederates during the Peninsular Campaign.

Taylor, Major General Richard, CS

The son of General and President Zachary Taylor, Richard was one of the last Confederate commanders to surrender his troops after the Southern capitulation at Appomattox. He was commanding 15,000 troops in Mobile, Alabama, before he finally surrendered to Union general E. R. S. Canby on May 4, 1865. With Taylor's capitulation, General Edmund Kirby Smith in Texas and Brigadier General Stand Watie, a Cherokee Indian, were left as the only Confederate commanders still fighting the war. Taylor served as secretary to his father during the Mexican War before joining the Confederacy. Taylor commanded the District of Western Louisiana and fought during the Red River Campaign. He led the victorious Rebel attack on a numerically superior Union force at the Battle of Mansfield and participated in the unsuccessful attack at Pleasant Hill. Earlier he commanded a brigade during General Stonewall Jackson's Shenandoah Campaign and fought in the Seven Days Battles. (See: Mansfield, Battle of; Smith, General Edmund Kirby, CS; and Watie, Brigadier General Stand, CS.)

Tecumseh, USS
When this ill-fated single-turret ironclad was sunk at the Battle of Mobile Bay, it was a shock to Union Navy brass, who had believed that monitor-class ships were virtually unsinkable. The *Tecumseh* went to the bottom so quickly after striking a floating mine that only 21 of the 114 men on board escaped with their lives. *Tecumseh* captain Tunis A. M. Craven went down with his ship after stepping aside so his pilot could escape and remarking, "I leave my ship last." (See: Mobile Bay, Battle of.)

Telegraph
During the Civil War the telegraph made it possible for the first time in history for commanders to communicate almost instantaneously over long distances. An invention that was less than 20 years old (1844) when the war began, the telegraph continued to be supplemented by mounted couriers, but the new device was an invaluable tool used by commanders such as General Grant for directing the activities of multiple units on widely dispersed fronts. Although the telegraph was used by both sides, because of political and other considerations in the South the North made the best use of it. (See: Federal Military Telegraph System.)

Telescopic Sights
Invented in 1848 by Morgan James of Utica, New York, the long-tube telescopic sights used by many Civil War snipers were four-power or less but in the hands of an expert marksman were deadly at long range.

Tennessee, CSS
The pride of the Confederate Navy was blasted into a floating wreck and surrendered after Union admiral David G. Farragut's flotilla ganged up on it at the Battle of Mobile Bay. The ill-fated dreadnaught was put out of action in its first naval engagement, after construction and launching at the South's iron foundry in Selma, Alabama. The *Tennessee* was heavily armored and carried six powerful guns, as well as being

outfitted with a ram. But it was slow and insufficiently powered. J. D. Johnston was the ship's commander. (See: Buchanan, Admiral Franklin, CSN; and Mobile Bay, Battle of.)

Tennessee, State of
Sentiments concerning secession were sharply divided in Tennessee, with support for the Union especially strong in the eastern areas of the state. After Tennessee finally joined the South, 450 Civil War battles were fought in the state.

Territories
At the beginning of the war, the North controlled seven territories in addition to the loyal Union states. Some territories were composed of large areas that were later broken up and admitted to the Union as more than one state. The territories were: Arizona, Colorado, New Mexico, Utah, Nebraska, Washington, and the Indian Territory.

Texas Counties
Naming counties after Civil War heroes was common on both sides of the conflict, but Texas may hold the record with 18 counties named after fallen warriors and former statesmen who served the Confederacy.

Thanksgiving
The last Thursday in November was designated as the national holiday of Thanksgiving by proclamation of President Lincoln.

Thirteenth Amendment
After Lincoln's election to a second term, he resumed efforts to officially abolish slavery by constitutional amendment. Despite his efforts to extend an olive branch to Democrats with a proposal for financial compensation to slave owners, the opposition party stubbornly resisted the president's attempts to win approval of the amendment during his first term. This time the House was under firm control of the Republicans and voted 38–6 for the amendment. But Senate Democrats were still dragging their feet, and the first vote

failed to gain the necessary two-thirds support needed for passage. So Lincoln called for a second vote, and the amendment was passed in January 1865 by a close 119–56 margin. Lincoln signed the amendment the next day, and it was ratified by eight states within a week. But it was eight months before the rest of the states followed suit and December 18, 1865, before the amendment outlawing slavery was officially ratified. (See: D.C. Emancipation Bill.)

Thomas, Major General George Henry, U.S.

This towering 200-pound giant called on his bulldog determination and courage three times to pull the Union's major general W. S. Rosecrans's fat from the fire, at the battles of Murfreesboro, Chickamauga, and Chattanooga. The fighting general whose admiring men called him Old Pap before he became nationally known as "the Rock of Chickamauga" was already used to fighting hard and winning. A Virginian, West Pointer, and Indian fighter who also served in the Mexican War, Thomas remained loyal to the Union. He was on leave and recovering after an Indian shot an arrow through his chin during a skirmish on the frontier when he requested an immediate return to active duty. Thomas commanded a brigade at the First Battle of Bull Run. After recruiting and organizing volunteers in eastern Kentucky, he devised a unique fighting technique that resulted in the first Union victory of the war. Defending against a fierce assault at Logan's Cross Roads, Thomas waited until the Rebels began to run out of steam, then launched a devastating counterattack. The same tactic calling on patience and timing was later used effectively at Brice's Cross Roads and at Nashville, where Confederate general John Bell Hood's Confederate Army of Tennessee was demolished. (See: Chattanooga, Battle of; Chickamauga, Battle of; Cumberland Pontoons; and Rock of Chickamauga.)

Thruston, Private Henry C., CS

Believed to be the tallest soldier on either side, this Texas private was a towering seven feet, seven and one-half inches tall. His four brothers who enlisted with him in a Morgan County company were all at least six feet, six inches tall. (See: Buskirk, Captain David, U.S.)

Todd, Lieutenant David H.
The commandant of Libby Prison in Richmond, Todd was a half brother of President Lincoln's wife, Mary Todd Lincoln. (See: Lincoln In-Laws.)

Tompkins, Captain Sally Louisa, CS
Barely five feet tall, this Richmond, Virginia, widow was the only woman to hold a military commission in the Confederacy. President Jefferson Davis made her a captain of cavalry to circumvent a regulation stipulating that all hospitals be under the operation of military personnel. When the government issued a plea for help caring for the wounded from the First Battle of Bull Run, Mrs. Tompkins drew on her considerable inheritance to open a private hospital in a house donated by Dr. John Robertson. From its opening until a few weeks after the war ended, 1,333 Confederate soldiers were treated at Robertson Hospital. During its 45 months of operation, the recovery rates for patients were so exceptionally high that officers competed to get their most critically injured men placed there under her care. When Davis ordered all private hospitals in Richmond to be closed, Tompkins talked him into making an exception of Robertson, leading to her commission as a cavalry officer. The commission allowed her to draw government rations and a salary, which she put back into hospital operations. "Captain Sally" continued her charity work after the war and, with her inheritance totally exhausted, moved into the Confederate Womens' Home in Richmond, where she remained until her death in 1916.

Torpedoes
The torpedoes of the Civil War were nothing like those used to arm modern submarines, but were the first floating water mines. They were released by the Confederates to protect rivers, harbors, and bays, and liberally sprinkled around areas

expected to attract enemy shipping or invasion forces. The torpedoes were very effective weapons for the blockaded South, and were credited with the sinking of 27 Union ships. (See: Farragut, Admiral David Glasgow; Minesweepers; Mobile Bay, Battle of; and Spar Torpedoes.)

Tracy, Benjamin F.

Commandant of the notorious Union prison camp at Elmira, N. Y., Tracy, 36, was the local district attorney and head of the New York Volunteers. In addition to the prison, Tracy was also in charge of a barracks at the other end of the small town housing Union draftees, and his administration of the facility was plagued by a high rate of desertions. (See: Elmira Prison.)

Traveller

All cavalrymen and many officers in both blue and gray practically lived on their horses, and most developed a deep mutual trust and affection. General Robert E. Lee and his trusted Confederate gray stallion, Traveller, were prime examples. Lee first spotted the horse during his West Virginia campaign in 1861 and a year later bought the 16-hand-high mount from its owner for $200. The handsome stallion was originally named after Confederate president Jeff Davis, but Lee changed the name to Traveller. Horse and master traveled together, covering thousands of miles, throughout the remainder of the war. Traveller recovered from a serious wound suffered at the Wilderness and outlived his master by several years before succumbing to lockjaw. His skeleton is preserved at the Washington and Lee Museum. (See: Lee, General Robert E., CS.)

Tredegar Iron Works

Nearly half of all the artillery produced in the South, 1,099 cannon, were produced by the Richmond foundry that became known as the mother arsenal of the Confederacy.

Trenches

World War I and the Crimean War may be better known for trench warfare, but the groundwork for widespread use of the new defensive system was laid during the Civil War by Confederate James Longstreet. Known as "Old Peter" to his men, this deliberate, cautious military leader constructed a sophisticated trench system along the Rappahannock River that could have provided a model for those used in the conflict in Europe a half-century later. A devastatingly effective maze of Confederate trenches at Cold Harbor was dug in a zigzag pattern so that an attacking enemy could be fired on from the front and the sides at the same time. The use of trenches quickly spread and was thereafter used by both sides. (See: Longstreet, Lieutenant General James, CS.)

Trent Affair

In a daring move to win foreign recognition of the Confederacy, a blockade runner slipped out of Charleston Harbor on the dark night of October 11, 1861, with two envoys to England and France aboard—setting the stage for one of President Lincoln's most ticklish diplomatic quandaries of the war. The blockade runner duly delivered James Mason, CSA envoy to England, and associate John Slidell to Havana, Cuba, where they transferred to a British mail steamer, the *Trent,* for the final leg of the journey across the Atlantic to London. The *Trent* was barely under way before it was intercepted by the U.S. Navy ship *San Jacinto,* and boarded after two shots were fired across the bow of the steamer. Although the acts were clearly against international maritime law, *San Jacinto* captain Charles Wilkes demanded surrender of the two CSA diplomats, and the *Trent* was directed to anchor at Boston, where the men were arrested and jailed. Britain was outraged, and Prime Minister Lord Palmerston drew a line in the sand, demanding the Union release Mason and Slidell or face war with Britain. Palmerston backed up his ultimatum by moving 8,000 troops to Canada. Lincoln wisely threw in the towel, and on January 1, 1862, the CSA diplomats were released to British officials and permitted to complete their journey to London unmolested.

Trimble, Major General Isaac Ridgeway, CS

Trimble once told Stonewall Jackson, "Before this war is over, I intend to be a major general or a corpse." He wound up as a major general and eventually as an incomplete corpse after losing a leg to an ankle wound suffered during Pickett's Charge at Gettysburg. Before the loss of the leg, capture, and exchange ended his career as a field officer, Trimble fought gallantly under Stonewall Jackson in the Shenandoah Campaign, and at Second Bull Run, where he was also wounded. After the war, Trimble returned to his native Baltimore, where he died in 1888. (See: Cross Keys, Battle of.)

Turchin, Brigadier General Ivan, U.S.

Better known to his troops and many enemies in the Union's officer corps as "the Mad Russian," Turchin was a veteran warrior who graduated from the Imperial Military School in St. Petersburg, Russia, and fought in Hungary and the Crimean War before marrying his commander's daughter and immigrating with her to the United States. After settling in Chicago, he Americanized his name from the Russian Ivan Vasilevich Turchinov, and when the Civil War began he joined the Union Army. Commissioned a colonel of the 19th Illinois Volunteers, he wrote the manual *Brigade Drill,* used throughout the army. Turchin fought gallantly in Missouri, Kentucky, and Alabama, and in December 1861 he was named to command the 8th Brigade in General Don Carlos Buell's Army of the Ohio. But Buell ordered his court-martial for inflicting Old World atrocities on innocent civilians, as well as other violations of the military code, and Colonel Turchin was dishonorably discharged on August 6, 1862. He was restored to duty a few months later and fought in Tennessee and Georgia before resigning on October 4, 1864, because of poor health and returning to Chicago. He died in an Illinois insane asylum at the age of 79. (See: Athens, Rape of; and Turchin, Madam.)

Turchin, Madam

The ultimate military wife, Madam Turchin not only took over temporary command of her ailing husband's regiment but also later got him his job back along with a promotion after he was sacked from the Union Army for violating the military codes. Madam Turchin, whose first name seems to have been lost to history, was the daughter of Turchin's commandant when they married in Russia. Years later when he was wounded while leading the 19th Illinois Regiment in Tennessee in 1862, she took over command for one day or several—depending on which account is most accurate. Then when Turchin was kicked out of the army for encouraging his troops to pillage Athens, Alabama, she personally called on Abraham Lincoln and talked him into restoring her husband to command. She did such a brilliant sales job that the president even approved Turchin's promotion to brigadier general. (See: Athens, Rape of; and Turchin, Brigadier General Ivan, U.S.)

Twiggs, Major General David Emanuel, CS

An officer who served in four American wars, Twiggs was a general in the U.S. Army and the Confederate Army and died brokenhearted because he was labeled a traitor in the North. Twiggs fought in the Black Hawk War, the Seminole Wars, the War of 1812, and the Mexican War before he was named commander of the Department of Texas, with responsibility for protecting settlers from Indians. He was 66 and a major general. A native Georgian, as the Civil War shaped up Twiggs wrote General Winfield Scott and asked to be relieved of his command because he was a Southerner and would join the Confederacy when his home state seceded. He was instructed merely to protect government property while avoiding aggressive action. When 10,000 Texans surrounded the 160-man Federal garrison in San Antonio on February 18, 1861, Twiggs had no choice but to surrender. He was immediately labeled a traitor by the North and dishonorably discharged from the army. Although he was named a major general in the Confederate Army, he never saw combat in the war and died in 1862.

U

Unconditional Surrender Grant

When Ulysses S. Grant captured Fort Donelson in Kentucky, it marked the Union's first notable victory of the Civil War after a series of demoralizing defeats and made him a Northern hero. The victory also earned him a nickname when his old friend and West Point classmate Brigadier General Simon Bolivar Buckner asked about the terms being offered to turn over his garrison. Grant responded with a curt two-word reply: "Unconditional surrender." Admirers in the press and public quickly coined a new nickname for the general, playing on his first and middle initials, and began calling him Unconditional Surrender Grant. (See: Buckner, Lieutenant General Simon Bolivar, CS.)

Underground Railroad

A loose system of safe houses, the Underground Railroad was established by abolitionists before the war to help runaway slaves escape from their Southern owners to free states in the North. Some runaways traveled all the way to Canada, which refused to deport escaped slaves.

Uniforms, South

The Confederacy had more cotton than it knew what to do with at the beginning of the war but was short on manufacturers to turn out the thousands of uniforms needed for the men flocking to the Stars and Bars. To augment the new government's sluggish production of uniforms, some Johnny Rebs went to war wearing the same clothes they wore at home.

Others dressed in uniforms lovingly sewn by female relatives or other women anxious to help the war effort. Early in the war, state militias formed the backbone of the Southern fighting forces and governors were given the right to choose the style and colors of uniforms for their troops. And most governors left the matter up to the men themselves. Predictably, the men chose a wide variety of fighting togs that had some units showing up dressed gaudily as Zouaves, French chasseurs, Scottish highlanders, or simple frontiersmen in buckskin or butternut brown. As the conflict wore on, shortages intensified and it was especially difficult for soldiers to get shoes and woolen coats and blankets for cold weather. In desperation, many ill-clothed fighting men resorted to stripping their fallen comrades or the enemy of their clothes and equipment.

Union

In 1860 just before South Carolina seceded, the nation was composed of 34 states and eight territories. During the war West Virginia and Nevada joined the Union as free states, swelling the number lined up against the South to 25 states. After secession by the 11 Southern states, the North controlled almost three-fourths of the land that made up the previous United States of America. Based on the national census of 1860, the North had a population of nearly 22 million, including 4 million men of fighting age. With nearly 100,000 factories, the North also had a huge advantage in industrial capacity and other economic advantages, including 81 percent of the nation's bank deposits and $56 million in gold. Union states were: California, Connecticut, Illinois, Indiana, Iowa, Kansas, Maine, Massachusetts, Michigan, Minnesota, Nevada, New Hampshire, New Jersey, New York, Ohio, Oregon, Pennsylvania, Rhode Island, Vermont, West Virginia, and Wisconsin. Slavery was legal in the border states of Kentucky, Maryland, Missouri, and Delaware, but the proportion of slaves to free whites was only about half that of states that had already seceded. Although the border states eventually remained with the Union, residents were sharply divided in their loyalties and contributed manpower and other resources to both sides. (See: Border States; Confederate States of America; and Conscription, Union.)

United Confederate Veterans

Established in 1889, this association's first commanding general was Andrew B. Gordon, who served until 1904. The UCV was disbanded in the mid-1940s. (See: Grand Army of the Republic.)

Utoy Creek, Battle of

Efforts to flank the Confederate lines and sever the Macon & Western Railroad during the Siege of Atlanta led to a series of sharp clashes on August 5–7, 1864, that ended in bloody Union defeats. While two of Union general William Sherman's generals bickered with each other, Confederate general William S. Hardee extended his defensive lines and built strong entrenchments on a ridge near Utoy Creek. On August 5 the Yankees launched an attack against the famous Orphan Brigade, which was thrown back with heavy Union losses. On August 6 a second attack was repulsed with even heavier losses. On May 7 the Federals finally broke off the fight, after suffering several hundred casualties. The Confederates lost a few dozen men.

V

Vallandigham, Clement

A former member of the Ohio State House of Representatives, elected to Congress in 1858, Vallandigham was a Northerner who strongly supported states' rights and slavery. When the Civil War began, he quickly emerged as a leading critic of President Lincoln and became a cofounder of the Peace Democrats—the Copperheads. After a defeat for reelection in 1862, he made a series of inflammatory speeches against Lincoln that led to his arrest and conviction for treason by a military commission. The testy Ohio lawyer was imprisoned, but Lincoln soon commuted his sentence and banished him to behind Confederate Army front lines. Vallandigham returned to Ohio after the war and on June 17, 1871, accidentally shot himself to death while handling a pistol that was an exhibit in a murder trial.

Van Dorn, Colonel Earl, CS

When Van Dorn assumed command in Texas he reneged on Confederate promises to allow Federal troops who surrendered in February 1861 to march unmolested out of the state carrying their arms and equipment. Uncomfortable with the idea of 1,600 armed Yankees moving through the state, he issued an order on April 11 declaring them to be prisoners of war. Yankee officers were paroled, and the enlisted men went to prison camps. A few weeks after issuing the order, Van Dorn was promoted to the rank of general in the Confederate Army.

Van Lew, Elizabeth "Crazy Bet"

Crazy Bet was fervently and openly abolitionist and crazy like a fox. She used her perceived eccentricity to allay the suspicions of Richmond neighbors when she railed against slavery and the Confederacy, while spying for the Union. They thought her ranting was merely a sign of her insanity. Bet was a frequent visitor to Union inmates at Libby Prison, where she gathered information on Confederate strength and troop movements and helped organize escapes. She even infiltrated Confederate president Jefferson Davis's home by arranging for one of her former servants to get a job on the household staff. Bet died in 1900, honored in the North and hated in the South.

Velasquez, Loreta Janeta

An adventuress whose exciting life reads more like fiction than reality, this Cuban-born widow of a Confederate soldier left her Louisiana home, disguised herself as a man, and recruited and equipped an infantry unit called the Arkansas Grays. Using the alias Harry Buford, she fought at First Bull Run, in Kentucky, and in Tennessee and was wounded twice and cited for gallantry before she was exposed as a woman and arrested as a suspected Union spy while serving in Richmond. Convincing authorities of her loyalty to the South, she then worked as a real spy—against the North.

Venereal Disease

Hordes of prostitutes who serviced Civil War soldiers spread venereal disease, and in 1861 doctors reported that one in every twelve Billy Yanks was infected with one or more of the ailments. Some regiments were hit harder than others, and on the Southern side the 10th Alabama reported 68 cases of venereal disease in a single month while stationed in Richmond.

Veteran Reserve Corps

Even the Union struggled under the crushing manpower demands of the war, and in 1863 it created the VRC so men who were hospitalized or disabled could serve in one of two special battalions that supported their more able brothers in the front lines. One battalion was composed of men who could still use weapons, and the other was designated for men who had lost an arm or a leg.

Vicksburg, Battle of

The Confederacy was already reeling from Lee's demoralizing defeat at Gettysburg on July 3, 1863, when the heavily fortified city of Vicksburg on the Mississippi River surrendered to General Ulysses S. Grant the next day. The victory came after Grant's earlier failure in November and December 1862 to take the critically located Mississippi fortress located on a high bluff overlooking a bend in the river. With the loss of Vicksburg, the Union had control of the Mississippi and the Confederacy was cut in half. Texas, Arkansas, Missouri, and most of Louisiana were isolated from the rest of the South and unable to contribute critical supplies or troops to Richmond. Grant had several options in developing his strategy for capturing the city, almost all bad. After careful consideration, he settled on a bold plan to move his army south on the west bank of the river just below the city. A flotilla of ships under the command of Admiral David Dixon Porter would then link up with Grant and ferry the Yankee troops to the opposite bank. Then he could march his men over dry land and attack the city from the rear. The plan was a dangerous one that not only required Grant to split his forces and temporarily cut himself off from his supply lines but also required Porter's transports and gunboats to race right past the strongly defended fort's batteries without winding up on the muddy bottom of the river. Porter's flotilla made its gallant run on the night of April 16, with the loss of only one transport. Grant then had General William T. Sherman with 10,000 men high on the bluffs overlooking the city, 1,700 men led by Colonel Benjamin Grierson rampaging through central Mississippi destroying rail centers and supply depots, and his own men in place for the main assault. Confederate commander Lieutenant General John Clifford

Pemberton led a defending force of 40,000 men, compared to the 34,000 assembled by Grant and Sherman. But in trying to deal with Grant's complicated attack plan, Pemberton spread his forces around so thin in an effort to defend everything and everywhere that the Yankees attacked them piecemeal and inflicted heavy casualties. Confederate general Joseph E. Johnston then arrived with a small force of 5,000 men to defend Jackson, Mississippi, which was also under attack. Johnston gave up Jackson without a fight and ordered Pemberton to move out of Vicksburg and attack. After a fierce clash at Champion's Hill, the Yankees drove him back into the city. Grant launched two major attacks against the fortress that were both driven back, then settled down to a siege. Sherman headed east with 50,000 men to keep an eye on Johnston, whose army had been reinforced to 35,000 men. As Grant's artillery and the navy ships kept up a steady bombardment against the fortress, Confederate food supplies dwindled, sickness began to spread, and civilians fled to dugouts and caves. On July 1 Johnston made a valiant effort to smash through Sherman's defenses and break the siege but was beaten back. Two days later, on July 3, Pemberton asked Grant for surrender terms. Grant responded as he always did with a firm, impossible to misunderstand: "Unconditional surrender." Pemberton surrendered the city on the Fourth of July.

Virginia, CSS
See *Merrimac,* CSS.

Virginia Military Institute
The Confederacy had so few fighting men left when Union major general Franz Sigel roared down the Shenandoah Valley at the head of a huge army that teenage cadets at VMI were called on for help. On Sunday, May 15, 1864, the 247 boys were in the front line at New Market when the Confederate's right collapsed, and the cadets charged a Federal battery. Fighting hand to hand, they followed their white-and-gold flag and took the battery, turning the tide of battle. Ten cadets

were killed and 47 wounded in less than one hour of heavy fighting. Lieutenant Colonel Scott Shipp, a professor who taught the 15- to 17-year-olds at VMI, led them in the battle. (See: Four Apostles, the.)

Vivandiere

Women who acted as a form of sutler, peddling provisions, vivandiere accompanied soldiers into battle, carrying small kegs of water or rum for the wounded on shoulder straps. Some vivandiere performed feats of heroism, and one of the most famous was "French Mary," who was wounded while braving 13 battles. Often the wives of soldiers, vivandiere dressed in distinctive costumes of a quasi-military type modeled on the French pattern, with a short military-type jacket and a short skirt over pantaloons.

Volunteers

Ironically, some generals were more impressed with the fighting mettle of the raw farm boys, small shopkeepers, and freshly arrived immigrants under their command than the seasoned professional soldiers. After commanding a division at the Battle of Chickamauga, Union general Thomas J. Wood declared, "The regulars are too sharp. They know when they are whipped, but the volunteers don't. They will fight as long as they can pull a trigger."

Von Borcke, Major Heros Johann August, CS

An aristocratic Prussian who served with J. E. B. Stuart's cavalry, Von Borcke was a giant who weighed 250 pounds, was six feet, four inches tall, and spoke heavily accented English. But he was a member of the Southern cavalry leader's inner circle and one of his most trusted officers. Von Borcke and Stuart were conferring with other officers just west of Middleburg during the Gettysburg Campaign on June 19, 1863, when the big Prussian was shot in the back of the neck by a Union sniper. The bullet severed his windpipe and lodged in a lung, but he miraculously survived even though the injury put him out of the war permanently. In Europe the awesome Prussian had served with the 2d Brandenburg Dragoons.

Von Fritsch, Captain Baron Frederick, U.S.

A native of Weimar, Germany, von Fritsch was a soldier of fortune who served in the Saxton cavalry and in Mexico with forces opposing the French. He obtained a commission in the Union Army through the influence of Colonel Bourry d'Ivernois, of the 68th New York Infantry. Von Fritsch served with the 68th under Colonel Leopold von Gilsa.

Vote, Soldier

Soldiers were allowed to vote in the field for the first time during the Civil War, but a few states still required them to travel home to cast ballots. During Indiana's off-year state election of 1863, President Lincoln was so concerned about taking advantage of an anticipated big soldier vote for politicians who favored seeing the war through to a successful conclusion that he wrote General Sherman and asked him to furlough all Hoosiers who could be spared by his command. Somehow, a large number of soldiers from Vermont accompanied their Hoosier buddies on furlough and voted in the Indiana elections.

W

Wachusett, USS

This Federal steam sloop was moored in the neutral harbor at Bahia, Brazil, when the local U.S. consul convinced the commander to ignore international law and sink the Confederate raider the CSS *Florida,* which was anchored nearby. On October 7, 1864, the *Wachusett* suddenly loomed out of the pitch-darkness of the night and rammed the *Florida.* The Confederate raider's mizzenmast was snapped and the starboard bulwarks crushed, but it remained afloat, so the *Wachusett*'s commander, Napoleon Collins, ordered his crew to board it and seize the crew. Collins sailed his prize to Hampton Roads, Virginia, amid a storm of international protests in Brazil and in Europe. The United States had apologized and diplomats were arranging for the *Florida*'s return to Brazil when the ship collided with a U.S. Army transport and sank. (See: *Florida,* CSS.)

Waddell, Captain James Iredell, CSN

A few days before being convinced that the Civil War was indeed over, the captain of the Confederate raider CSS *Shenandoah* hatched a wild scheme to sail to San Francisco and hold the city hostage under the ship's powerful guns. Although Waddell called off his plan to move on San Francisco after British sailors convinced him that hostilities had ceased, he refused to surrender to Union authorities because he was afraid he would be hanged for piracy. That wasn't an illogical fear, because Waddell had captured or sunk 38 Union merchantmen and whalers, including several that were attacked

after the war was over. And Confederate captain Raphael
Semmes had been arrested and indicted for piracy after
ravaging Union shipping with the commerce raider CSS
Alabama. So Waddell sailed 17,000 miles to Liverpool and
surrendered to British authorities. (See: Semmes, Captain
Raphael, CSN; and *Shenandoah,* CSS.)

Waddill, Joanna Fox

Born in Pennsylvania but reared in Mississippi, Joanna Fox
was 22 when a Yankee fleet captured Natchez while on its
way upriver to attack Vicksburg. This adopted daughter of
the South hid a Confederate flag under her petticoat to prevent its capture by the Yankees. Then she volunteered for
hospital service. While tending to sick and injured Mississippi Rebels she met and married George Waddill, who served
with the Pelican Rifles before switching to the healing arts.
(See: Vicksburg, Battle of.)

Wainwright, Commander Jonathan Mayhaw, Jr., USN

In command of the gunboat USS *Harriet Lane* at the Battle
of Galveston, Wainwright was wounded, then killed with a
fatal shot in the head during ferocious hand-to-hand fighting.
(See: Galveston, Battle of.)

Walker, Mary

An 1855 graduate of Syracuse Medical College, at a time
when it was almost unheard of for a woman to aspire to a career in medicine, this young doctor practiced in Rome, New
York, until the Civil War began and she traveled to Washington to volunteer her services to the Union Army. After working far behind the lines as a volunteer nurse, she was finally
sent to the combat area in September 1863 and a short time
later was appointed by General George Thomas as an assistant surgeon in the Army of the Cumberland. The only woman
in the Union Army, she served at Fredericksburg, Chickamauga, and Atlanta. After capture by the Rebels, she spent four-

months in a Richmond prison, from April to August 1864, before she was released to care for the sick and injured. Dr. Walker later claimed she used the opportunity to spy for the Union. In 1865 she was awarded the Medal of Honor, becoming the only woman who served in the Civil War to be so honored by Congress. After the war she was arrested at least twice for posing as a man, and Congress revoked the medal. It was restored in 1977 by President Jimmy Carter.

Wallace, Major General Lewis "Lew," U.S.

This Mexican War veteran from Indiana fought at Forts Henry and Donelson in Kentucky and at Shiloh, but his battlefield judgment led to his temporary removal from field command. He was put in charge of organizing defenses at Cincinnati when Confederate major general Edmund Kirby Smith launched an invasion of Kentucky. Wallace returned to field command and fought at Monocacy and in the Shenandoah Valley Campaign of 1864 but was most notable during the Civil War for his service on military tribunals. He presided at the convictions and pronouncing of death sentences of conspirators in the Lincoln assassination and of Captain Heinrich Wirz, commandant of the Confederate's notorious Andersonville Prison camp. After the war, Wallace served as governor of New Mexico and minister to Turkey, but he is best known as the author of the novel *Ben-Hur: A Tale of the Christ.* (See: Wirz, Captain Heinrich "Henry," CS.)

Ward, Captain Minott

The captain of the former blockade runner SS *General Lyon,* Ward complained about the poor condition of his boilers and overloaded ship before the vessel burned and sank on April 2, 1865, causing the deaths of some 600 passengers. Ward panicked after the ship caught fire in a fierce storm, and leaped into the first lifeboat but drowned when it was struck by the *Lyon*'s propeller. (See: *General Lyon,* SS; and *General Sedgwick,* SS.)

Washington, Captain George, CS

A Caddo Indian chief, Washington led an Indian unit that fought for the Confederacy. Some Indians on both sides rode to war wearing war paint and armed only with bows and arrows, tomahawks, or war clubs.

Washington Light Infantry

Young men from the richest and most aristocratic families in and around Charleston, South Carolina, volunteered for the infantry regiment. Armed with Mississippi rifles, many of the privates and officers marched off to war accompanied by personal servants, picnic hampers, and other comforts of home.

Watie, Brigadier General Stand, CS

The only American Indian to achieve the rank of general while fighting with the Confederacy, Stand Watie is best remembered for his performance as a colonel with the 1st Cherokee Mounted Rifles, CSA. Born near Calhoun, Georgia, Watie—whose Indian name was De-ga-do-ga—joined with other slave-owning Cherokee aristocrats to sign a treaty with Washington giving up all claims to their land in the East in return for land west of the Mississippi. Cherokee opponents of the move assassinated other members of the Watie faction after the tribe reached the Indian territory, but he escaped, sided with the Confederacy, and was commissioned as a colonel. Watie and his irregulars ambushed trains and Yankee cavalry, burned a Federal steamboat, battled Cherokee and other Indians loyal to the Union, and fought beside Confederate allies in Arkansas with Major General Earl Van Dorn's victorious 16,000-man army in the Battle of Pea Ridge. On June 23, 1865, more than two months after Lee's capitulation at Appomattox, Watie became the last Confederate general to surrender his troops. (See: 1st Cherokee Mounted Rifles; Indian Allies of the Confederacy; and Van Dorn, Colonel Earl, CS.)

Waynesboro, Battle of

The sharp clash on March 2, 1865, between forces led by Southern general Jubal Early and the North's general Philip Sheridan led to a Union victory that ended major military action in Virginia's Shenandoah Valley.

Wedge Tents

The most common portable shelters used by Union soldiers, wedge tents were simple six-foot pieces of canvas draped over horizontal poles and staked down at the sides. The same design also saw limited use by the South.

Weitzel, Major General Godfrey, U.S.

After leading troops into the Confederate capital on April 3, 1865, Weitzel sent off a wire to Washington announcing: "We entered Richmond at 8 o'clock this morning." Earlier in the war the West Point–educated engineer worked on fortifications and led troops as a field commander. He also served under General Benjamin Butler as the military commander of New Orleans during the Union occupation.

Wells, Gideon

Although Wells was a journalist and Connecticut politician with no experience with naval matters, he was picked by the president for the job of secretary of the navy because Lincoln wanted New England represented in his cabinet. Wells was intelligent and energetic and proved a surprisingly good choice. He oversaw the Union blockade of Southern ports and pressed for the construction of ironclad ships. Wells continued in the post until 1869.

West Point Foundry

Robert Parrott turned out thousands of powerful rifled cannon, reinforced with wrought-iron coils, for Union artillerists at the Northern foundry. The 300-pound cannon, using a 16-pound powder charge, could fire a ball nearly five miles. The foundry was producing several classes of Parrott guns at the beginning of the war: 10-, 20-, 30-, 60-, 100-, and 200-pounders. (See: Parrott Guns.)

West Virginia

West Virginia was admitted to the Union as a state on June 20, 1863, exactly two years after seceding from Virginia. While Virginia's slaveholding aristocracy was voting overwhelmingly for secession, the mountainous western counties were turning a firm thumbs-down on the referendum. When Virginia voted to join the other secessionist states, despite the disapproval of the residents of the farming and mining area west of the Alleghenies, residents of an area now covering 55 counties gathered at a convention in Wheeling and established their own state. The new pro-Union state was eagerly accepted by the Lincoln administration, and senators and congressmen were elected from West Virginia to fill seats that were vacated when Virginia seceded. (See: Kanawha.)

Wheat's Tiger Rifles

One of the most famous Zouave regiments, Major Roberdeau "Rob" Wheat's Tiger Rifles was formed from brawling, hard-drinking riverboatmen, longshoremen, and laborers recruited for the Confederacy from the New Orleans waterfront. The Tigers once charged the 11th New York Infantry with bowie knives and captured two artillery pieces. (See: Zouaves.)

Wheeler, Major General "Fighting Joe," CS

It wasn't only the Union that had a prominent general known as "Fighting Joe" during the Civil War. The South had its own, and "Fighting Joe" Wheeler commanded Confederate troops in 127 battles and more than 500 skirmishes. He didn't get along with Nathan Bedford Forrest, and the two Confederate cavalry officers had a serious falling-out during the unsuccessful Southern effort to save Fort Donelson from capture by Union forces. Forrest was so incensed by their differences that he swore he would never serve under Wheeler again. Despite Forrest's enmity, "Fighting Joe" played a valiant and unique role in America's wars. When the West Pointer was promoted to major general of volunteers during the Spanish-American War, he became the only former Rebel to attain the same rank in the U.S. Army as he held during the conflict between the states. Wheeler also served in the Far East as a brigadier general during the Philippine Insurrection. (See: Hooker, Major General Joseph "Fighting Joe," U.S.; and Horses and Mules.)

White Oak Swamp, Battle of
General Thomas "Stonewall" Jackson was hurrying to reinforce Confederates at the Battle of Glendale during the Peninsular Campaign when his divisions were attacked by the retreating Union's rear guard under the command of Major General William Franklin in the boggy marshes of White Oak Swamp. The June 30, 1862, clash in Henrico County, Virginia, quickly developed into an artillery duel. Total casualties in the battle numbered about 500 men, and there was no clear-cut winner. Many historians consider the artillery duel at White Oak Swamp part of the Battle of Glendale.

White's Comanches
Officially known as the 35th Virginia Cavalry, this Confederate battalion was initially recruited for border service in Virginia and Maryland and led by Elijah V. "Lige" White. There is no evidence that any of the volunteers, who fought throughout the war in many battles far removed from the Maryland-Virginia border as part of the Laurel Brigade, were Comanche or had ever seen one.

Whitman, Walt
This famous American poet worked as a volunteer dressing wounds and visiting with injured Federal troops in and around Washington, D.C.

Whitworth Rifles
These artillery pieces were widely used by the Confederates. Manufactured in Manchester, England, and smuggled through the Union blockade, the 12-pounders featured a hexagonal

bore. The unique rifling system allowed a faster spin on the projectile, providing greater accuracy. Most were breech-loaders, another artillery innovation observed during the war.

Widow Blakely, the

This 7.5-inch rifle became one of the most widely traveled of the Civil War's artillery pieces after the conflict was ended. It acquired its unusual nickname because it was the only gun with the Confederate batteries at Vicksburg that had been designed by British captain Theophilus A. Blakely. But its main claim to fame occurred after the war when it was transported to West Point, where it was mistakenly identified as the famous Confederate cannon Whistling Dick. When the error was discovered, the Widow Blakely was returned to its rightful home, on the bluffs at Vicksburg.

Wig-Wag Signaling

Edward Porter Alexander and Albert J. Meyer teamed up when they were young U.S. Army signal officers in the 1850s to develop a communication system designed to transmit military messages by waving flags during the day and torches at night. When the Civil War broke out, Alexander resigned his commission to join the Confederate Army and Meyer remained with the Union. (See: Alexander, Brigadier General Edward Porter, CS; and Signal Corps, U.S.)

Wilcox, Major General Admus Marcellus, CS

A West Point graduate, this native North Carolinian fought in the Mexican War and served at frontier posts before joining the Confederacy in July 1861. Named a brigadier general in October, he fought at Seven Pines, in the Seven Days Battles, and at Second Bull Run, Fredericksburg, Chancellorsville, Salem Church, the Wilderness, and Spotsylvania and took part in Pickett's Charge at Gettysburg. Wilcox ended the war as a major general and after returning to civilian life became chief of the railroad division of the U.S. Government Land Office.

Wilderness, Battle of the

The Battle of Chancellorsville, which was fought out in the same dense forests and nasty thickets of scrub brush, had already proven that the Wilderness was a nasty place for a fight, but that's exactly where Union soldiers and Confederates met on May 5–7, 1864, in one of the most hellish clashes of the war. The fight in Virginia's Rapidan basin was the first confrontation between Ulysses S. Grant and Robert E. Lee and the beginning of a bloody 40-day campaign. Newly appointed as the Union's general in chief, Grant hoped to stage a final brutal battle between General George G. Meade's Army of the Potomac and Lee's Army of Northern Virginia that would destroy the Confederacy's will and ability to continue the war. When the Union forces crossed the Rapidan River at Germanna's Ford they planned to continue south through the Wilderness and flank Lee's army, confronting the Rebels near Chancellorsville, where the Confederacy had won its biggest victory almost exactly a year earlier. But Lee had other plans for the approaching battle. With his 60,000-man army outnumbered nearly two to one by Meade's 115,000-man force, Lee planned to even the odds a bit by using the Wilderness to his advantage. Grant's forces were still trying to negotiate the thick undergrowth with supply wagons and artillery while they attempted to ignore the bleached bones of men who had fallen in the earlier battle when Lee struck before they could emerge from the forest and reach clearer ground that would favor the Union's superior numbers. The two corps then available to Lee, quickly reinforced by another corps led by General James Longstreet, smashed into the Union forces in what bitter Bluecoats later described as "bushwhacking on a grand scale." The first day of fighting was a huge brawl. Soldiers could hardly see who they were fighting as fires were ignited by the burning powder of small arms and smoke obscured their vision. Officers couldn't stay in close contact with their men, individual soldiers and entire units were separated from their commands, orders were lost and never delivered, and artillery was useless. Men on both sides were killed by friendly fire as nervous soldiers shot at anything that moved. The fighting deteriorated into individual firefights with rifle and musket, and the small blazes set here and there mushroomed into a full-fledged forest fire that roasted the injured and dead where they fell. By nightfall Grant had weakened Lee's right flank, and at dawn the next day Grant opened an assault on the Confederate center. The Bluecoats pushed the enemy back and had almost reached Lee's field headquarters when Longstreet and others arrived in the nick of time with reinforcements. General Lee grabbed a battle flag from one of Longstreet's Texas brigades and rushed to the front of the line to lead a charge. United to a man, the Confederates refused to allow him to take such a risk, shouting, "General Lee to the rear!" Longstreet quickly convinced Lee to listen to the men, then joined Brigadier General John Gregg, in command of Hood's Texas Brigade, to lead the counterattack. The Confederates were pushing back the Federals when Longstreet was accidentally shot and wounded by one of his own men, breaking the momentum. By nightfall the Federals had regained almost all the lost ground, but the two days of battle had cost the Union a ghastly toll of 17,500 casualties, more than twice the 7,750 Confederates who fell or were taken prisoner. After the terrible bloodletting of the first two days, fighting the next morning and afternoon was confined to light skirmishes. Although the Confederates pronounced the confrontation to have been a victory for the South, most military historians marked it up as a tactical draw. And Grant was still in a fighting mood. Spotsylvania Court House was just down the road and a day away. (See: Spotsylvania, Battle of.)

Williams, Walter Washington, CS

Williams was recognized by the U.S. government as the last living veteran of the war from either side when he died at the age of 113 in Franklin, Texas, on December 19, 1959. But subsequent research of census records and other documents indicated that he would have been only 5 years old when he reputedly enlisted. John Sallings, another apparently false claimant to being the oldest living Confederate veteran when he died on March 19, 1959, in Virginia, would have been only 2 years old when he reputedly marched off to fight in the Great Rebellion. Confederate records were often nonexistent, incomplete, or destroyed during the war, so it is more difficult for historians to document their service than that of Union soldiers. (See: Crump, Private Pleasant Riggs, CS; and Woolson, Private Albert H., U.S.)

Wilson, Major Jurgen, U.S.

A European immigrant, Wilson worked as a Wisconsin store clerk and a sailor shipping out of New Orleans before returning to the Dairy State just in time to enlist in the Scandinavian Regiment. Appointed second lieutenant of Company B, Wilson participated in the raid on Union City, Tenneessee, and campaigned through Tennessee, Mississippi, and Alabama before being promoted to full lieutenant. He led Company H at the Battle of Chaplin Hills and was wounded at the Battle of Murfreesboro. Wilson had returned to duty and been promoted to major when he was shot three times while the Scandinavian Regiment was being savaged at the Battle of Chickamauga. After being nursed back to health in Wisconsin, Wilson took temporary command of the regiment and led his troops at the battles of Rocky Face Ridge, Resaca, and Pickett's Mill. Wilson stayed with the regiment after turning over command to Colonel Ole Johnson and by the end of the war had fought in 26 military engagements. (See: Heg, Colonel Hans Christian, U.S.; and Johnson, Colonel Ole C., U.S.)

Wilson's Creek, Battle of

Confederates won control of southwestern Missouri when they scored a victory at the Battle of Wilson's Creek on August 10, 1861. The battle, about 12 miles west of Springfield, pitted Union brigadier general Nathaniel Lyon's Army of the West against Confederate troops led by Brigadier General Ben McCulloch. The Federals suffered 1,235 casualties, including their commander, and the South had 1,095 fighting men put out of action. (See: Lyon, Brigadier General Nathaniel, U.S.)

Winchester, Virginia

More Civil War battles occurred in Virginia than any other state, and much of the action took place around the northern Shenandoah Valley town of Winchester. As armies of the North and South foraged for food and marched or rode up and down the valley chasing each other, Winchester changed hands 76 times.

Winder, Brigadier General John Henry, CS

The first commander at the notorious Andersonville Prison, Winder was previously provost marshal of Richmond. The position was established at the beginning of the war, and as provost marshal Winder was responsible for the defense of Richmond, military discipline in the Confederate capital area, and counterespionage. The West Point graduate and Mexican War veteran was also in charge of captured Bluecoats and other inmates at the Libby and Belle Isle military prisons. When Andersonville was constructed as the Confederacy's main prison for captured Union soldiers, Winder moved to Georgia and became its first commandant. (See: Andersonville Prison.)

Winslow, Rear Admiral John A., USN

Born in Wilmington, North Carolina, Winslow became a midshipman in 1827 and was promoted to lieutenant in 1839 and to commander after being cited for gallantry in Tabasco during the Mexican War. When the Civil War started, he was assigned as executive officer of the Western Gunboat Flotilla, but he was injured in the fall of 1861 while commanding the gunboat *Benton* and spent several months recovering. Shortly after promotion to captain in July 1862, he took command of the sloop-of-war USS *Kearsarge*. For 18 months Captain Winslow and his crew patrolled European waters searching for Confederate raiders, leading to one of the most famous naval battles of the war, between the *Kearsarge* and the CSS *Alabama*. Winslow earned promotion to commodore for his performance sinking the *Alabama*. Five years after the end of the war he was promoted to rear admiral and was assigned as commander of the Pacific Squadron, a job he kept until 1872. Admiral Winslow died in 1873. (See: *Alabama, CSS,* and *Kearsarge, USS, Battle of;* and Semmes, Captain Raphael, CSN.)

Wire Entanglements

Military use of wire entanglements was introduced during the Civil War when three Rebel brigades stormed Union-held Fort Sanders on the night of November 29, 1863, during the Knoxville Campaign. Union general Ambrose Burnside's defenders had stretched telegraph wires through a maze of tree stumps, which slowed the attack, and the Rebels were repulsed with heavy losses after running into an even more formidable barrier, a wide, deep ditch dug around the fort.

Wirz, Captain Heinrich "Henry," CS

A native Swiss who served nine years in various European armies before immigrating to Louisiana, Wirz became one of the most widely hated men in the Confederacy because of his behavior as commandant of the notorious Andersonville Prison. Ironically, the brutal disciplinarian and bully who was later to become known as "the Beast of Andersonville" and "the Andersonville Savage" was a Louisiana physician before joining the Confederate Army. After suffering a disabling injury to his left arm at Seven Pines in 1862 and being left in constant pain, Wirz was assigned to take over the hell-hole at Andersonville. The nasty-tempered commander's brutality and hatred for his charges compounded the built-in miseries already created by lack of space and absence of proper sanitation, food, and supplies at the jam-packed prison camp. (See: Andersonville Prison; Old Capitol Prison; Seven Pines, Battle of; Wallace, Major General Lewis "Lew," U.S.; and Winder, Brigadier General John Henry, CS.)

Women Soldiers

No one is really certain how many women disguised themselves as men and served as soldiers during the Civil War, but estimates place the numbers on both sides as being in the hundreds—and possibly a thousand or more. Women enlisted for adventure, to escape unhappy marriages, to accompany husbands or lovers, and even for the bounty payments available in the North for taking the place of someone else who had been drafted. The secrets of females in blue or gray were most often found out when they were wounded or became ill and submitted to medical care or when their bodies were found on the battlefield. A few became pregnant, and others left after their husbands were killed. (See: Edmonds, Sarah Emma.)

Woolson, Private Albert H., U.S.

The last authenticated survivor of the Civil War, Woolson died in Duluth, Minnesota, on August 2, 1956, at the age of 109. Seventeen on October 4, 1864, when he enlisted for one year, he served the Union Army as a drummer on garrison duty at Chattanooga, Tennessee. Woolson was attached to Battery C, 1st Minnesota Heavy Artillery, and never saw combat. He was mustered out of service on September 27, 1865. There is no question that Woolson was the last Union survivor, but his status as the last living man to have fought on either side is muddied by dubious claims that he was outlived by three Confederates. (See: Crump, Private Pleasant Riggs, CS; Lundy, William, CS; Salling, John, CS; and Williams, Walter Washington, CS.)

Worden, Lieutenant John, USN

Chosen to command the USS *Monitor* because of his excellent seamanship and aggressiveness, Worden was knocked out of action during the battle with the CSS *Merrimac* when a shell struck the pilothouse as he was peering through the eye slits. Worden reeled back, blinded in his left eye and temporarily blinded in his right eye. Half of his face would be black for the rest of his life. As Worden was helped to his

wardroom, Lieutenant S. Dana Greene assumed command.
(See: Hampton Roads, Battle of.)

Wright, Major General Horatio Governeur, U.S.

A former engineering instructor at West Point, Wright was
the engineer in charge of efforts to destroy the Norfolk Navy
Yard in April 1861 before it was taken over by the Confederates. Captured at Norfolk, Wright was quickly exchanged
and served as chief engineer for a division during the First
Battle of Bull Run. Promoted to brigadier general in September, he commanded a brigade at Port Royal, South Carolina,
and in 1862 led a division that was defeated at Secession-
ville. He fought at Gettysburg, Rappahannock Station, Mine
Run, Spotsylvania, the Wilderness, Cedar Creek, and Cold
Harbor and in the Petersburg Campaign and was commissioned a major general on May 12, 1864. After the war he directed the completion of the Washington Monument.

Wyndham, General Sir Percy, U.S.

Although Britain was strongly pro-Confederacy, Wyndham
didn't share those sentiments and volunteered to fight for the
Union. Born aboard ship in the English Channel, Wyndham
was a soldier of fortune who first went to war when he was
15 and fought in the French Revolution, then in the French
navy, and served with the 8th Austrian Lancers and with the
Italian Army before offering his services to the Union.
Named to command the 1st New Jersey Cavalry on February 9, 1862, he was sent to the Shenandoah Valley to help
run down Stonewall Jackson. The Federals caught up with
Jackson near the town of Strasburg and briefly skirmished
with his rear guard, led by Colonel Turner Ashby. But Ashby
and the Englishman weren't through with each other. Wyndham was a courageous, brash warrior who reveled in baiting
the enemy and had boasted that he would capture Jackson,
Ashby, and other members of the Confederate command. So
they decided to capture him and laid an ambush near Port
Republic. When Wyndham realized he had ridden into a trap,

he charged the enemy, but his soldiers scattered under the withering Union fire and he found himself cut off with 63 of his men. Wyndham surrendered, and was exchanged two months later. After fighting at Second Bull Run, he was given command of Major General Franz Sigel's cavalry and his brigade was stationed at Fairfax Court House. Wyndham soon reverted to his old tricks and let it be known that he considered Confederate partisan raider John Singleton Mosby to be nothing but a horse thief. Mosby decided to repeat the earlier feat by Jackson and Ashby and capture the flamboyant braggart. Wyndham was at a party in nearby Washington the night Mosby led a postmidnight raid into Fairfax, and escaped possible capture or death. Mosby captured another Union general in Wyndham's place. Undeterred by the close call, Wyndham led a raid into Virginia, destroying bridges, supplies, and canal boats and capturing the city of Columbia. On June 9, 1863, he led his brigade in the Battle of Brandy Station, where he was shot in the leg. Sent to Washington to recuperate, he was placed in command of cavalry defending the capital. Wyndham then fought at Gettysburg before returning again to Washington, where he was named to command the cavalry depot. After being mustered out of the Union Army as a brigadier general at the end of the war, Wyndham returned to Italy to join Giuseppe Garibaldi's staff. Later Wyndham traveled to India, then to Burma, where he was killed when a hot air balloon he was flying burst and he plunged 300 feet into a lake. (See: Ashby, Brigadier General Turner, CS; and Mosby, Colonel John Singleton, CS.)

Y

Yancey, William I.
Chosen to lead the first diplomatic mission to seek European recognition for the Confederacy, Yancey set sail on the eve of the attack on Fort Sumter. He secured meetings with Britain's Lord John Russell, secretary of state for foreign affairs, and with France's Napoléon III in Paris. Although the European powers did not agree to extend official recognition to the Confederacy, they issued a proclamation of neutrality, which granted the South the rights of a belligerent.

Yellow Tavern, Battle of
The Army of the Potomac and the Army of Northern Virginia were clawing at each other at Spotsylvania Court House when cavalry led by the South's major general Jeb Stuart and Union major general Philip H. Sheridan clashed at Yellow Tavern on May 11, 1864. Sheridan was leading his cavalry on a raid toward Richmond, ripping up Southern road, rails, and communications, when the two forces met. The Confederates put up a fierce fight but were outnumbered three to one, and before they were routed their commander was fatally wounded with a single shot from a .44-caliber pistol fired by a dismounted Union soldier during a Confederate charge. Before Stuart was taken away to Richmond, where he died the next day, he turned over command to General Fitz Lee. The horse-drawn ambulance was barely under way when Stuart spotted some Southern troopers leaving the field and shouted to them to return to the fight and do their duty.

Estimated total casualties on both sides were about 800 men. The Union not only won the skirmish but also deprived the South of one of its most gifted military leaders. (See: Sheridan, General Philip Henry, U.S.; and Stuart, Major General James Ewell Brown "Jeb," CS.)

Young, Major General Pierce Manning Butler, CS

Young resigned from West Point three months before graduation to fight for the Confederacy. He was commissioned a lieutenant of the Georgia Militia but quickly transferred to the Confederate Army. After a few weeks in Pensacola, Florida, he was sent to Richmond, where he became adjutant of Cobb's Legion, then was promoted to major in the force's cavalry. Following a brief illness, he returned to combat duty with Brigadier General Wade Hampton's cavalry brigade. While fighting in Maryland in 1862 Young was wounded twice, once at Burkittsville and a second time near Middletown, where he suffered a serious chest injury. Quickly back in the saddle, he fought bravely at the Battle of Brandy Station and in the Hunterstown, Pennsylvania, area during the Gettysburg Campaign. Young was wounded for the third time during action south of the Rappahannock River in northeastern Virginia, and after recovery he was promoted to brigadier general. In 1864 while fighting at Ashland, Virginia, he was wounded for the fourth time. After returning to duty Young participated in the Hampton-Rosser Cattle Raid and two months later traveled to Georgia to obtain remounts, recruit troops, and join in the defense of Augusta and Savannah. At the end of the war, Young was a major general and division leader, serving with Hampton in the Carolinas Campaign. After the war Young served four years in Congress and was consul general at St. Petersburg, Russia, and U.S. minister to Guatemala and the Honduras.

Young Napoléon

A nickname used early in the war for the Union's major general George Brinton McClellan. He was also sometimes called Little Mac. (See: McClellan, Major General George Brinton, U.S.)

Z

Zigler's Grove

The copse of trees located at the extreme right of General Meade's lines on Cemetery Ridge at Gettysburg.

Zollicoffer, Brigadier General Felix Kirk, CS

After mistakenly riding into Federal lines during the Battle of Fishing Creek, Zollicoffer was fatally shot when he discovered his mistake and attempted to escape. Commander of one of two brigades under Brigadier General George B. Crittenden, Zollicoffer launched a dawn attack on a large encampment of Federals at Mill Springs, Kentucky, on January 19, 1862, during a blinding rainstorm. After leading an attack with the 19th Tennessee that was driving the enemy back, Zollicoffer mistakenly thought part of his command was firing on their own men. But when he rode through the rain to give a cease-fire command he realized he was surrounded by the enemy. He was wheeling his mount around when he was shot to death by Colonel Speed S. Fry of the 4th Kentucky (U.S.), who Zollicoffer had mistakenly thought was his own officer. (See: Crittenden, Major General George B., CS.)

Zouave, USS

This Federal gunboat was the first to spot and fire on the CSS *Merrimac* (*Virginia*) when the Confederate ironclad sailed down the Elizabeth River into Chesapeake Bay on May 8, 1862, and launched an attack on wooden blockaders. The uneven battle against the Union blockaders led early the next day to the historic confrontation between the *Merrimac* and the USS *Monitor* just off Hampton Roads, Virginia. (See: Hampton Roads, Battle of; *Merrimac,* CSS; and *Monitor, USS.*)

Zouaves

These volunteer regiments on both sides of the conflict were conspicuous for uniforms inspired by the military dress of the original Zouaves in French colonial Algeria. The Zouave look was most apparent early in the war and included various color combinations. The uniform usually consisted of a turban or fez with tassel, baggy pants, leggings, and a short open jacket. Some of the most famous of these regiments were Duryee's Zouaves, Hawkins's Zouaves, Collis's Zouaves, and the 73d New York "Fire" Zouaves made up of New York City firemen. (See: Wheat's Tiger Rifles.)

Civil War Time Line

1860

November 6   Republican Abraham Lincoln is elected president of the United States.

December 20   South Carolina votes at a state secession convention to secede.

December 27   The Federal arsenals in Charleston and Fort Moultrie in Charleston Bay are seized by South Carolina troops.

1861

January   Alabama, Florida, Georgia, Louisiana, and Mississippi secede.

January 29   Kansas is admitted to the Union as a free state.

February 4   The Confederate States of America (CSA) is formed as a provisional government by the six breakaway states.

February 9   The Provisional Congress selects Jefferson Davis as president and Alexander Stephens as vice president of the CSA.

February 23   Texas secedes.

March 4   Abraham Lincoln takes the oath of office as the 16th president of the United States.

March 16   A Constitution is adopted by the Confederate congress. It is similar to the U. S. Constitution, except that it prohibits any law that interferes with slavery.

April 12   The bombardment of Fort Sumter in Charleston is opened by South Carolina troops.

April 13   U. S. Army major Robert Anderson surrenders Fort Sumter.

April 15   President Lincoln declares a state of insurrection and calls for 75,000 volunteers to serve for three months.

April 17 Virginia secedes from the Union.

April 19 Union volunteers are attacked by Southern sympathizers while marching through Baltimore on their way to defend Washington, D.C. On the same day as the Baltimore Riot, Lincoln orders a blockade of Southern ports.

May 6 Arkansas and Tennessee join the Confederacy.

May 13 Great Britain announces its neutrality in America's fratricidal conflict.

May 20 North Carolina secedes and becomes the eleventh and final state to join the Confederacy.

May 29 With the arrival of Jefferson Davis, Richmond becomes the capital of the Confederacy. The Old Dominion city replaced Montgomery, Alabama, which was the provisional capital.

July 21 The first major battle of the war is fought at Manassas, Virginia. Known in the North as the First Battle of Bull Run, the fight ends with a Union defeat.

July 27 Union general George B. McClellan becomes commander of the Army of the Potomac, replacing General Irvin McDowell.

October 21 The Union suffers another stunning defeat at the Battle of Ball's Bluff.

November 1 Lincoln accepts the resignation of aging general in chief Winfield Scott. General McClellan becomes the new general in chief.

November 8 A diplomatic crisis threatens to bring Great Britain into the war on the side of the South when Confederate agents are removed from the British ship, *Trent,* by Union forces. The incident is known as the Trent Affair.

1862

January 11 Simon Cameron is replaced as Lincoln's secretary of war by Edwin Stanton.

February 16 The Confederate garrison at Fort Donelson on the Tennessee River is forced to surrender to Union general Ulysses S. Grant.

February 25 Nashville, Tennessee, is occupied by Union troops.

March 9 The Battle of Hampton Roads is fought between the Union's USS *Monitor* and the Confederate's CSS *Virginia* (*Merrimac*). The historic duel is the first battle in naval history to occur between two ironclad ships, and ends in a draw.

March 11 Fed up with McClellan's reluctance to engage the enemy,

Lincoln demotes him from general in chief to commander of the Army of the Potomac.

April 4   A Union advance on Yorktown with the largest, best-equipped army ever assembled marks the beginning of the Peninsular Campaign.

April 6–7   Led by General Grant, the Union scores a huge victory at the two-day Battle of Shiloh, leading to a Confederate withdrawal from Pittsburg Landing, Tennessee.

April 7   Island Number 10, a Confederate fortress on the Mississippi River, falls to a combined Union force of army and navy. The Confederate loss leaves the river under Union control all the way from the island to Memphis.

April 10   Slavery is abolished in Washington, D.C.

April 25   New Orleans is surrendered to an overwhelming force led by Flag Officer David Farragut.

May 4   The Siege of Yorktown near the Southern end of the Virginia Peninsula ends when the city is evacuated by Southern troops.

May 5   Williamsburg, just across the peninsula from Yorktown and up the James River, also falls to the Union troops.

May 12   Natchez, Mississippi, surrenders to a strong force of Union gunboats led by Flag Officer Farragut.

May 31   General Joseph E. Johnston, commander of the Confederate forces in Virginia, is seriously wounded at the Battle of Seven Pines on the Peninsula.

June 1   Robert E. Lee replaces Johnston. He reforms his fighting force and names it the Army of Northern Virginia.

June 6   Memphis, Tennessee, falls to the Union.

June 25–July 2   The Seven Days Battles lead to the withdrawal of Union forces from the Virginia Peninsula and end the immediate threat to Richmond.

July 11   Henry Halleck is named general in chief by President Lincoln.

August 28–30   The Union suffers a crushing defeat in the Second Battle of Bull Run.

September 17   The bloodiest single day of the war occurs when the North and South fight to a draw at the Battle of Antietam. Although there is no clear winner of the Maryland scrap, Lee is forced to abandon his plans for an invasion of the North.

October 8   General Don Carlos Buell leads Union forces to a victory over Confederates led by General Braxton Bragg at the Battle of Perryville. The victory keeps the border state of Kentucky firmly in the Union.

November 5   After failing to pursue Lee's army from the battlefield at

Antietam, McClellan is replaced by General Ambrose Burnside as commander of the Army of the Potomac.

December 13 The Union is soundly defeated at the Battle of Fredericksburg in Virginia.

December 31 The Battle of Murfreesboro (Stones River) begins in Tennessee.

1863

January 1 President Lincoln issues the Emancipation Proclamation.

January 2 The Battle of Murfreesboro ends with capture of the vital rail junction by the Federals.

January 25 Burnside is replaced by General Joseph Hooker as commander of the Army of the Potomac.

March 3 The first Conscription Act is signed by President Lincoln.

May 1–4 A smashing Confederate victory at the Battle of Chancellorsville in Virginia is diminished by the death of General Thomas "Stonewall" Jackson.

May 22 The lengthy siege of Vicksburg begins after General Grant launches an attack on the heavily fortified city and Confederate fortress overlooking the Mississippi River.

June 22 West Virginia is admitted to the Union as a free state, after several Virginia counties sympathetic to the North seceded from the Old Dominion.

June 27 General Joseph Hooker is replaced with General George Meade as commander of the Army of the Potomac.

July 1–3 The Union scores a costly victory at the Battle of Gettysburg that delivers a decisive blow to the Confederacy's chances for independence. Meade fails to pursue Lee's retreating army into Virginia.

July 4 On Independence Day, one day after the disheartening Confederate defeat at Gettysburg, Vicksburg is unconditionally surrendered to General Grant. The loss of Vicksburg gives the Union control of the vital Mississippi River and cuts the Confederacy in half.

July 13–16 Troops are called out to put down savage riots that break out in New York and several other Northern cities in reaction to the unpopular Conscription Act.

July 17 Confederate troops pull out of Jackson, Mississippi.

September 19–20 The Confederates win the Battle of Chickamauga, but the failure of General Braxton Bragg to take advantage of his opportunities prevents an even more decisive victory.

October 16 General Grant is named commander of the united armies of the west by President Lincoln.

November 19 Lincoln delivers the Gettysburg Address.

November 23–25 General Grant arrives from Vicksburg and propels the Union to victory at the Battle of Chattanooga. And when the Confederates abandon Knoxville, Tennessee is left totally in Union control.

1864

February 3–14 Union General William Tecumseh Sherman captures Meridian, Mississippi, kicking off his policy of total warfare to destroy anything that can be used to support the Confederacy.

March 10 In response to Grant's victory at Chattanooga, Lincoln appoints him as general in chief of all Union armies.

April 12 Black and white Union soldiers are executed after the capture of Fort Pillow, Tennessee, by troops led by Confederate General Nathan Bedford Forrest.

May 3 Leading 120,000 troops, Grant begins his campaign to take Richmond. Lee's Army of Northern Virginia has 60,000 men to defend the Confederate capital.

May 4 General Sherman, at the head of an army of 110,000 men, begins his march to Atlanta.

May 5–6 The armies led by Grant and Lee battle to a draw at the Battle of the Wilderness in Virginia's Rapidan basin.

May 8–12 The two armies fight to another draw at Spotsylvania, Virginia.

June 1–3 Grant uncharacteristically makes crucial errors of judgment that enable General Lee to win the Battle of Cold Harbor in Virginia.

June 7 Despite widespread dissatisfaction with the way Lincoln has handled the war, the Republican Party nominates him for a second term as president.

June 15–18 After an assault by Grant on Petersburg, Virginia, is replused by Lee, the Union begins a siege of the city.

June 27 More than 2,000 Union casualties are suffered in a Confederate victory over General Sherman at the Battle of Kennesaw Mountain in Georgia.

July 14 Washington is thrown into a panic when Confederate general Jubal A. Early reaches the outskirts of the city with his cavalry. Union general Lewis "Lew" Wallace halts the advance and Early is forced to withdraw when Federal reinforcements arrive.

August 5	Advanced to the new navy rank of admiral, David Farragut captures Mobile, Alabama.
September 2	Atlanta is surrendered to General Sherman.
September 4	General Sherman orders the evacuation of all civilians in Atlanta.
September 19–October 19	Confederate general Jubal A. Early is driven from Virginia's Shenandoah Valley by Union Cavalry General Philip T. Sheridan. The "breadbasket of the Confederacy" remains in Union hands throughout the rest of the war.
October 31	Nevada is admitted to the Union as the thirty-sixth state.
November 8	Helped by a steady stream of Union victories, Lincoln is overwhelmingly elected to a second term over his main opponent, Democrat George B. McClellan.
November 16	Sherman leaves Atlanta and begins his famous March to the Sea at Savannah, Georgia.
November 30	The South wins its last major victory of the war at the Battle of Franklin in Tennessee, but at a terrible cost. General John B. Hood's Army of Tennessee has six generals killed among nearly 6,300 casualties.
December 15–17	Hood loses the Battle of Nashville and nearly 4,500 more men from his rapidly dwindling army.
December 22	Sherman wires Lincoln that he is presenting Savannah to him as a Christmas gift after marching unopposed into the city.

1865

January 15	Fort Fisher is captured from the Confederates by combined land and sea forces. The fort protected Wilmington, North Carolina.
January 31	The U. S. House of Representatives passes the 13th Amendment abolishing slavery and it is sent to the states for ratification.
February 1	Illinois becomes the first state to ratify the 13th Amendment.
February 3	President Lincoln and his secretary of war meet with the Confederate vice president and secretary of war at the Hampton Roads Conference at the mouth of the James River to talk peace. The conference breaks up after four hours with no agreement reached.
February 22	Wilmington, North Carolina, becomes the last port in the Confederacy to be captured by the Union.

THE COMPLETE HANDBOOK 345

March 3 The Bureau of Refugees, Freedmen, and Abandoned Lands is established by the U. S. Congress.

March 4 Lincoln is inaugurated for his second term.

March 13 Jefferson Davis signs a bill authorizing blacks to serve in the Confederate Army.

April 1 General Philip Sheridan leads his troops to victory at the Battle of Five Forks in Virginia.

April 2 General Lee ends the lengthy Siege of Petersburg by withdrawing his forces and notifies Jefferson Davis that Richmond can no longer be defended.

April 2 The *General Lyon,* a side-wheel steamboat, burns and sinks on the Mississippi River, killing about 600 Union soldiers and civilian refugees from the South.

April 3 Union troops occupy Petersburg and Richmond.

April 5 Lincoln tours Richmond.

April 6 The Army of the Potomac and the Army of Northern Virginia meet at Sayler's Creek in Virginia in their last clash of the war. The Union beat the exhausted Confederates, who were vainly attempting to protect supply wagons with food for their starving troops.

April 9 Robert E. Lee surrenders Confederate forces to Union General Ulysses S. Grant at Appomattox Court House.

April 14 President Lincoln is fatally shot by actor and Confederate sympathizer John Wilkes Booth while watching a play at Ford's Theatre in Washington.

April 15 Early in the morning, President Lincoln dies from his head injury.

April 15 Vice President Andrew Johnson, a Democrat, takes the oath as the nation's 17th president.

April 18 In North Carolina, Confederate general Joseph E. Johnston surrenders the last remnants of his Army of Tennessee to Union general William T. Sherman.

April 27 The SS *Sultana,* a side-wheel steamer packed with between 2,000 and 2,500 Union soldiers and civilians, burns and sinks off Cape Hatteras, North Carolina. There are fewer than 600 survivors.

May 4 Major General Richard Taylor, son of former president Zachary Taylor, surrenders 15,000 Confederate troops in Alabama to Union major general Edward R. S. Canby.

May 12–13 Isolated in the West and unaware of Lee's surrender, Confederate lieutenant general Edmund Kirby Smith wins the last land battle of the war, at Palmetto Ranch in West Texas.

May 25 Lieutenant General Edmund Kirby Smith is in Galveston attempting to recruit more troops for the Confederate Army's Trans-Mississippi Department when his forces are

surrendered in New Orleans by a subordinate, Lieutenant
General Simon Bolivar Buckner.

June 23 Brigadier General Stand Watie, a Cherokee Indian, surrenders his irregulars to the Union. They are the last
Confederates to surrender.